Jewish Fundamentalism in Israel

Pluto Middle Eastern Studies

Also available

Jewish History, Jewish Religion
The Weight of Three Thousand Years
Israel Shahak

Open Secrets
Israeli Foreign and Nuclear Policies
Israel Shahak

Jewish Fundamentalism in Israel

Israel Shahak and Norton Mezvinsky

Pluto Press

LONDON • STERLING, VIRGINIA

First published 1999 by Pluto Press
345 Archway Road, London N6 5AA
and 22883 Quicksilver Drive,
Sterling, VA 20166–2012, USA

British Library Cataloguing in Publication Data
A catalogue record for this book is available from the
British Library

ISBN 0 7453 1281 0 hbk

Library of Congress Cataloging in Publication Data
Shahak, Israel.
    Jewish Fundamentalism in Israel / Israel Shahak and Norton
Mezvinsky.
        p.   cm. — (Pluto Middle Eastern series)
    Includes bibliographical references and index.
    ISBN 0–7453–1281–0 (hbk.)
    1. Orthodox Judaism—Israel—Controversial literature.
2. Orthodox Judaism—Political aspects—Israel. 3. Political
violence—Israel. I. Mezvinsky, Norton. II. Title. III. Series.
BM390.S486   1999
296'.095694'09045—dc21   99–30525
                                                              CIP

Designed and Produced for Pluto Press by
Chase Production Services, Chadlington, OX7 3LN
Typeset from disk by Stanford DTP Services, Northampton
Printed in the EC by TJ International, Padstow

Contents

Preface

Virtually identified with Arab terrorism, Islamic fundamentalism is anathema throughout the non-Muslim world. Virtually identified with ignorance, superstition, intolerance and racism, Christian fundamentalism is anathema to the cultural and intellectual elite in the United States. The recent significant increase in its number of adherents, combined with its widening political influence, nevertheless, make Christian fundamentalism a real threat to democracy in the United States. Although possessing nearly all the important social scientific properties of Islamic and Christian fundamentalism, Jewish fundamentalism is practically unknown outside of Israel and certain sections of a few other places. When its existence is acknowledged, its significance is minimized or limited to arcane religious practices and quaint middle European dress, most often by those same non-Israeli elite commentators who see so uncompromisingly the evils inherent in Jewish fundamentalism's Islamic and/or Christian cousins.

As students of contemporary society and as Jews, one Israeli, one American, with personal commitments and attachments to the Middle East, we cannot help seeing Jewish fundamentalism in Israel as a major obstacle to peace in the region. Nor can we help being dismayed by the dismissal of the perniciousness of Jewish fundamentalism to peace and to its victims by those who are otherwise knowledgeable and astute and so quick to point out the violence inherent in other fundamentalist approaches to existence.

This book is a journey of understanding – often painful, often dreary, often disturbing – for us as Jews who have a stake in Jewry. With our hearts and minds we want Jews, together with other people, to recognize and strive for the highest ideals, even as we fall short of them. We see these ideals as central to the values of Western civilization and applicable throughout the civilized world. We believe these values do not stand in the way of peace anywhere. That a perversion of these values in the name of Jewish fundamentalism stands as an impediment to peace, to the development of Israeli democracy and even to civilized discourse outrages us, both as Jews and as human beings. To identify and lessen, if not purge, this outrage, we have written this book and undertaken this journey in the hope that it may bring understanding to our readers as it has brought understanding to us. Our assumption is that peace in the Middle East cannot be achieved until the currents and cross-currents of contemporary life in the region are understood. In this most historical and most religious area, understanding entails an exploration of the past that continues to impinge upon the attitudes, values, assumptions and behaviors of all the people of this beautiful and troubled land. Jewish opposition in Israel to Jewish fundamentalism greatly increased after a Jewish, fundamentalist, religious fanatic, Yigal Amir, who insisted that he was acting in accordance with dictates in Judaism, shot and killed Prime Minister Yitzhak Rabin. That numerous groups of religious Jews after the assassination supported this murder in the name of the "true" Jewish religion aroused interest in Israel in past killings by Jews of other Jews who were alleged to be heretics or sinners. In our book we cite present and past investigations by Israeli scholars documenting that for centuries prior to the rise of the modern nation state, Jews, believing they were acting in accordance with God's word and thus preparing themselves for eternal paradise, punished or killed heretics and/or religious sinners. Contemporary Jewish fundamentalism is an attempt to revive a situation that often existed in Jewish communities before the influence of modernity. The basic principles of Jewish fundamentalism are the same as those found in other religions: restoration and survival of the "pure" and pious religious community that presumably existed in the past.

In our book we describe in some detail the origins, ideologies, practices and overall impact upon society of fundamentalism. We emphasize mostly the messianic tendency, because we believe it to be the most influential and dangerous. Jewish fundamentalists generally oppose extensions of human freedoms, especially the freedom of expression, in Israel. In regard to foreign policy, the National Religious Party, ruled by supporters of the messianic tendency of Jewish fundamentalism, has continuously opposed any and all withdrawals from territories conquered and occupied by Israel since 1967. These fundamentalists opposed Israeli withdrawal from the Sinai in 1978, just as twenty years later they continued to oppose any withdrawal from the West Bank. These same Jews printed and distributed atlases allegedly showing that the land of Israel, belonging only to the Jews and requiring liberation, included the Sinai, Jordan, Lebanon, most of Syria and Kuwait. Jewish fundamentalists have advocated the most discriminative proposals against Palestinians. Not surprisingly, Baruch Goldstein and Yigal Amir, the most sensational Jewish assassins of the 1990s, and most of their admirers have been Jewish fundamentalists of the messianic tendency.

In the 1990s, Israeli sociologists and scholars in other academic fields have focused more attention than ever before upon the social effects in Israeli society of Jewish fundamentalists. The overwhelming opinion of these scholars is that the adherents of Jewish fundamentalism in Israel are hostile to democracy. The fundamentalists oppose equality for all citizens, especially non-Jews and Jewish "deviants" such as homosexuals. The great majority of religious Jews in Israel, influenced by fundamentalists, share these views to some extent. In a book review published on October 14, 1998, Baruch Kimmerling, a distinguished Israeli sociologist, citing evidence from a study conducted by other scholars, commented:

> The values of the [Jewish] religion, at least in its Orthodox and nationalistic form that prevails in Israel, cannot be squared with democratic values. No other variable – neither nationality, nor attitudes about security, nor social or economic values, nor ethnic descent and education – so influences the attitudes of [Israeli] Jews against democratic values as does religiosity.

Citing additional evidence, Kimmerling commented further that secular, Israeli Jews who had acquired college or university education had the greatest attachment to democratic values and that religious Jews who studied in yeshivot (religious schools) most opposed democracy. It is clear that fundamentalist antagonism to democratic values, as well as to most aspects of secular culture and life style, is deeply instilled in Israel's religious schools.

The documentation of fundamentalist antagonism to the secular life style of a majority of Israeli Jews is clear. The September 20, 1998, edition of *Yediot Ahronot*, the largest circulation, Hebrew-language, daily Israeli newspaper, for example, contained a "cultural profile" survey of Israeli Jewish society. The survey revealed that the major Israeli consumers of culture, who visit museums and attend concerts and the theater, had finished high school and defined themselves as either secular or not Orthodox (religious). The Israeli religious press and pronouncements by Israeli rabbis, condemning cultural activity, have confirmed the survey's findings.

Jewish fundamentalists have displayed severe enmity against Jews who adopt a different sexual life style. Many Israeli rabbis and the Israeli religious political parties in the 1990s reacted sharply against the increased visibility and power of the homosexual and lesbian communities in Israel. According to the Halacha (Jewish religious law), homosexuality is punishable by death by stoning, and, although the punishment is not clear, lesbian relations are forbidden. The Israeli secular press emphasized in the 1990s some of the more outrageous rabbinical proposals for dealing with homosexuals; these included a "compulsory healing treatment" and/or a period of "education in a closed institution." Many rabbis, when interviewed, indicated that they favored imposition of the death penalty for Jewish homosexual men. (The rabbis tended to leave lesbians alone.) In their televised election advertisements, Israeli religious political parties usually have emphasized that homosexual Jews constitute one of the greatest dangers facing Israel. The religious parties have been successful in their attempts to eliminate in public school courses any mention of Hebrew homosexual love poems, some of which contain beautiful Hebrew lyrics. This censorship is evidence of fundamentalist influence.

Conflicts in Israeli society between adherents and opponents of Jewish fundamentalism rank among the most important issues in Israeli politics. In this book we do not attempt to discuss all of these problems and/or issues. Rather, we focus upon what we consider to be the most vital problems and issues of Jewish fundamentalism.

Defenders of the "Jewish interest" often attack persons who write critically about Jews and/or Judaism for not emphasizing in the same text positive features that may have nothing or little to do with the substance under focus. Some of these defenders, for example, attacked Seffi Rachlevsky after the publication of his best-selling book, *Messiahs' Donkeys*. In his book, Rachlevsky correctly claimed that Rabbi Kook, the Elder, the revered father of the messianic tendency of Jewish fundamentalism (who is featured in our book), said "The difference between a Jewish soul and souls of non-Jews – all of them in all different levels – is greater and deeper than the difference between a human soul and the souls of cattle." The Rachlevsky detractors did not attempt to refute substantively the relevance of the Kook quotation. Rather, they argued that Rabbi Kook said other things and that Rachlevsky, by neglecting to mention them, had distorted the teachings of Rabbi Kook. Rachlevsky pointed out that Rabbi Kook's entire teaching was based upon the Lurianic Cabbala, the school of Jewish mysticism that dominated Judaism from the late sixteenth to the early nineteenth century. One of the basic tenants of the Lurianic Cabbala is the absolute superiority of the Jewish soul and body over the non-Jewish soul and body. According to the Lurianic Cabbala, the world was created solely for the sake of Jews; the existence of non-Jews was subsidiary. If an influential Christian bishop or Islamic scholar argued that the difference between the superior souls of non-Jews and the inferior souls of Jews was greater than the difference between the human soul and the souls of cattle, he would incur the wrath of and be viewed as an anti-Semite by most Jewish scholars regardless of whatever less meaningful, positive statements he included. From this perspective the detractors of Rachlevsky are hypocrites. That Rabbi Kook was a vegetarian and even respected the rights of plants to the extent that he did not allow flowers or grass to be cut for his own pleasure neither distracted from nor added anything to his position regarding the comparison of the souls of Jews and non-Jews. That Kook deprecated unnecessary Jewish brutality against non-Jews should not minimize criticism of his expressed delight in the belief that the death of millions of soldiers during World War One constituted a sign of the approaching salvation of Jews and the coming of the Messiah.

The detractors of Rachlevsky and those who may level similar criticisms against our book and us are not the only hypocrites in this area. Shelves of bookshops in English-speaking and other countries groan under the weight of books on Jewish mysticism in general and on Hassidism and the Lurianic Cabbala more specifically. Many of the authors of these books are widely regarded as famous scholars because of the minutiae of their scholarship. The people who read only these books on these subjects, however, cannot suspect that Jewish mysticism, the Lurianic Cabbala, Hassidism and the teachings of Rabbi Kook contain basic ideas about Jewish superiority comparable to the worst forms of anti-Semitism. The scholarly authors of these books, for example Gershon Scholem, have willfully omitted reference to such ideas. These authors are supreme hypocrites. They are analogous to many authors of books on Stalin and Stalinism. Until recently, people who read only the books written by Stalinists could not know about Stalin's crimes and would have false notions of the Stalinists' regimes and their real ideologies.

The fact is that certain Jews, some of whom wield political influence, consider Jews to be superior to non-Jews and view the world as having been created only or primarily for Jews. This belief in Jewish superiority is most dangerous when held by Jews who love their children, are honest in their relations with other Jews and perform, as do fundamentalists in all religions, various acts of piety. This belief is less dangerous when held by Jews who are not overwhelmingly concerned about religion and/or corruption. A parallel worth citing here is that in a secular, totalitarian system, a dedicated party worker or a convinced nationalist is usually more dangerous and harmful than a corrupt member of the same ideological system.

Our final point in this preface is both personal and universal. As Jews, we understand that our own grandparents or great-grandparents probably believed in at least some of the views described in our book. This same statement may apply to other contemporary Jews. In the past many non-Jews, as individuals and as members of groups, held anti-Semitic views, which, especially when the circumstances were propitious, influenced the behavior of others towards Jews. Similarly, in the past, slavery was universally practiced and justified, the inferior status of women was a global phenomenon and the belief that a country belonged to an individual or family and was heritable was common. Jewish fundamentalists still believe, as they have in the past, in a golden age when everything was, or was going to be, perfect. This golden age is so much of a reality for them that, when faced with issues of pernicious beliefs and practices, they take refuge by invoking God's word, by falsely describing the past and by condemning non-Jews for harboring feelings of superiority and having contempt for Jews. The fundamentalists also justify their own belief in Jewish superiority and their feeling of contempt for non-Jews; they seek to reproduce the mythical golden age in which their views would dominate. We have written this book in order to reveal the essential character of Jewish fundamentalism and its adherents. This character threatens democratic features of Israeli society. We believe that awareness is the necessary first step in opposition. We realize that by criticizing Jewish fundamentalism we are criticizing a part of the past that we love. We wish that members of every human grouping would criticize their own past, even before criticizing others. This, we further believe, would lead to a better understanding between human groups and would be followed, perhaps slowly and hesitantly, by better treatment of minorities. Most of our book is concerned with basic beliefs and resultant policies in Israeli Jewish society. We believe that a critique of Jewish fundamentalism, which entails a critique of the Jewish past, can help Jews acquire more understanding and improve their behavior towards Palestinians, especially in the territories conquered in and occupied since 1967. We hope that our critique will also motivate other people in the Middle East to engage in criticism of their entire past in order to increase their knowledge of themselves and improve their behavior towards others in the present. All of this could constitute a major factor in bringing peace to the Middle East.

Glossary

Agudat Israel ("Association of Jews" in Hebrew): A former name of the Askenazi Haredi party now called Yahadut Ha'Torah.

Aron Ha'kodesh ("Cupboard of the Holiness" in Hebrew): Place in synagogue where the Scrolls of Law are stored, to be taken out only on specific occasions. Regarded as the holiest place in the synagogue.

Ashkenazi ("German" in pre-modern Hebrew): A common name for Jews whose ancestors lived in northern France, England, Germany, Poland, Russia and other countries of central and eastern Europe.

Bar Mitzva ("capable of [fulfilling] commandments" in Hebrew): A ceremony usually accompanied by a feast, to celebrate the occasion when a Jewish boy reaches the age of thirteen, is then obliged to fulfill all religious commandments and becomes capable of sinning. According to traditional Judaism the father is responsible for all sins committed by sons below the age of thirteen.

Black Panthers: In the context of this book this term refers to a small and ephemeral, but highly publicized, organization of Oriental Jews in Israel during the 1970s, which protested discrimination of Oriental Jews.

Bnei Brak: Israeli town near Tel Aviv, inhabited almost only by Haredim, mainly Ashkenazi.

Border guards: A paramilitary unit of the Israeli police.

Cabbala ("The received [thing]" in Hebrew): The usual name for Jewish mysticism; used especially for the Jewish mystical groups that have developed since the eleventh century.

Davar ("Matter," in Hebrew): A Hebrew newspaper that ceased to appear in the mid-1990s.

Degel Ha'Torah ("Flag of the Torah" in Hebrew): A faction of Mitnagdim within the party, Yahadut Ha'Torah.

Der'i, Aryeh: Chief politician of the Shas party, born in 1959. In April, 1999, he was convicted for taking bribes and sentenced to four years of imprisonment. The punishment was suspended pending his appeal.

Ga'on ("genius" in Hebrew): Title of the two chief rabbis in Iraq from about 650 to 1050, each of whom was acknowledged by all Jews as the supreme religious authority. In the last two hundred years also used in a vague manner to designate (or to flatter) any important rabbi.

Ge'onim: Plural of Ga'on.

Goren, Rabbi Shlomo: An important Israeli rabbi. Appointed by Prime Minister David Ben Gurion as the first Chief Rabbi of the

Israeli army. Subsequently a Chief Rabbi of Israel in the 1960s and 1970s.

Gush Emunim ("Block of Faithful" in Hebrew): The ideological and settling messianic movement (see chapters four and five). Founded in early 1974.

Ha'ain Hashvi'it ("the seventh eye" in Hebrew): Bimonthly issued by the Israeli Institute for Democracy and devoted to media criticism.

Haaretz ("The land" in Hebrew): The most prestigious Hebrew newspaper, read mainly by the elite.

Hadashot ("News" in Hebrew): A radical Hebrew newspaper of the 1980s and early 1990s.

Ha'ir ("The town" in Hebrew): A Friday, widely read, Hebrew newspaper of Tel Aviv and neighboring towns with radical tendencies.

Halacha ("Accepted" in Hebrew): The term as two meanings in Hebrew. 1. The entire body of the Jewish religious law. 2. A single regulation of that law. To avoid confusion in this book we used the term only in its first meaning. Where it occurred in our Hebrew sources in the second meaning (for example, in references in quotations to books codifying Jewish religious law), it was translated as "rule."

Haredim ("Fearful" in the meaning "God-fearing" in Hebrew): Name of those Jewish fundamentalists who refuse modern innovations. Haredi is the singular form and is also an adverb.

Ha'Shavua ("The week" in Hebrew): An extreme Haredi weekly.

Heder ("Room" in Hebrew): Name for the pre-modern Jewish school system.

Hesder ("Arrangement" in Hebrew): Name for religious units in Israeli army that serve by a special arrangement.

Israel A and Israel B: Popular Israeli terms designating the two parts of Israeli Jewish society that often oppose each other: the former leaning to the right and the second leaning to the left and less influenced by religion.

Karo, Rabbi Yoseph: 1488–1575, the author of Shulhan Aruch, commentaries on Maimonides and other religious works. Regarded as the most important rabbinic authority of the sixteenth and seventeenth centuries.

Kashrut ("proper manner" in Hebrew): A set of rules governing the types of food that religious Jews can eat according to the Halacha and the proper manner of their preparation.

Kitzur Shulhan Aruch ("abridgment of Shulhan Aruch" in Hebrew): A popular book containing the most necessary rules of Halacha, used in the education of Haredi children and by the uneducated Haredim. Written by rabbi Shlomo Gantzfried in early nineteenth century.

Kollel ("entire" or "inclusive" in Hebrew): An institution for the studying of Talmud by adults who have finished their Yeshiva studies.

Kook, Rabbi Avracham Yitzhak Hacohen: 1865–1935, also called and referred to in this book as "Rabbi Kook the elder." After filling various rabbinic posts he was the Chief Rabbi of Palestine 1920–35. A prolific author, many of whose works were posthumously edited from his notes. The founder of the messianic ideology (chapters four and five). Held in great regard by Gush Emunim followers and to some extent by all Zionists.

Kook, Rabbi Tzvi Yehuda Hacohen: 1890–1982, a son of Rabbi Avraham Yitzhak Kook. Called and referred to in this book as "Rabbi Kook the younger." Took over the leadership of the adherents of messianic ideology after the death of his father. All important Gush Emunim rabbis are his students.

Kosher: Yiddish expression used in Hebrew with ironic undertones to refer to food, chosen and prepared according to rules of Kashrut. The proper Hebrew word "Kasher" is used mainly in polite discourse.

Kuneh: A Yiddish word meaning a particular type of stocks used by Jews in Eastern Europe. Adopted in Hebrew historical and religious works.

Labor: Proper name The Israeli Labor Party. The largest and also the oldest Israeli left party.

Likud ("consolidation" in Hebrew): The largest Israeli right party.

Lurianic Cabbala: The most important branch of Cabbala since the early seventeenth century. Founded by Rabbi Isaac Luria (1538–72) and his disciples, it has dominated all subsequent Jewish mysticism.

Maariv ("eventide" in Hebrew): The Hebrew daily paper with the second largest circulation.

Maimonides: Used in this book, following Hebrew usage, in two meanings: 1. Rabbi Moshe son of Maimon, called in European languages Maimonides, 1138–1204, author of many books of commentary on the Halacha. Also, the greatest philosopher of Judaism. 2. The largest codex of Halacha composed by Maimonides; the proper name is "Mishneh Torah" ("second rank Torah"). It includes all commandments and beliefs of Jewish religious law. It is divided into books that are in turn divided into tractates, entitled according to the issues with which they deal; they tractates in turn are divided into chapters and individual rules. In our references following the Hebrew usage, only the tractate, chapter and the number of the rule are given.

Maskilim ("the enlightened ones" in Hebrew): Name adopted by the Jews who introduced modern influences into Judaism in late eighteenth and nineteenth centuries.

Mishnah ("repetition" in Hebrew): The basic and easier part of Talmud, often studied by itself and equipped with special commentaries.

Mitnagdim ("opponents" in Hebrew): The most extreme right-wing party now represented in the knesset.

National Religious Party: Often referred to by its acronym NRP. Represents the fundamentalist Jews in Israel who are not Haredim.

Oriental Jews ("mizrahim" in Hebrew): Collective name used at present for Israeli Jews who are not Ashkenazi.

Orthodox: In Israel and elsewhere, a common name for Jews who keep the rules of Halacha, or at least most of them. Orthodoxy refers to the behavior and practices of Orthodox Jews. (Contrary to Christianity,

Orthodox and orthodoxy in Judaism refer mostly to practices and not to beliefs.)

Palestinian Talmud (called incorrectly in Hebrew "Jerusalem Talmud"): The less authoritative and extensive of the two Talmuds.

Pentateuch: The first five books of the Bible, believed to have been written by Moses and regarded as more sacred than the rest of the Bible.

Purim: A lesser Jewish holiday that occurs about one month before Passover. It has many features of the carnival but is also characterized by increased hostility to non-Jews.

Rabenu ("our rabbi" in Hebrew): An unofficial title given to specially important rabbis.

Rebbe ("rabbi" in Yiddish): Kept to this day by the holy men of Hassidic sects as one of their titles. Used in Hebrew in this connotation.

Sages: The customary English translation of the Hebrew term "our wise men of blessed memory." Used primarily to designate all rabbis mentioned in the Talmud, but also to refer more vaguely to all past Orthodox rabbis.

Sephardi ("Spanish" in Hebrew): Until the late 1970s used in Israel instead of the term, Oriental Jews.

Sha'atnez: A Hebrew word denoting the forbidden mixture of wool and flax in a textile.

Shach, Rabbi Eliezer: 1898–, the spiritual leader of the Degel Ha'Torah faction and one of the most influential rabbis in Israel.

Shas: The party of Oriental Jewish Haredim.

Shishi ("Sixth" or "Friday" in Hebrew): Name of a defunct Hebrew weekly.

Shofar: Ram's horn used for sacred blowing during some synagogue services and especially on the New Year.

Sholem, Professor Gershon: 1897–1982, founder of the modern study of Cabbala; wrote many authoritative books on Jewish mysticism.

Shulhan Aruch ("prepared table" in Hebrew): A summary of a longer work, Bet Yoseph, by Rabbi Yoseph Karo but shorter than the Maimonides version, because it omits many less important subjects. It is regarded as authoritative by most Orthodox Jews. Usually the differences between the Shulhan Aruch and the Maimonides version are minor.

Tal, Professor Uriel: Died in 1985. Professor of German history at Tel Aviv University.

Talmud ("study" in Hebrew): Although there are two Talmuds, Palestinian and Babylonian, the term "Talmud" without qualification always refers to the Babylonian Talmud, regarded as the most authoritative text by Orthodox Jews. The Palestinian Talmud (much shorter and inferior in its arrangement) enjoys only a supplementary authority. The basic part of both Talmuds is the Mishnah, a collection of terse laws written in Hebrew. The other part, called "Gemarah" consists of a discussion of those laws mixed with many legends. The Gemarah is much longer than the Mishnah and is written in both Aramaic and Hebrew. Both Talmuds are divided into sixty tractates. The Babylonian

Talmud is always printed in standard editions with the same division of pages so that all references are to the names of tractate and page numbers.

Torah Sheba'al Peh ("oral Torah" in Hebrew): Term used, especially by Orthodox Jews, to refer to the sacred Jewish literature other than the Bible.

Tractate: A major division of the Talmud. Each tractate has a name, usually roughly describing its main contents.

Tsomet ("junction" in Hebrew): Secular right-wing party headed by Reserve General Raphael Eitan and allied with Likud. Tsomet has been politically powerful in the early 1990s.

Yahadut Ha'Torah ("Judaism of the Torah" in Hebrew): Party of Ashkenazi Haredim, comprised of two almost independent factions: one Degel Ha'Torah and the other a coalition of Hassidic sects.

Yated Ne'eman ("faithful tent peg" in Hebrew): Weekly of Degel Ha'Torah.

Yediot Ahronot ("last news" in Hebrew): The Hebrew newspaper with by far the largest circulation.

Yerushalaim ("Jerusalem" in Hebrew): A Hebrew Friday paper published in Jerusalem. Belongs to Yediot Ahronot.

Yeshiva ("sitting" or "meeting" in Hebrew): Institution for higher Talmudic studies. The plural is Yeshivot.

Yom Kippur (Day of Atonement in English): The most sacred day of the Jewish religious calendar.

Yoseph, Rabbi Ovadia: The spiritual leader of the Shas party.

Introduction

This is a political book about Jewish fundamentalism in Israel. It includes some original scholarly research but is based to a great extent upon the scholarly research of others. Hopefully, this book is analytical.

We have inserted in the text many and copious quotations from serious articles that have appeared in the Israeli Hebrew press. The majority of articulate Israeli Jews have learned about Jewish fundamentalism and some of the reactions thereto during the past ten to fifteen years from these articles. Some of these articles provided summaries of and analyses by leading scholars who have researched in-depth aspects of Jewish fundamentalism.

We have quoted and have usually explained texts from talmudic literature. Such texts have been and still are often used in Israeli politics and often quoted in the Israeli Hebrew press. We have concluded that in the usual English translations of talmudic literature some of the most sensitive passages are usually toned down or falsified – as a result, we have ourselves translated all of the texts from talmudic literature that we have quoted in the book. The quotations from the Bible, however, follow the standard translations, sometimes in more modern English, except when specifically noted otherwise.

We realize that we have presented a number of lengthy quotations. We determined that this was necessary in order to explain our points adequately. We believe the quotations deserve to be and should be read in full. Instead of footnoting each quotation separately in the traditional scholarly manner, we decided to mention in the text from where each quotation was taken. Although this may at times appear to be a bit redundant, it makes the flow of understanding easier.

Although our book deals primarily with recent developments in Jewish fundamentalism, it is rooted in Jewish history. A brief overview of Jewish history, especially for readers who may lack adequate knowledge thereof, is necessary in order to provide the contextual framework for the subject matter. Fundamentalists of all religions wish to restore society to the "good old times" when the faith was allegedly pure and was practiced by everyone. Fundamentalists believe that in the "good old times" all the evils associated with modernity were absent. To gain an understanding of Jewish fundamentalism, it is imperative to identify the historical period that fundamentalists believe should be re-established. In order to do this, we must specify the various periods of Jewish history.

Jewish history is usually divided into four major periods. The first is the biblical period during which most of the Jewish Bible (Old Testament in the Christian tradition) was written. Although its beginning time is uncertain, this period lasted until about the fifth century BC. Judaism, at least in its major characteristics, did not exist in this time period. The Hebrew word "yehudim" ("Jews" in post-biblical Hebrew) and its cognates in the Jewish Bible only denotes the inhabitants of the small kingdom of Judea and is used to distinguish these inhabitants from all the other people, called Israelites or "sons of Israel" or, rarely, "Hebrews." The Bible anyway is not the book that primarily determines the practices and doctrines of Orthodox Jews.[1] The most fundamentalist Orthodox Jews are largely ignorant of major parts of the Bible and know some parts only through commentaries that distort meaning. Controversies, moreover, consumed the biblical period. The majority of Israelites, including inhabitants of Judea, practiced idolatry throughout much of this period. Only a minority of Israelites followed those tendencies from which Judaism subsequently arose. In short, Judaism, as it came to be known, did not exist during the biblical period.

The second period of Jewish history, usually called the Second Temple period, began in the fifth century BC and lasted until the destruction of the Second Temple by the Romans in AD 70. This was the formative period of Judaism with its subsequent characteristics. The term "Jews," which denotes those people who followed the distinctive religion of Judaism and the name Judea, which denotes the land wherein Jews lived, appeared in this period. Near the end of this period, after Jews had conquered most of Palestine, the Romans adopted the term "Judea" in describing Palestine.[2] The two most important new Jewish characteristics that developed in this period were Jewish exclusiveness and the resultant separation of Jews from all other nations. For the first time the persons of other nations were referred to by the collective name of gentiles.[3] The second new characteristic was based upon the assumption that the Jews must follow biblical law, that is, the true interpretation of the law. During most of this period, however, disputes centering upon differing and rival interpretations of the law occurred. At times, these disputes erupted into civil wars. The long-lasting quarrel between the Pharisees and Saducees was but one example of such disputes. Shortly after the beginning of this period, Alexander the Great conquered Palestine. States influenced by Hellenism ruled Palestine for almost a thousand years thereafter; even the short-lived independent Jewish state of the Hasmonean dynasty was in most essentials a type of Hellenistic state. Consequentially, Jewish society and the Hebrew language, even though keeping their Jewish characteristics were transformed by the influences of Hellenism. Hellenism influenced even more deeply the Jewish diaspora in Mediterranean countries. Jews in those countries often spoke and prayed in Greek. Unfortunately most of the Jewish literature in Greek, which was produced in this period, was subsequently lost by the Jews; only that part preserved by various Christian churches has remained.

Most historians date the beginning of the third period in AD 70 with the destruction of the Second Temple. Other historians prefer to date the beginning of the third period in AD 135, when the last major Jewish rebellion against the Roman Empire ended. This period ended at different times in different countries with the onset of modernity and the rise of modern nation states. Modernity began when Jews were granted rights as citizens equal to those granted to non-Jews and consequently when their autonomy, which entailed subjection to the rabbis, ended. This occurred in the United States and France, for example, by the end of the eighteenth century; this did not occur in Russia until 1917 or in Yemen until the 1950s. The Jewish rebellions against the Romans resulted in a permanent loss of Jewish population in Palestine; the importance of the Jewish diaspora thus increased. This change became fully operative in the fifth century AD. Additionally, the failure of rebellions caused the Jews to lose hope that the Temple would be rebuilt and that the animal sacrifices performed in the Temple, previously the heart-center of the Jewish religion, would be restored before the coming of the Messiah. The repeated defeats caused most Jews to accommodate themselves to the ruling authority of Rome and of other states in return for the limited autonomy directed by the rabbis. Thus, in the Roman empire of the fourth century AD, in a system created much earlier, all the Jews were in religious matters subject to the Patriarch who had the power to punish them by flogging, by levying fines for religious offenses and by imposing taxes. The dignitary called Patriarch in Roman sources was called President ("Nassi" in Hebrew) in Jewish sources. He presided over the Sanhedrin, the supreme Jewish court, and in Palestine appointed court members and other religious functionaries. The Patriarch, whose post was hereditary, held a high official rank in the hierarchy of Roman state officials. A similar arrangement simultaneously existed in Iraq where the top official was called the head of the diaspora. Both the patriarch and the head of the diaspora claimed to have been descended from the family of King David. The office of the patriarch lapsed shortly after

AD 429; the office of the head of the diaspora lasted until about AD 1100. Both offices provided the framework for models of Jewish autonomy. This autonomy, which persisted until the modern era, and later repercussions thereof, contributed to the rise of Jewish fundamentalism. The great abundance of literature produced in the third period, the longest in the entire course of Jewish history, was written mostly in Hebrew but also in Aramaic, Greek, Arabic, Yiddish and other languages. The major theme was religion; the minutiae of religious observances were mainly emphasized. Poetry, philosophy and science, predominantly of the Aristotelian variety, appeared at some times in some places but were neither universal nor continuous. In many diaspora areas, particularly in central Europe, the only literature produced until 1750 was religious. From the perspective of Jewish fundamentalism the most important occurrence in the third period was the growth of Jewish mysticism, usually referred to by the name of Cabbala. Jewish mysticism transformed Jewish beliefs without changing, except for a few details, Jewish observance. Between 1550 and 1750, the great majority of Jews in western Europe accepted the Cabbala and its set of beliefs. This was the end of the third period of Jewish history, which immediately preceded the rise of modern nation states and the beginning of modern influences. Mysticism is still accepted by and constitutes a vital part of Jewish fundamentalism, being especially important in the messianic variety. As shown in our book, the ideology of the messianic variety of Jewish fundamentalism is based upon the Cabbala. In spite of making occasional references to the Bible, Jewish fundamentalists generally have consistently pinpointed and described the last part of this third period as the golden age that they wish to restore. It is important to note that, beyond the spawning of Jewish fundamentalism, the wide circulation of religious literature in this third period created a strong sense of Jewish unity, based upon a common religion and the Hebrew language. (Almost all educated Jews, regardless of what language they spoke, understood and employed Hebrew as a written language for their religion.)

The fourth and modern period of Jewish history is the one in which we live. It began at different times in different countries; many Israeli Jews passed directly from pre-modern to modern times. As discussed in Chapter 3 of our book, this phenomenon has been especially important for Oriental Jews. Our book emphasizes that Jewish fundamentalism arose as a reaction against the effects of modernity upon Jews. The influence of Jewish fundamentalism upon the Israeli Jewish community can only be understood adequately within the context of the entire course of Jewish history.

Jewish Fundamentalism Within Jewish Society

Almost every moderately sophisticated Israeli Jew knows the facts about Israeli Jewish society that are described in this book. These facts, however, are unknown to most interested Jews and non-Jews outside Israel who do not know Hebrew and thus cannot read most of what Israeli Jews write about themselves in Hebrew. These facts are rarely mentioned or are described inaccurately in the enormous media coverage of Israel in the United States and elsewhere. The major purpose of this book is to provide those persons who do not read Hebrew with more understanding of one important aspect of Israeli Jewish society.

This book pinpoints the political importance of Jewish fundamentalism in Israel, a powerful state in and beyond the Middle East that wields great influence in the United States. Jewish fundamentalism is here briefly defined as the belief that Jewish Orthodoxy, which is based upon the Babylonian Talmud, the rest of talmudic literature and halachic literature, is still valid and will eternally remain valid. Jewish fundamentalists believe that the Bible itself is not authoritative unless interpreted correctly by talmudic literature. Jewish fundamentalism exists not only in Israel but in every country that has a sizeable Jewish community. In countries other than Israel, wherein Jews constitute a small minority of the total population, the general importance of Jewish fundamentalism is limited mainly to acquiring funding and garnering political support for fundamentalist adherents in Israel. Its importance in Israel is far greater, because its adherents can and do influence the state in various ways. The variety of Jewish fundamentalism in Israel is striking. Many fundamentalists, for instance, want the temple rebuilt on the Temple Mount in Jerusalem or at least want to keep the site, which is now a holy Muslim praying place, empty of visitors. In the United States most Christians would not identify with such a purpose, but in Israel a significant number of Israeli Jews who are not fundamentalists identify with and support this and similar demands. Some varieties of Jewish fundamentalism are clearly more dangerous than others. Jewish fundamentalism is not only capable of influencing conventional Israeli policies but could also substantially affect Israeli nuclear policies. The same possible consequences of fundamentalism feared by many persons for other countries could occur in Israel.

The significance of fundamentalism in Israel can only be understood within the context of Israeli Jewish society and as part of the contribution of the Jewish religion to societal internal divisions. Our consideration of this broad topic begins by focusing upon the ways sophisticated observers divide Israeli Jewish society politically and religiously. We then proceed to the explanation of why Jewish fundamentalism influences in varying degrees other Israeli Jews, thereby allowing fundamentalist Jews to wield much greater political power in Israel than their percentage of the population might appear to warrant.

The customary two-way division of Israeli Jewish society rests upon the cornerstone recognition that as a group Israeli Jews are highly ideological. This is best evidenced by their high percentage of voting, which usually exceeds 80 per cent. In the May 1996 elections, over 95 per cent of the better educated, richer, secular Jews and the religious Jews in all categories of education and income voted. After discounting the large number of Israeli Jews who live outside Israel (over 400,000), most of whom did not vote, it can be safely assumed that almost every eligible voter in these two crucial segments of the population voted. Most Israeli political observers by now assume that Israeli Jews are divided into two categories: Israel A and Israel B. Israel A, often referred to as the "left," is politically represented by the Labor and Meretz Parties; Israel B, referred to as the "right" or the "right and religious parties," is comprised of all the other Jewish parties. Almost all of Israel A and a great majority of Israel B (the exception being some of the fundamentalist Jews) strongly adhere to Zionist ideology, which in brief, holds that all or at least the majority of Jews should emigrate to Palestine, which as the Land of Israel, belongs to all Jews and should be a Jewish state. A strong and increasing enmity between these two segments of Israeli society nevertheless exists. There are many reasons for this enmity. The reason relevant to this study is that Israel B, including its secular members, is sympathetic to Jewish fundamentalism while Israel A is not. It is apparent from studies of election results over a long period of time that Israel B has consistently obtained a numerical edge over Israel A. This is an indication that the number of Jews influenced by Jewish fundamentalism is consistently increasing.

In his article "Religion, Nationalism and Democracy in Israel," published in the Autumn 1994 issue of the periodical, *Z' Manim* (no. 50–51), Professor Baruch Kimmerling, a faculty member of Hebrew University's sociology department, presented data pertaining to the religious division of Israeli Jewish society. Citing numerous research studies, Kimmerling showed conclusively that Israeli Jewish society is far more divided on religious issues than is generally assumed outside of Israel, where belief in generalizations, such as "common to all Jews," is challenged less than in Israel. Quoting the data of a survey taken by the prestigious Gutman Institute of the Hebrew University in Jerusalem, Kimmerling pointed out that whereas 19 per cent of Israeli Jews said they prayed daily, another 19 per cent declared that they would not enter a synagogue under any circumstances.[1] Influenced by the Gutman Institute analysis and similar studies, Kimmerling and other scholars have concluded that Israel A and Israel B contain hard-core believers who hold diametrically opposed views of the Jewish religion. This conclusion is almost certainly correct.

More generally, the attitude towards religion in Israeli Jewish society can be divided into three parts. The religious Jews observe the commandments of the Jewish religion, as defined by Orthodox rabbis, many of whom emphasize observance more than belief. (The number of Reform and/or Conservative Jewish in Israel is small.) The traditional Jews keep some of the more important commandments while violating the more inconvenient ones; they do honor the rabbis and the religion. The secularists may occasionally enter a synagogue but respect neither the rabbis nor the religious institutions. The line between traditional and secular Jews is often vague, but the available studies indicate that 25 to 30 per cent of Israeli Jews are secular, 50 to 55 per cent are traditional and about 20 per cent are religious. Traditional Jews obviously belong to both the Israel A and Israel B categories.

Israeli religious Jews are divided into two distinctly different groups. The members of the religiously more extreme group are called Haredim. (The singular word is Haredi or Hared.) The members of the religiously more moderate group are called religious-national Jews. The religious-national Jews are sometimes called "knitted skullcaps" because of their head covering. Haredim usually wear black skullcaps that are never knitted, or hats. The religious-national Jews otherwise usually dress in the more usual Israeli fashion, while the Haredim almost always wear black clothes.

The Haredim are themselves divided into two parties. The first, Yahadut Ha'Torah (Judaism of the Law) is the party of the Ashkenazi Haredim who are of East European origin. Yahadut Ha'Torah itself is a coalition of two factions. The second is Shas, the party of the Oriental Haredim who are of Middle Eastern origin. (The differences between the two types of Haredim will be more specifically discussed in Chapter 3.) The religious-national Jews are organized in the National Religious Party (NRP). By analyzing the 1996 electoral vote and making some necessary adjustments, we can estimate the population percentages of these two groups of religious Jews. In the 1996 election the Haredi parties together won 14 of the 120 total Knesset seats. Shas won ten seats; Yahadut Ha' Torah won four. The NRP won nine seats. Some Israeli Jews admittedly voted for Shas because of talismans and amulets distributed by Shas that were supposedly valid only after a "correct" vote. Some NRP members and sympathizers, moreover, admittedly voted for secular right-wing parties. Everything considered, the Haredim probably constitute 11 per cent of the Israeli population and 13.4 per cent of the Israeli Jews; the NRP adherents probably constitute 9 per cent of the Israeli population and 11 per cent of the Israeli Jews.

The basic tenets of the two groups of religious Jews need some introductory explanation. The word "hared" is a common Hebrew word meaning "fearful." During early Jewish history, it meant "God-fearing" or exceptionally devout. In the mid-nineteenth century it was adopted, first in Germany and Hungary and later in other parts of the diaspora, as the name of the party of religious Jews that opposed any modern innovation. The Ashkenazi Haredim emerged as a backlash group opposed to the Jewish enlightenment in general and especially to those Jews who refused to accept the total authority of the rabbis and who introduced innovations into the Jewish worship and life style. Seeing that almost all Jews accepted these innovations, the Haredim reacted even more extremely and banned every innovation. The Haredim to date have insisted upon the strictest observance of the Halacha. An illustrative example of opposition to innovation is the previously mentioned and still current black dress of the Haredim; this was the dress fashion of Jews in Eastern Europe when the Haredim formed themselves into a party. Before that time Jews dressed in many different styles and were often indistinguishable in dress from their neighbors. After a brief time, almost all Jews except for the Haredim again dressed differently. The Halacha, moreover, does not enjoin Jews to dress in black and/or to wear thick black coats and heavy fur caps during the hot summer or at any other time. Yet, Haredim in Israel continue to do so in opposition to innovation; they insist that dress be kept as it was in Europe around 1850. All other considerations, including climatic ones, are overridden.

In contrast to the Haredim, the religious-nationalist Jews of the NRP made their compromises with modernity at the beginning of the 1920s when the split between the two large groupings in religious Judaism first appeared in Palestine. This can be immediately observed in their dress, which, with the exception of a small skullcap, is conventional. Even more importantly, this is evident in their selective observance of the Halacha, for example, in their rejection of many commandments regarding women. NRP members do not hesitate to admit women to positions of authority in many of their organizations and in the political party itself. Before both the 1992 and 1996 elections the NRP published and distributed an advertisement, containing photographs of various public figures including some women supporting the party, and boasted more broadly on television of female support. Haredim did not and would not do this. Even when Haredim, who ban television watching for themselves, decided to present some television election programs directed to other Jews, they insisted that all participants be male. During the 1992 campaign the editors of a Haredi weekly consulted the rabbinical censor about whether or not to publish the above-mentioned NRP advertisement. The rabbinical censor ordered the paper to publish the advertisement with all photographs of the NRP women blotted out. The editors did what the censor ordered. Outraged, the NRP sued the newspaper for libel and sought damages in Israeli secular courts, disregarding the rulings of Haredi rabbis prohibiting using secular courts to settle disputes among Jews.

The religious-nationalist Jewish compromises with modernity regarding women are exceedingly complicated in many ways. The Halacha forbids Jewish males to listen to women singing whether in a choir or solo regardless of what is sung. This is stated directly in the halachic ruling that a voice of a woman is adultery. This is interpreted by later halachic rulings stipulating that the word "voice" here means a woman's singing not speaking. This rule, originating in the Talmud, occurs in all codes of law. A Jewish male who willingly listens to a woman's singing commits a sin equivalent either to adultery or fornication. The great majority of NRP faithful members, nevertheless, listen to women singing and thus commit "adultery" routinely. Some of the most strict NRP members, especially among the religious settlers in the West Bank, have not only puzzled over this problem but at times have tried to solve the problem of how to adjust by developing creative approaches. In the early 1990s some of the settlers founded a new radio station, Arutz, or Channel, 7. For their station to become successful and to appeal as broadly as possible to Israeli Jews, the settlers understood that the songs of the fashionable singers of the day, some of whom were women, would have to be broadcast. The rabbinical censor, however, has refused to allow a breach of the Halacha whereby male listeners would hear female singers and thus commit "adultery." After further consultation with the censor, the settlers devised an acceptable solution that is still being employed. Men sing the songs, made popular by women; the male voices are then electronically changed to the female pitch and are broadcast accordingly over Arutz 7. A part of the traditional public is satisfied by this expedient, and the learned NRP rabbis insist that no adultery is committed when men listen to the songs being sung.

The Haredim obviously have rejected and condemned this accom-
modation and to date have refused to listen to Arutz 7. Even more
importantly, the Haredim, after increasing somewhat their political
power in the 1988 elections, were able to impose their position in
this regard upon the whole state by forcing a change in the opening
of the new Knesset session. The opening ceremony previously
began with the singing of "Hatikva," the Israeli national anthem,
by a mixed male–female choir. After the 1988 election, in deference
to Haredi sensitivities, a male singer replaced the mixed choir. After
the 1992 election, won by Labor, an all-male choir of the Military
Rabbinate sang "Hatikva."

How can the Haredim, who altogether constitute only a small
percentage of Israel's Jewish population, at times, either alone or
even with the help of the NRP, impose their will upon the rest of
society? The facile explanation is that both the Labor and Likud
parties kowtow to the Haredim for political support. This
explanation is insufficient. The kowtowing continued between
1984 and 1990 during the time that Labor and Likud had formed
a coalition. Currying favor from the Haredim for alignment purposes
was then politically unnecessary. The offered explanation,
furthermore, does not adequately take into account the special
affinity of all the religious parties, perceived since 1980 as fundamentalist, to Likud and other secular right-wing parties. This
affinity, especially between Likud and the Haredi religious parties,
based upon a shared world outlook, is at the crux of Israeli politics.
(This affinity is analogous to that existing between Christian and
Muslim fundamentalists and their secular right parties.) The
relatively simple case of the NRP illustrates this well. The NRP
recognizes, although does not always follow, the same halachic
authorities as do the Haredi parties. The NRP also adheres to the
same ideals relating to the Jewish past and, more importantly, to
the future when Israel's triumph over the non-Jews will allegedly
be secure. The differences between the NRP and the Haredim stem
from the NRP's belief that redemption has begun and will soon
be completed by the imminent coming of the Messiah. The Haredim
do not share this belief. The NRP believes that special circumstances
at the beginning of redemption justify temporary departures from
the ideal that could help advance the process of redemption. NRP
support in some situations for military service for talmudic scholars
is a relevant example here. These deviant NRP ideas have been
undermined since the 1970s by the expanding Haredi influence
upon increasing numbers of NRP followers who have resisted
departures from strict talmudic norms and have favored Haredi
positions. This process has been counter-balanced to some extent
by the growth in prestige of the NRP settlers who are esteemed as
pioneers of messianism even though the assassination of Prime

Minister Rabin by a messianist may have momentarily increased Haredi prestige.

The religious influence upon the Israeli right-wing of Israel B is attributable both to its militaristic character and its widely shared world outlook. Secular and militaristic right-wing, Israeli Jews hold political views and engage in rhetoric similar to that of religious Jews. For most Likud followers, "Jewish blood" is the reason why Jews are in a different category than non-Jews, including, of course, even those non-Jews who are Israeli citizens and who serve in the Israeli army. For religious Jews, the blood of non-Jews has no intrinsic value; for Likud, it has limited value. Menachem Begin's masterful use of such rhetoric about Gentiles brought him votes and popularity and thus constitutes a case in point. The difference in this respect between Labor and Likud is rhetorical but is nevertheless important in that it reveals part of a world outlook. In 1982, for example, when the Israeli army occupied Beirut, Rabin representing Labor, although advocating the same policies as favored by Sharon and Likud, did not explain the Sabra and Shatila Camp massacres by stating, as did Begin: "Gentiles kill Gentiles and blame the Jews." Even if Rabin had himself been capable of saying this, he knew that most of his secular supporters in Labor, who distinguish between Gentiles who hate Jews and those who do not, would not have tolerated such a statement. They would have repudiated such rhetoric as being both untrue and harmful.

Religious influence is evident in the right's general reverence for the Jewish past and its insistence that Jews have an historic right to an expanded Israel extending beyond its present borders. More than other secular Israelis, members of the Israeli right insist upon Jewish uniqueness. During many centuries of their existence, the great majority of Jews were similar in some ways to the present-day Haredim. Thus, those Jews who today revere the Jewish past as evidence of Jewish uniqueness respect to some extent religious Jews as perpetuators of that past. An essential part of the right's emphasis upon uniqueness is its hatred of the concept of "normality," that is, that Jews are similar to other people and have the same desire for stability as do other nations. Some cultural affinities between secular and religious Jews of the Israeli right are not primarily ideological. Many Likud supporters, whether Sephardic or Ashkenazi in origin, are traditionalists; they view rabbis as glamorous figures and are affected by childhood memories of the patriarchal family in which education was dominated by the grandfather and the women "knew their place." Although most pronounced in those of the religious vanguard, such considerations also affect secular Jews of the right. The right often exaggerates the beauty and superiority of the Jewish past, especially when arguing for the preservation of Jewish uniqueness.

The religious and secular members of the right share fears as well as beliefs. In an October 6, 1993, article, published in *Haaretz*, Israel's most prestigious daily Hebrew-language newspaper, Doron Rosenblum, relying upon varied sources, illustrated this by quoting pronouncements of Likud leaders that were designed to show Israelis the grave nature and risks of the peace process and at the same time to continue the boasting that Likud had initiated the process.

Rosenblum quoted the following statement by Likud Member of the Knesset (MK) Uzi Landau, who after the 1996 elections was appointed chairperson of the Knesset Committee for Defense and Foreign Affairs:

> If Rabin's policies toward Syria are followed, one morning they [Israeli Jews] will awaken to see columns of Syrian tanks descending from the Golan Heights like herds of sheep ... The settlements of the Galilee will then be attacked by fire-power stronger than that used in [the war of] 1973 ... Since the idea of extermination of Israelis remains a topic in the Syrian consciousness ... any [Israeli] withdrawal from the Golan Heights will only precipitate the moment that the Syrian knife will approach the throat of every inhabitant of the Galilee ... Syrian policies are fixed by a genetic code not subject to rapid changes.

Apparently keeping to its double-standard approach, the Western media, which would almost certainly have blasted any non-Jewish politician for attributing Israeli policies to a Jewish genetic code not subject to rapid changes, avoided commenting upon the Landau statement.

Rosenblum also quoted MK Benny Begin, a major Likud leader, who expressed the fear that Syria would make a frontal attack upon Israel. This fear is commonly expressed by members of most Israeli political parties. What is characteristic of Israel B, however, is that, as Benny Begin specifically declared, the aims of a Syrian invasion will be the same as "the aims of Pogromists of Kishinev to cut Jewish throats."[2] Begin added that this time nuclear scientists would help in the Syrian venture. Comparing the unarmed Jewish community, a small minority in the Russian Empire, with Israel and its army illustrates a common attitude to the Jewish past held by the secular right-wing Israeli parties and the religious Jews. This attitude takes no cognizance of historical development. Jews in whatever condition are always the real or potential victims of Gentiles.

Rosenblum, who is a member of Israel A, perceived all such imagery as incongruous. Observing that Landau regarded the Syrians as sheep, he asked: "Can it be that he [Landau] means to say that we are wolves?" Rosenblum then offered his analysis of why this rhetoric has nevertheless been so persuasive:

> The suspicion is long-standing that members of the national camps [that is, the secular right] use power-mad rhetoric to cover their subliminal existential fear of the entire world. This fear was not dispelled in the slightest when the state of Israel was founded. Labor, in spite of all its faults, has succeeded by whatever means to cast aside such fear and replace it with a constructive and pragmatic world outlook. Likud, which resumed its historical note with ease, has not.

Those chauvinistic Jews who speak with utmost confidence about Israel's power and ability to impose its will upon the Middle East are most susceptible to such fears. The same people who predict that a second Holocaust will almost immediately occur if Israel makes any concession to the Arabs also often state categorically that the Israeli army, if not restrained by politicians, by Americans, or by leftist Jews, could conquer Baghdad within one week. (Ariel Sharon actually made this claim a few months before the outbreak of the October 1973 war.) The fear and the self-confidence co-exist harmoniously. The belief in Jewish uniqueness enhances this co-existence. Most foreign observers do not realize that a sizeable segment of the Israeli Jewish public holds these chauvinistic views. The schizophrenic blend of inordinate fears and exaggerated self-confidence, common to the Israeli secular right and religious Jews, resembles ideas held by anti-Semites who usually view Jews as being at the same time both powerful and easy to defeat. This is one of the reasons why attitudes of Israeli right-wing individuals toward the Gentiles, especially toward the Arabs, resemble so closely the attitudes of anti-Semites toward the Jews.

The secular right and the religious Jews also share other fears. They fear the West and its public opinion. They fear and condemn Jewish leftists, a term sufficiently broad to include most Labor followers, for not being sufficiently Jewish, for preferring Arabs to Jews and for living lives of delusion. They view the left as dangerous because of its ability to attract new recruits, especially from the ranks of the country's intellectual elite.

The issue of normalcy most divides the Israeli right from the left. The left longs for normalcy and wants Jews to be a nation like all other nations. The entire Israeli right, on the other hand, is united in its resentment of the idea of normalcy and its belief, along the lines of the Jewish religion, that Jews are exceptional – different from other people and nations. Reverence for the national past allegedly solidifies this uniqueness. Religious Jews believe that God made the Jews unique; many of the secular right believe that

Jews are doomed to be unique by their past and have no free choice in this matter.

Another, but somewhat less important, reason for the affinity between the secular right and religious Jews is that the latter are capable of providing "convincing" arguments for perpetual Jewish rule over the land of Israel and for the denial of certain basic rights to the Palestinians. These arguments are not only put in terms of national security but more importantly in terms of the God-given right to these territories. The secular Likud scholars and politicians are often far too alienated from the Jewish past and Jewish values to talk competently, or indeed even to understand properly, such matters. Only the religious can provide an in-depth rationale for Likud's policies, which are grounded not in short-term strategic considerations but rather in the long history of the special relationship between God and his chosen people.

Although far more intense among members of Israel B, these same sentiments can be discerned among members of Israel A. This fact provides the explanation for the political concessions made to the religious parties. (Foreign observers have too often incorrectly attributed these concessions merely to the size and/or the lobbying power of the religious parties.) These sentiments have also affected Jewish historiography and education. Since the late 1950s, and especially after the 1967 war, Israeli Jewish historians, scholars in allied fields and popularizers, although generally less dishonest in their writings than most of their diaspora colleagues, have too often unduly beautified and romanticized past Jewish societies and have carefully avoided normal criticism. This type of apologia constituted a new trend. From the late nineteenth century until the mid-twentieth century, early Zionists and others in modern Jewish movements were severely critical of many aspects of their own religious cultural tradition and tried to change, in many cases even to destroy, parts of that tradition. Since the late 1980s, some younger Israeli historians, perhaps prompted by a growing polarization of Israeli Jewish society, have written and published some critical works that have shaken to some extent the still current apologetic trend.

The comparison of the world outlook and fears of the secular right with those of the Haredim requires more explanation. Standard Haredic perceptions of the world can only be understood as relics of pre-modern times. Menachem Friedman, a Westernized observant Jew, a highly regarded authority on the Haredim in both mandatory Palestine and the state of Israel and a professor at the religious Bar-Ilan University, provided an excellent description of these Haredic perceptions in a *Davar* article published on November 4, 1988. Friedman wrote this article to explain the electoral fiasco that developed from the unsuccessful attempt of some candidates on the religious list of 1988 to advocate some moderation regarding the treatment of Palestinians. Friedman explained:

> The Haredi world is Judeocentric. The essence of Haredi thought is the notion of an abyss separating the Jews from the Gentiles. This is why any coalition between Labor and Haredi doves is impossible. There actually is no such thing as a Haredi dove. People who speak about the Haredi world usually do not know how to read its signs. They do not understand that world nor its prominent personalities. The distance between Haredi doves and hawks is not great. Haredi doves and hawks share a common point of departure. Both see the relationship between non-Jews and Jews as they had seen them before Israel was established. They assume that non-Jews and Jews are poles apart. Non-Jews want to kill and destroy the Jews; the rightful differences between Jews should only be about how they should react to the ever-present non-Jewish desire. Currently, these are two alternative Haredi reactions to that common assumption. Rabbi Shach [the spiritual leader of one of the two Haredi factions] says that since the non-Jews hate us we need to keep quiet and refrain from provoking them by not reminding them of our existence. The Lubovitcher Rebbe says that we should be strong. [The Lubovitcher Rebbe, Rabbi Menachem Schneerson, died in 1992.] Those are two alternative answers, both arising from the common concept that a gap separates Jews from non-Jews. Rabbi Shach is not a dove in the same sense as Shulamit Aloni [a former Meretz Party leader] is a dove. Aloni is a dove, because she believes in a humanism that emphasizes the fundamental equality of all human beings and nations and the capability of different human beings and nations to communicate. Rabbi Shach believes that communicating with non-Jews is not possible and that they may only be able to forget that Jews exist. The Lubovitcher Rebbe states that we should be strong in order to defend ourselves against the non-Jews who always want to destroy us. [The difference between the two leaders] can be illustrated by their respective attitudes toward the peace [treaty] with Egypt. They both say that there is no peace and there can never be one, because the Egyptians want to exterminate us. Rabbi Shach, however, adds that we should try to minimize [Jewish casualties] by keeping quiet. The Lubovitcher Rebbe says that, because the peace does not exist in any case, we should refuse to make any concessions. The Haredi dove does not believe in any kind of peace, and, therefore, all the talk about a narrow coalition, headed by Labor [and including Haredim] is completely baseless.

Subsequent political developments in Israel, including the election of Netanyahu in May 1996, have confirmed the truth of Professor Friedman's analysis. From another Haredi perspective Rabbi Ovadia Yoseph, the spiritual authority of the Shas Party, corroborated this article. Rabbi Yoseph argued in a September 18, 1989 article in *Yated Ne'eman* that since Israel is too weak to demolish all Christian churches in the Holy Land it is also too weak to retain all the conquered territories. Using this reasoning, Rabbi Yoseph advocated that Israel make territorial concessions in order to avert a war in which Jewish lives will be lost. Rabbi Yoseph did not mention Palestinians nor even their most rudimentary rights. The Haredi world view is similar to the view held by the Israeli secular right. The world view of Likud politicians, enthusiastically supported by followers, is basically the classic world view of religious Jews; it has undergone significant secularization but has kept its essential qualities.

The alliance between the religious and secular parties of the right produced the Netanyahu victory in the 1996 election. This alliance was forged in spite of two deep political differences between the parties. The first difference concerns democracy, especially as illustrated by the structure of Israeli parties; the second difference revolves around Zionism.

All Israeli political parties except for the Haredi were and remain structured along the lines of parties in Western countries, especially those in the United States. Most of the Israeli parties, for example, introduced primaries in order to choose their candidates for the Knesset elections. The Haredi party structure, however, is different and peculiar, perhaps analogous only to what has happened in Iran. All the Haredi parties have a two-tier structure. The tier that is lower in importance includes the acting politicians, who, even if they are ministers or Knesset members, humbly profess in public that they are merely serving the party's rabbinical sage councils whom they consult for directions before making any decisions. None of the Haredi politicians of any one party accept direction from rabbinical councils of other Haredi parties. The councils' deliberations are kept secret; their decisions are not subject to any appeal since they are regarded as divinely inspired. The council members are not elected either by rabbis or lay people. If a council member dies, his successor is appointed by the remaining members. The rabbinical members of Haredi party councils, usually referred to by their followers as sages, make all decisions and view with suspicion the usual party structure, because it is viewed as innovative and modern. The modern political party structure, including membership, branches, internal elections and a host of other items that exist in the NRP, is totally absent in the Haredi parties. The disagreement and sometimes even hatreds of one another by Haredi parties stem from recognition of different rabbinical "sages" as final authorities. The Haredi political structure has preserved a male monopoly. To date, there have been no female Haredi politicians. Haredi disunity has prevented more rapid Haredization of parts of Israeli society. Structure similar to the Haredi was common in Jewish communities from the second century of the common era until the abolition of Jewish communal autonomy in modern nation states. The aim of Haredi practices has been and still is to preserve the Jewish way of life as it existed prior to modern times. Haredi parties, in their attempt to preserve an ancient Jewish regime, have to date constituted a political backlash directed against the tide of modernity that engulfed the NRP. The Haredi reaction, like many others, is often disguised as a romantic desire to return to a past that was allegedly happier and more emotionally secure for Jews than the modern life with its doubts and uncertainties. The Haredi-indoctrinated community strives to suppress all doubts of members and believes that happiness is thus achieved.

The disagreement between Haredim and most other Israeli Jews over Zionism is complex. The Haredim and the Zionists agree about the centrally important Zionist principle that anti-Semitism is an eternal quality common to all non-Jews and is different from xenophobia and/or any hatred of other minorities. This view is, of course, similar to that held of Jews by anti-Semites. (This similarity probably accounts for the political contact between some Zionists, beginning with Herzl, and "moderate" anti-Semites, who only wanted to rid their societies of Jews or limit the numbers of Jews in their societies without killing them.) The views concerning and the fears of anti-Semitism shared by the secular right and the Haredim accord with this central principle of Zionism better than do the views currently held by the left Labor and Meretz parties, which are frequently accused by Likud of not being sufficiently Zionist.

Haredi ideology nevertheless clashes with Zionism on certain other principles. Two major examples are the Zionist aims to concentrate all Jews, or as many as possible, in and to establish a Jewish state in Palestine. These aims or dogmas contradict the Haredi interpretations of the Talmud and talmudic commentaries. Because of the perceived contradiction, Haredim have consistently proclaimed, and still proclaim, their strong opposition to Zionism; they claim that the state of Israel is merely another diaspora for Jews, and they avoid using Zionist symbols. Every Israeli political party other than the Haredi, including the NRP, end or begin their conventions with the singing of "Hatikva," the Israeli national and the world Zionist movement anthem; the Haredi parties and organizations do not do this but instead recite Jewish prayers. The media often condemns the Haredim for not singing "Hatikva" on official occasions. At all international Zionist conventions held in Israel only the Israeli flag is displayed. At Haredi conventions held in Israel all flags of the nation states from which delegates came, including Israel, are displayed in alphabetical order.

The Haredi objection to Zionism is based upon the contradiction between classical Judaism, of which the Haredim are the continuators, and Zionism. Numerous Zionist historians have unfortunately obfuscated the issues here. Some detailed explanation is therefore necessary. In a famous talmudic passage in *Tractate Ketubot*, page 111, which is echoed in other parts of the Talmud, God is said to have imposed three oaths on the Jews. Two of these oaths that clearly contradict Zionist tenets are: 1) Jews should not rebel against non-Jews, and 2) as a group should not massively emigrate to Palestine before the coming of the Messiah. (The third oath, not discussed here, enjoins the Jews not to pray too strongly for the coming of the Messiah, so as not to bring him before his appointed time.) During the course of post-talmudic Jewish history, rabbis extensively discussed the three oaths. Of major concern in this discussion was the question of whether or not specific Jewish emigration to Palestine was part of the forbidden massive emigration. During the past 1,500 years, the great majority of traditional Judaism's most important rabbis interpreted the three oaths and the continued existence of the Jews in exile as religious obligations intended to expiate the Jewish sins that caused God to exile them.

In recent years, a number of Israeli Jewish scholars, who in general have developed a more honest Jewish historiography, have focused upon the essence of rabbinical interpretations of the three oaths. In his highly regarded scholarly book, *Messianism, Zionism and Jewish Religious Radicalism* (published in Hebrew in Israel in 1993), Aviezer Ravitzky, for example, provided a good summary of rabbinical interpretations of the three oaths from the fifth century AD (or CE – Common Era). In his analysis Ravitzky noted that in the ninth century Rabbi Shmuel, son of Hosha'ana, an important leader of Palestinian Jewry, in a poetic prayer quoted the following as God's words. "I took the oath of my people not to rebel against Christians and Muslims, told them to be silent until I myself will overturn them as I did in Sodom." In the thirteenth century during the time that some rabbis and poets emigrated to Palestine for religious reasons,[3] Ravitzky continued, other rabbis in many parts of the world quoted the three oaths theory to warn against the spread of this potentially dangerous phenomenon. Rabbi Eliezer, son of Moshe, the spiritual leader of a Jewish congregation in Wurtzburg, Germany, in the thirteenth century warned Jews who wrongly emigrated to Palestine that God would punish them with death. At about the same time, Rabbi Ezra of Gerona, Spain, a famous cabbalist, wrote that a Jew emigrating to Palestine forsakes God who is only present in the diaspora, where a majority of Jews live, and not in Palestine. In his book Ravitzky stressed that similar and even more extreme views continued to be expressed until the nineteenth century. The celebrated German rabbi, Yehonathan Eibshutz, wrote in the mid-eighteenth century that massive immigration of Jews to Palestine, even with the consent of all the nations of the world, was prohibited before the coming of the Messiah. In the early nineteenth century, Moses Mendelsohn and other supporters of the Jewish Enlightenment, as well as their opponents such as Rabbi Rafael Hirsch, the father of modern orthodoxy in Germany, agreed and continued to derive this prohibition from the three oaths. Hirsch wrote in 1837 that God had commanded Jews "never to establish a state of their own by their own efforts." Rabbis in Central Europe were even more extreme. In 1837, the same year that Hirsch prohibited Jews from declaring a Jewish state, an earthquake in northern Palestine killed a majority of the inhabitants of Safad, of which many were Jews, some of whom had recently immigrated. Rabbi Moshe Teitelbaum, a leading Hungarian rabbi, attributed the earthquake to God's displeasure with excessive Jewish emigration to Palestine. Teitelbaum stated: "It is not God's will that we should go to the land of Israel by our own efforts and will." Rabbi Moshe Nachmanides, who died in 1270, was the one exceptional Jewish leader who opined that Jews should not only emigrate to but should also conquer the land of Israel. Other important rabbis of that time and for many centuries thereafter ignored or strongly disagreed with the view of Nachmanides.

In the 1970s, seven centuries after his death, Nachmanides became the patron saint of the NRP and the Gush Emunim settlers. NRP rabbis also have claimed that the three oaths do not apply in messianic times and that, although the Messiah has not yet appeared, a cosmic process called the beginning of redemption has begun. During this period some of the previous religious laws should allegedly be disregarded; others should be changed. Thus, the dispute between the NRP and the Haredim has centered upon the issue of whether Jews are living in normal times or in the period of the beginning of redemption. Having made some political gains and becoming more self-confident after the 1988 national election, the Haredim strengthened their principled opposition to Zionism and to the NRP. In 1989, the two most important Haredi rabbis, Rabbi Shach and Rabbi Yoseph, held an anti-Zionist convention in Bnei Brak, Israel. Their speeches, devoted to expressions of principled opposition to Zionism and the beginning of redemption doctrine, were published in the Haredi newspaper, *Yated Ne'eman*, on September 18, 1989. The two rabbis from an halachic perspective also addressed the vital Israeli political issue of whether some areas of the land of Israel should be given to non-Jews, that is, to Palestinians. They refuted the NRP and Gush Emunim view that in accordance with the beginning of redemption no land of Israel should be given to non-Jews. Rabbi Yoseph and Shach argued that Jews still live in normal times when visible help of God cannot always be expected to save Jewish lives.

Rabbi Yoseph, renowned for his halachic erudition, presented in-depth analysis and correctly noted that Rabbi Shach here agreed fully with him. Rabbi Yoseph began by disagreeing with the NRP and Gush Emunim rabbis who argued that the beginning of redemption and God's commandment to conquer the land of Israel were more important than the saving of Jewish lives that would be lost in the war of conquest. Rabbi Yoseph acknowledged that in messianic times Jews would be more powerful than non-Jews and would then be obligated to conquer the land of Israel, to expel all non-Jews and to destroy the idolatrous Christian churches. Rabbi Yoseph, however, asserted that the messianic time of redemption had not yet arrived. He wrote:

> The Jews are not in fact more powerful than the non-Jews and are unable to expel the non-Jews from the land of Israel because the Jews fear the non-Jews ... God's commandment is then not valid ... Even non-Jews who are idolaters live among us with no possibility of their being expelled or even moved. The Israeli government is obligated by international law to guard the Christian churches in the land of Israel, even though those churches are definitely places of idolatry and cult practice. This is so in spite of the fact that we are commanded by our [religious] law to destroy all idolatry and its servants until we uproot it from all parts of our land and any areas that we are able to conquer ... Surely, this fact continues to weaken the religious meaning of the Israeli army's conquests [in 1967].

The quotation cited above illustrates well a part of Israel's *realpolitik*. Before the 1996 election, both Peres and Netanyahu regarded Rabbi Yoseph as an important political figure and often courted him openly. This was done in spite of Yoseph's publicly declared doctrine that Jews, when sufficiently powerful, have a religious obligation to expel all non-Jews from the country and destroy all Christian churches. Leftists and most peace advocates in Israel lauded Yoseph and Shach for agreeing to withdrawal from the occupied territories but neglected to mention and actually suppressed the major thrust of the Yoseph and Shach position. For the most part the Western media avoided reporting the most essential points of the Yoseph speech. The reality here is that the

Yoseph–Shach view constitutes one part of the hawkish heart of Israeli politics.

In his speech Rabbi Yoseph also acknowledged the halachic prohibition of selling real estate to non-Jews in the land of Israel, but he limited this prohibition to a time when doing so would not cause the loss of Jewish life. In the same manner he dealt with the issue of whether Jews should trust only in the hope of God's help or should take their own precautions against danger or war. Yoseph contended that this issue is analogous to the question of whether a Jew who is ill on Yom Kippur should be given food to save his or her life. In the latter case, according to Rabbi Yoseph, the Jew who is ill should be given food even if the medical experts disagree with one another about the danger to life that would exist if the fast were observed. Following this line of reasoning, Rabbi Yoseph opined that, even if the military experts disagreed with one another as to whether withdrawal from the territories would avert war, the government should order withdrawal. Rabbi Yoseph, not influenced by the trusting-in-God argument, pointed out that Jews had been killed in previous wars and that the miraculous coming of the Messiah establishing God's rule over the world would occur without the loss of a single Jewish life. Rabbi Yoseph also noted that the state of Israel is filled with Jewish sinners who provoke God. He quoted numerous rabbinical authorities who agreed with him that the three oaths were still valid.

Rabbi Yoseph's view did not interest Rabin, Peres or Netanyahu. His dazzling display of erudition, occupying three large pages of small print, moreover, did not convince a single NRP rabbi. Rabbis Yoseph and Shach, who a bit later became enemies, continued to oppose Zionism and the beginning of redemption doctrine; they continued to advocate their variety of Jewish fundamentalism and to command the allegiance in 1996 of fourteen members of the 120-member Knesset. Rabbi Shach, who is more extreme in his opposition to Zionism than is Rabbi Yoseph, prohibited the Knesset members of his political party, Yahadut Ha'Torah, from becoming ministers in Netanyahu's Zionist government. Shach, however, ordered his party's Knesset members to support the Netanyahu government. Netanyahu rewarded Yahadut Ha'Torah by creatively giving it control of the ministry of housing. Netanyahu made himself the housing minister and signed almost blindly anything submitted by Deputy Minister Ravitz of the Yahadut Ha'Torah Party. This procedure was obviously employed to obviate the necessity of Yahadut Ha'Torah's formally joining a Zionist government while nevertheless enjoying its benefits. Contrary to Rabbi Shach, Rabbi Yoseph ordered members of his party to become ministers in the Netanyahu government. These facts illustrated the political importance of Rabbis Yoseph's and Shach's views.

Rabbi Yoseph's clearly expressed views on the territories not only reflect the Haredi view but also clearly resemble a great part of the actual foreign policy of the state of Israel. Rabbi Yoseph has argued that Jews have a religious duty to expel all Christians from the state of Israel only if doing so would not endanger Jewish life. Rabbi Yoseph has postulated that any Jewish concessions to non-Jews in the state of Israel has to be based solely upon the consideration of whether denial thereof could prove harmful for Jews. Rabbi Yoseph would almost certainly have favored a permanent occupation of all the territories if he were convinced that this would not provoke Arabs to harm Jews. Israeli governmental leaders with almost full support of Israeli Jews believed after the June 1967 war that the Arabs were incapable of harming Israel and therefore refused to make any concessions. Only after suffering grievous losses in the October 1973 war, and fearing another war, did the government of the state of Israel, again with almost the full support of Israeli Jews, agreed to return the Sinai to Egypt. In 1983, even after the massacres at Sabra and Shatila, the Israeli leaders contemplated permanent occupation of one-third of Lebanon and domination of the remaining two-thirds. Sharon concluded a peace treaty, based upon those terms, with the then puppet Lebanese government. The guerilla warfare, conducted by the Lebanese in 1984 and 1985, which resulted in consistent Israeli casualties, caused the Israeli leaders to abandon those plans and to retreat. Israeli foreign policy, although usually conceived and conducted by secular Jews, has to date displayed an essence derived in part from the Jewish religious past. Indeed, the Zionist movement, which underwent a partial secularization, also kept many basic Jewish religious principles. Rabbi Yoseph, Ben-Gurion, Sharon and all major Israeli politicians share a common ground in policy advocacy.

2

The Rise of the Haredim in Israel

Although expanding steadily from the early 1970s, Jewish religious fundamentalism in Israel attracted relatively little interest in the dominant secularly oriented Israeli society until 1988. Members of the various Haredi sects, generally self-contained in residentially segregated areas of Israeli cities, led lives absorbed by concerns and preoccupations that appeared exotic at best to outsiders. Although some members of these sects clashed sharply over specific issues with the secular part of Israeli society and at those times acquired a bit of public attention, they were mostly ignored. The sensational Haredi political success in the Israeli parliamentary elections of 1988, predicted by none of the professional pollsters, surprised many people. Because of their continued political successes in succeeding elections through the 1990s, the Haredim put themselves into a position at various times to be able to dictate to the Israeli secular majority.

The Haredi political successes not only caused many Israeli Jews to look more closely at and to be more concerned with the Haredim but also sparked increased attention abroad, especially in the United States. The interest generated in the United States prompted the writing and publication of many new books and articles in English that focused upon the folkloristic aspects of the Haredim but unfortunately largely ignored their basic ideology and world outlook. The following discussion will attempt to analyze, particularly for those readers who are not literate in Hebrew, the political importance of the Haredi upsurge. A crucial part of this analysis is the acceptance of the well-documented proposition that an understanding of the entire Israeli political right is to some extent dependent upon an understanding of the basic elements of Heredi politics, apart from the disagreements, splits and reunification efforts of many Heredi individuals and sects. The two major questions to be analyzed are:

- How have the Haredi parties secured their political influence?
- What organizational structure have the Haredi employed for maximum political success?

Concern with education has provided the major answer to both questions. The Haredi have on balance successfully educated their own children and other Jewish children, over whom they have obtained custody, in a manner guaranteeing maximum continuity. The Haredi have influenced many Israeli Jews in addition to their own by acquiring direct authority over several school networks and by indirectly influencing numbers of other schools.

Throughout the twentieth century, the Haredim have attempted to continue Jewish education as it had mostly existed in the diaspora before the Enlightenment influenced Jewish society. The governments in the countries in which the Haredim lived, however, have at times insisted upon some modernized curricular content that was inconsistent with and in opposition to what had previously been taught in Jewish schools. This was the case in Israel until 1980. Since 1980, helped by generous Israeli governmental subsidies, the Haredim have attempted with some success to reimpose the earlier type of Jewish education and the earlier school networking system in many poorer provincial Israeli towns and in slum areas of larger Israeli cities. The Haredi goal has obviously been to perpetuate their educational influence upon an increasing segment of younger-generation Israelis.

Historically, Jewish schooling began with the heder for Jewish male children aged three or four. (The heder, a word meaning 'room' in Hebrew, was the name of the traditional Jewish elementary school as it existed from talmudic times in the earliest centuries of the Common Era until the formation of the first modern nation-states at which time many Jews strove to modify or abolish the heder.) The heder was previously for males only. According to the Talmud and the Halacha, females do not need education and are explicitly forbidden from some forms of study. Until modern times, most Jewish women received no formal education and were mostly illiterate. This stood in striking contrast to Jewish males. Faced with governments of modern nation states and with many Jews themselves reacting against and abolishing the exclusion of females from formal education, the Haredim established special institutions to train, more precisely to indoctrinate, young Haredi girls to accept and to agree to inferior education. Heder education consists only of sacred, Jewish studies. Secular subjects, including arithmetic, foreign languages, science, literature and Hebrew grammar are excluded. Most of the Bible is included among subjects not taught. After studying the Pentateuch with the help of a commentary by Rashi (Rabbi Shlomo Yitzhaki who died in 1099), the students proceed directly to study of the easier parts of the Talmud. After studying about eight years, the less capable students are sent to various places to learn a craft, trade or some other occupation; the more capable are admitted to an institution of higher learning called a yeshiva. (Yeshiva in Hebrew means sitting or meeting.) Usually, several levels of "yeshivot" (plural) exist. The weeding-out process of students continues at each level. Those students who are found to be less capable are directed to moneymaking pursuits and somewhat later to involvement in religious services as minor rabbis or as supervisors of religious kashrut rules in restaurants, hospitals, the army and other institutions. The more capable students proceed in their learning by going from one yeshiva level to another. After graduating from the highest yeshiva and marrying, the best of the students spend their lives in an institution called a kollel (a term derived from the word meaning "entire") and spend their time studying only talmudic literature. A few of the most capable are later appointed to high rabbinic positions or become heads of yeshivot or kollels.

As mentioned previously, traditional Jewish education, described above, does not include any secular or humanistic studies. It is worth re-emphasizing that this exclusion of secular subjects includes not only mathematics, all sciences and foreign languages but also Hebrew literature, which includes poetry dealing with religious subjects, grammar and Jewish history. It is thus no surprise that Hebrew religious poetry, even the medieval masterpieces, are unknown to the Haredim. Only the sacred studies (a pre-modern term in Judaism) are taught with the greatest possible intensity. The sacred studies consist mostly of the Talmud and some subsequent talmudic literature. At the highest yeshiva level, one out of twelve to fourteen hours per day of sacred studies may be devoted to the study of morality, which primarily consists of lurid descriptions of the punishment, inflicted by God either in the life of this world or in hell, for even the smallest deviations from religious commandments. The teachings of the biblical prophets, the books of Job and Ecclesiastes and numerous other parts of the Bible are studied neither in the heders nor the yeshivot and are therefore unknown to the Haredim. Except for the Pentateuch, Haredim know only those parts of the Bible quoted in the Talmud and then only within the context of talmudic interpretation. Haredim generally lack knowledge of major parts of the Bible; this lack of knowledge constitutes one source of the differences between the Haredim and some other religious as well as most secular Israeli Jews. Yeshiva students are often deprived of sleep. After reaching the age of sixteen, Yeshiva students devote at least twelve to fourteen hours per day to study. The classes are noisy, because the students shout about what they are studying. Studying in silence is considered to be a sin. Chaos is often the result in the classroom; different students often shout about different passages of texts. Students may ask questions about the internal matters of what is being studied but never about the assumptions upon which inter-pretations are made or about the external world. Students are most often isolated from the outside world, especially from the secular world. Students are prohibited from contact with unbelievers. The teacher's authority is extensive and almost absolute. The main teacher or the head of the yeshiva usually will select the wives for students.

The type of education described above has shaped human character. It also inevitably has produced dissenters. The first Jewish dissenters from Judaism in modern times rebelled against this type of education and became principled opponents of the religion that from their perspectives tried to subject them to such totalitarian controls. Other individuals, schooled in the Haredi tradition, have ultimately yielded to temptations of modernity, such as watching television and attending movies. This usually has resulted in a weakening of commitment to Haredi Judaism but seldom to its renunciation. In Israel such persons have been and still are called "traditional" or "Mesorati." These people have usually remained – and still are – outwardly uncritical of what they learned; they have continued to worship the charismatic rabbis without paying any price for renunciating the prohibition of forbidden secular pleasures. Others who have strayed but have not undergone self-emancipation have after a temporary break returned to sacred studies to be again indoctrinated by their education.

The Haredim emphasize the sanctity and predominant importance of the sacred studies; they believe that the virtue emanating from those engaged in sacred studies is responsible for all good happenings for Jews. For that reason those who engage in sacred studies are not required to make their own livings, are granted numerous privileges and are exempted from communal duties. All of this originated and became universal among Jews in talmudic times. Living in autonomous communities, in which they retained local rule, Jews could and did determine that individuals engaged in sacred studies be exempted from paying taxes and from most other obligations and burdens for which members of the community were responsible. Additionally, the disciples of the sages, those who reached a specified high degree of proficiency in the sacred studies, were granted special privileges in many areas of life over which the Jewish community had control. During talmudic times (c. AD 200–500) in Iraq, for example, the disciples of the sages, who also were merchants, were granted the privilege of selling their merchandise before ordinary Jews were allowed to do so in the markets of Jewish towns. That meant that these disciples of the sages had no competition.

A burning issue in Jewish history, and in Israeli politics, is how rabbis and rabbinical students earn their livelihoods. In Israel the constantly increasing burden of support weighs heavily upon taxpayers, most of whom are not religious. This has provoked and continues to provoke resentment, especially when combined with the fact that a majority of rabbinical students do not have to serve in the army. Most Israeli religious Jews, especially the Haredim, attempt to justify state support and freedom from army service by arguing that the Jews and the Jewish state of Israel exist by virtue of their support of talmudic study. Their support is supposedly responsible in turn for God's support, which includes God's allowing Israel to win its wars. This argument, similar to arguments made by clergy of other religions and frequently emphasized in the Israeli media, alleges that God's help not soldiers win wars. This argument specifies that God provides other benefits as well. He, for example, grants good weather because of rabbis and students who spend most of their time studying Talmud. Engaging in such study is the best way, better than reciting prayers, giving charity or performing other good deeds, to gain entrance into paradise. Those who engage in talmudic study make it possible for themselves, their families, their financial supporters and, to some extent, other Jews to enter paradise.

Direct financial support of rabbis and students of Talmud is, nevertheless, a relatively new innovation in Judaism. During the lengthy period of Talmud composition, approximately 50 BC to AD 500, and for centuries thereafter, rabbis and students received no salaries or any other forms of financial support for talmudic study. (Elementary teachers who taught Bible to small children were paid.) Indeed, the Talmud itself prohibited payments for talmudic study. Some talmudic sages were working-class people who had well-known professions and earned their livelihoods from their labors. The only form of financial reward that was allowed for a talmudic sage was a recompense for not working. This can be illustrated by a talmudic anecdote about one of the most important sages, Abaye, who lived in Babylonia in the fourth century AD. Abaye was a farmer and cultivated his farm by himself. If asked a question by someone while working, he told the questioner: "Work on this irrigation canal for me while I ponder your question." The last important rabbi who fully supported such behavior was Maimonides, who died in 1204. Maimonides' ruling in his *Learning Torah Laws* (chapter 3, verse 10) is often quoted by secular, Jewish Israelis:

> Anyone supposing that he will engage in Torah [talmudic study] and not engage in labor, thus taking his livelihood from charity, should be considered a person who has extinguished the light of religion, put Torah to shame, caused evil to himself and lost his chance to enter paradise, since it is forbidden to make profit form the sayings of Torah in this world. The sages said: "Everyone who makes profit from the sayings of Torah loses his life." They

[the sages] have also ordered and said: "Do not make it [Torah] either a crown in which to boast or an axe with which to work." And they [the sages] have further ordered and said: "Love labor and hate the rabbinate." All Torah not accompanied by labor will be nullified, and the end of such a person [so engaged] will be that he will rob the people.

Many Israeli secular Jews use this statement of Maimonides to document their contention that all rabbis, especially rabbis in Israel, are robbers.

Why for centuries have almost all religious Jews not paid attention to the opinion of Maimonides, which is solidly based on many talmudic passages? The answer is that religious Jews read any sacred text, including the Talmud and the writings of Maimonides, only with the help of the most sacred commentaries that become the accepted religious opinions. Regarding the above-quoted passage of Maimonides, the most important, subsequent commentary is "Kesef Mishne" ("an addition of silver"), written by Rabbi Joseph Karo, who died in 1575. Karo, the author of *Shulhan Aruch* which to date is the most authoritative compendium of the Halacha, opposed the opinion of Maimonides on this issue. Almost all subsequent rabbis accepted the opposing position of Karo. In the beginning of his "Kesef Mishne," Karo mentioned that Maimonides in his commentary on Mishne wrote at length against salaries of rabbis and presented a sizeable list of talmudic rabbis who were laborers receiving no salaries for talmudic studies. Karo wrote:

He, let his memory be blessed [Maimonides], brought the example of Hillel, who was a wood-cutter while a talmudic student. This is not proof. We must assume that he [Hillel] engaged in labor only at the beginning of his studies. In his [Hillel's] time there were thousands of talmudic students; perhaps, they gave financial support only to the most famous among them ... But how can we assume that when Hillel became famous and was teaching the people they did not give him financial support?

Religious Jews in Israel use this form of reasoning, which without adequate proof attributes customs of current rabbis to the hallowed past. Secular Israeli Jews often have satirized such reasoning by telling a joke that is known to almost every Israeli Jew. This joke is based upon the fact that, although no halachic reference exists concerning an obligation of a male Jew to wear a head covering, there is no other visible custom to which religious Jews are universally so faithful. Indeed, the popular Hebrew saying for a formerly religious male that became secular is "He took off his skullcap." The joke centers upon a rabbi's being asked to provide the proof for the obligation that male Jews must wear head coverings. The rabbi in the joke answers: "The Bible says: 'And Abraham went' [to a certain place]. Can you imagine that he went without a head covering?" The joke's ridiculing of the usual mode of rabbinic reasoning is obvious.

Karo argued that all famous sages, described in the Talmud itself as laborers or craftsmen, must have been given financial support. Karo concluded by arguing that priests in the temple were paid for their work and that, therefore, rabbis, who are equivalent to priests, should be paid. Talmudic students should be paid, Karo maintained, because without students there would be no rabbis. "Those in control of the usual expenditures [in Jewish congregations] should be compelled to pay the rabbis," he stated. "The current custom is that all Jewish rabbis receive their salaries from the [Jewish] public." This was the general custom in the sixteenth century, except in some distant communities such as Yemen. The salaries of rabbis continually increased as did the occasions on which they took fees from their captive public. Evidence of rabbinic corruption in Jewish communities since the latter part of the seventeenth century is abundant. The rabbinate's alliance with rich people in oppressing poor people, especially in Ashkenazi communities, and the use of bribery and other undue influence in the appointments of rabbis are but two of the many aspects of this corruption. Corrupt practices of many Israeli rabbis, both Haredi and NRP, have been well-documented by the Israeli Hebrew press and are widely known in Israel. This corruption is a continuation of a long-term trend.

The granting of special privileges for pursuing sacred studies exists in modern Israeli society. One of the most controversial issues in the State of Israel has been, and continues to be, the deferments from military service for most students and graduates of yeshivot. These students and graduates first receive a draft deferment on the basis of declarations from heads of yeshivot. When their deferments expire, the students or graduates are either entirely exempted from army service or are inducted directly into the army reserve forces after undergoing only brief and cursory recruit training. They are disqualified from serving in any dangerous or even unpleasant capacities. Their chances of being killed or wounded in wartime are thus greatly reduced. Their deferments mean that these students or graduates do not have to serve in the army for the period of three years, which is compulsory for all other Israeli Jewish males who are between the ages of eighteen and twenty-one. In his analysis of this situation, Ehud Asheri reported in his August 22, 1996 article, published in *Haaretz*, that at that time 5 per cent of all Jewish males were so deferred.

The vehement passions aroused by and the debates over this issue have antagonistically deepened the split between Israeli Jewish secularists and the Haredim. Currently, many secular Jews complain, as they and others have in the past, that the Haredim do not share equally with other Israeli Jews the tasks and burdens imposed upon society. The Haredim argue, as they continually have in the past, that such reasoning is fallacious. Influenced by their education, the Haredim are convinced that all victories as well as defeats of the Israeli army are due to God's intervention and that without doubt God takes into consideration the numbers, progress in study and commitment of those Jews who engage in talmudic study. The Haredim cite numerous passages in the Talmud and in subsequent talmudic literature that are emphatic on this point. Not only the privileged students and graduates of yeshivot but also traditional Israeli Jews support the Haredim and the cited sacred Jewish writings on this point.

The attitude of many secular Israeli Jews towards sacred studies and the Talmud is the exact opposite of that held by the Haredim. Secularly oriented parodies of the Talmud have remained popular and still abound in Israeli society. Many of these parodies revolve around the Haredi rationale underlying the deferment and exclusion from military service. In December 1988, for example, during one of the recurrent disputations about the deferment from service of yeshiva students, the Haredim pointed to the talmudic version of the biblical account of the victories of Yo'av, the general of King David. The Haredim quoted the talmudic interpretation that these victories were attributable to David's sacred studies, since in their view Talmud in an oral form dated back to Moses and perhaps to Abraham and was written later. Some secular writers responded publicly that David rather remained at home and sent Yo'av to fight, because he was occupied in committing adultery with Bathsheba and causing the death of her husband, Uriah. One columnist in the Israeli press, certainly not Haredi-oriented, opined that David was probably more keen about studying Bathsheba's bodily curvature than he was about studying the Talmud. Such debate has had, and continues to have, a bearing upon Israel similar in some ways to the effect upon politics that similar debate had in Christian Europe in the eleventh and twelfth centuries. What many foreign observers of Israeli Jewish society have not grasped is that, even with the scientific and technological accomplishments in Israel, the Haredim and most other Israeli Jewish fundamentalists live figuratively in a time period that corresponds closely to European Christian societies many generations ago. These fundamentalists have not made the quantum leap, as have secular Israelis, into modern times. The tension between fundamentalist and secular Israelis, therefore, stems mostly from the fact that these two groups live in different time periods.

Haredim often propound theories even more extreme than those mentioned previously. Many Haredi rabbis, for example, assert that the Holocaust, including most particularly the deaths of one-and-a-half million Jewish children, was a well-deserved divine punishment, not only for all the sins of modernity and faith renunciation by many Jews, but also for the decline of Talmudic study in Europe. The Haredim and their traditional Jewish followers attribute the death of every Jew, including each innocent child, not to natural causes but to direct action of God. The Haredim believe that God punishes each Jew for his or her sins and sometimes punishes the entire Jewish community, including many who are innocent, because of the sins committed by other Jews. In 1985, when twenty-two children, twelve and thirteen years of age, were killed in the town of Petah Tikva in a traffic accident involving their bus, Rabbi Yitzhak Peretz, one of the heads of the Shas Party and the then Minister of the Interior, stated in a television appearance that the children were victims, because a movie house was allowed to remain open on the Sabbath eve. Many members of the Hebrew press, predominantly representing secular Jews, attacked Rabbi Peretz mercilessly for making this statement. The Shas Party, nevertheless, in the next election did not lose but rather gained votes in various places, including Petah Tikva. The Haredim held and advocate similar beliefs about God's punishing and rewarding Jews in many areas of life on the basis of Jews' either committing sins or following God's word.

In the late 1990s, the primary concern of the Haredim is to expand their educational system, especially in poorer localities wherein they successfully offer material inducements such as hot meals. The Haredim strongly lobby the non-Haredi public schools with their propaganda. In some places these lobbying efforts are successful. In other areas the fierce opposition by parents who are educated and politically effective thwarts the Haredi propaganda and lobbying efforts. Haredi influence is sometimes extreme in specific places. In Netivot, one of the most religious towns in Israel, for example, the Haredim have successfully opposed any public high school, because it would be obligated to provide instruction in secular subjects. Netivot is the only Jewish town in Israel without a high school.

In order to proselytize and to spread their superstitions, Haredim often exploit the distress of people. Relatives of terminally ill hospital patients, especially if they are traditional, are often approached by messengers of a charismatic rabbi, who first reiterate that the doctors cannot help and then suggest that the relatives buy some sacred water, consecrated by a certain rabbi, and smear the patient with it. The messengers relate stories about miracles that occur after the use of this sacred water, which is never distributed without a non-returnable payment. The messengers, of course, never mention the failure of sacred water miracles. The secular Hebrew press at times will report on the failure of these miracles, especially when a large amount of money is known to have been spent for the sacred water. Such reporting, however, most often only deepens the chasm between those who read and those who do not read but loathe the secular Hebrew press. In their own press the Haredim not only attack the secular press but also display their general hostility towards secular Israeli Jews. Until the later part of the 1980s, most of the Israeli Jewish public paid little attention to the Haredi press. Since then, general public attention has increased considerably. Dov Albaum, one of Israel's foremost experts on Haredi affairs, focused upon this point in two Hebrew-language articles, one published in the August 30, 1996 issue of the newspaper, *Yediot Ahronot*, the other published in the July–August issue of the bi-monthly periodical, *Ha'ain Hashvi'it* (*The Seventh Eye*), which is published by the Israeli Democracy Institute and is devoted to analyzing the Israeli press. Albaum discussed the structure of the Haredi press in *Yediot Ahronot* and then proceeded to a discussion in *Ha'ain Hashvi'it* of the Haredi attitude as a whole towards secular Israeli Jews. According to Albaum, the violent attacks in the Haredi press upon Aharon Barak, the president of the Israeli Supreme Court, attracted increased public attention. The Haredi press called Barak "the most dangerous enemy ever to face the Haredi public." Albaum pointed out that the earlier Haredi press attacks upon the left-wing kibbutzim, the Israeli army, the secular media and many other secular institutions and figures aroused little general interest. The attack upon the Supreme Court, long regarded as the holiest symbol of Israeli secular democracy, piqued the interest of many secular Jews. The violent Haredi press attacks upon Yitzhak Rabin, while he was prime minister, did not have the same effect. Shortly before Rabin's assassination an article in one of the most popular Haredi weekly publications, *Ha'Shavua* (*The Week*) predicted:

> The day will come when the Jews will bring Rabin and Peres to the defendant's bench in court with the only two alternatives being the noose or the insane asylum. This insane and evil pair have either gone mad or are obvious traitors. Rabin and Peres have guaranteed their place in the Jewish memory as evil Jews of the worst kind. They resemble the apostates or the Jews who served the Nazis.

Reiterating that secular Jewish interest in Israel heightened after the attack upon Barak and the Supreme Court, Albaum observed that increasing numbers of secular Israelis are insulted when they read in the Haredi press that their lives are garbage and their children are hallucinating, lifeless drug addicts. Albaum explained:

> Haredi journalists deliberately exaggerate all marginal phenomena in secular society. They describe all murders, cases of alcoholism and hard drug situations as characteristics of secular Jewish society. In addition, they allege as facts incorrect statements, engage in the wildest forms of slander and often use the most derogatory terminology. Their aim is to condemn absolutely the secular, Jewish lifestyle.

It is difficult to avoid considering such depiction as analogous to the Nazi methodology.

The structure of the Haredi press is significant. Albaum pinpointed as the main Haredi ideological trendsetter *Yated Ne'eman* (*Faithful Tent-Peg*), the official newspaper of the Degel Ha'Torah faction, headed and controlled by Rabbi Shach. Albaum explained that *Yated Ne'eman* is strictly monitored by a committee of five rabbis, all appointed by Rabbi Shach and headed by Rabbi Natan Zohavsky. At least one of the committee's rabbis is in the newspaper's office each evening except the Shabbat. Every word of every article, advertisement and announcement must be approved for publication by the rabbi(s) on duty. Certain words and expressions, such as aids or television, are not allowed to be printed. The term "Red Cross," supposedly associated with Christianity, is especially prohibited from usage.

Yated Ne'eman articles often ferociously attack rival Haredi factions. One example is that all advertisements about social events of the Shas Party, which is despised by Rabbi Shach, are not allowed to be printed. The importance of this prohibition was highlighted when, after an apparent lull in the spiritual war between Rabbi Shach and Shas, one of the newspaper's editors dared to publish an advertisement announcing the bar-mitzvah of Aryeh Der'i's son. (Aryeh Der'i is a Member of the Knesset and an important Shas leader.) Upon learning of this, Rabbi Shach strongly reprimanded Rabbi Zochovsky, the head of the overseeing committee of rabbis.

Spiritual censorship committees exist and monitor everything printed in other Haredi newspapers. Albaum asserted: "Freedom of the press is an unknown concept in the Haredi press." Haredi editors, according to Albaum, proclaim a different kind of freedom: "the right of our public not to know certain things." The censoring rabbis decide what the public should not know.

In reflecting the general Haredi attitude towards secular Jews, Haredi press articles often present arguments reminiscent of anti-Semitic statements about all Jews. Albaum pointed to a February 1996 article, for example, in which Israel Friedman reiterated the position that the land of Israel belongs only to the Haredim and that secular Jews and Palestinians should leave it. In addressing secular Jews, Friedman in his article stated: "Go away from here ... We tell you this in a friendly manner. Go away. American crime will easily absorb the criminal secular youth who are all enchanted by alcohol, drugs and earrings. They are bloodsuckers who drink our blood. They dare to live on land that belongs to us." In another article Albaum quoted Nathan Ze'ev Grossman, the editor of *Yated Ne'eman*, as attributing the rise of neo-Nazism in European countries "to the influence of the Rabin government." Grossman described all kibbutzim as Nazi institutions and proposed "to put them on trial according to the precedent of the Nuremberg trials."

The Haredim demand that other Jews should, at least in public and especially in regard to matters of symbolism, behave according to their dictates. Haredi demands, often supported by traditionalist Jews, so frequently cause political scandals that they can be described as a staple of Israeli politics. More Israeli government crises have occurred because of religious scandals than for any other reasons. To further their political interests, the Haredim insist upon employing certain symbols. This insistence has played an important role in Israeli politics. Many Israeli Jews, together with a much greater number of diaspora Jews, in deference to what they believe is Jewish tradition and the commandments of Judaism, support Haredi demands to keep and display symbols of religious observance. Such support has produced scandal. One particularly illustrative scandal occurred in Autumn 1992 and occupied Israeli politics for many months. During the time of this scandal, the Haredi Shas Party threatened to leave the Rabin government, not because of Rabin's plans to deal with the Palestinians nor because of possible concessions to the Syrians but rather because the then Minister of Education Shulamit Aloni, on a visit to Nazareth was photographed eating in a non-kosher, Arab restaurant and thus violating the religious symbol of the ritual purity of food. Only six months prior to the Aloni affair another scandal involving a Member of the Knesset had occurred; MK Yael Rayan was photographed on a Tel Aviv beach, dressed in a swimsuit and reading a book on Yom Kippur. All the religious political parties then protested furiously against what they termed this "profanation of Judaism." After hearing traditionally religious Labor Party Knesset members echo the same sentiments, Prime Minister Rabin, who was not traditionally religious, reinforced the accusation.

During her tenure as minister of education, Shulamit Aloni made numerous statements that were viewed as being in opposition to symbols in Judaism and thus blasphemous; these statements resulted in scandals. One month before arousing scandal by eating in an Arab restaurant, for example, Aloni publicly acknowledged that the denial of the world's being created in six days was a tenable hypothesis. She also publicly struck the controversial, although hardly earth-shattering, position that the teaching of Judaism in the state's secular schools should be slightly changed. (She was content to leave as it is the teaching of Judaism in the state's religious schools.) Aloni caused even more furore when she publicly slighted some biblical figures. Ranny Talmor, a respected Israeli journalist, rightly observed in her October 14, 1992 article in the newspaper, *Hadashot*;

> [Aloni] scarcely escaped Galileo's fate after he persisted in maintaining that the earth moved around the sun. Some supposedly enlightened, secular Jews whispered to one another: "Of course she is right, but why does she need to say this in public?" The Jewish Grand Inquisitors were delighted in their realization that they had scored another victory against the weak-minded infidels.

The Jewish Inquisitors harassed Aloni even more after Rabin forced her to apologize publicly in an open letter to Rabbi Ovadia Yoseph, the spiritual head of the Shas Party. Yoel Markus, a well-known Israeli journalist, reflected widely held opinion when he observed in his October 13, 1992 *Haaretz* article:

> As is well known, each concession in such matters only encourages the demand for more. This is why the abject surrender to Jewish religious demands by members of the Labor and Meretz Parties makes us wonder. Rabin has solemnly undertaken to check closely an intelligence report, submitted to him by the National Religious Party [NRP], describing how Aloni violated the Sabbath and ate non-kosher food in Israel and abroad. The Chairman of the Labor Party faction in the Knesset [Elie Dayan] publicly rebuked Aloni and Member of the Knesset Yael Dayan.

The NRP hired detectives to spy on ministers in order to discover what transgressions of Jewish religious commandments they committed. Such spying continued while the Rabin and Peres governments were in power. Rabin and Peres, while prime ministers, obtained all the findings of the detectives and continually attempted to keep their ministers from transgressing any religious laws in public.

In his *Haaretz* article, Yoel Markus articulated many fears, shared by a sizeable segment of the Israeli Jewish public:

> We can also expect demands that each minister and member of the Knesset be accompanied by a kashrut inspector, who holds a full-time job for this purpose and that similar inspectors be appointed to insure that kashrut is observed in every neighborhood and on every street in Israel. A demand may also be made to establish vice squads, authorized to raid private homes in order to ascertain whether kashrut is being observed and whether, God forbid, a wife does not by chance have sex with her husband in the period of impurity during and after the time of menstruation [lasting eight to fourteen days.]

Other Israeli journalists expressed similar fears and went further than did Markus in their published articles. Some attacked not only the religious but also the secular Jews who remained silent about the attacks upon them and their behavior and who would allow continual efforts by religious surveyors to brainwash systematically. Many Israeli Jews, whose opinions were represented by certain journalists, saw the activities and actual victories by religious factions as advancements towards a full-scale Jewish "Khomeinism" in Israel.

The discussion of the Aloni scandal continued for weeks in the Israeli press and became increasingly political. Nahum Barnea wrote in his October 23, 1992 *Yediot Ahronot* article:

> Rabin encouraged the torrents of anti-Aloni propaganda by advancing the slogan "either Aloni or peace." What connection can there be between Aloni's dietary preferences and peace ... On four separate occasions Rabin summoned the leaders of Meretz [Aloni's party] to his office in order to convey to them the complaints about Aloni made by Rabbi Ovadia Yosef, the spiritual head of the Shas Party.

In his October 23, 1992 *Davar* article, Amir Oren censured Rabin for being subservient to Rabbi Ovadia Yoseph and for equating the rabbi's power to be equal to that of Stalin's in his time. Oren opined that the Shas Party had begun to fulfil in Israel a role analogous to that of the Shi'ites in Lebanon. In Oren's view Israel, "far from being the only democracy in the Middle East was imitating Lebanon and Iran, becoming in effect half a state of anarchy and half a theocracy."

Amnon Abromovitz in his October 23, 1992 *Maariv* article put a somewhat different spin on the Aloni scandal. He wrote: "The vicious use of Aloni as a scapegoat by the religious Jews generated

public support for her. A repelling stench of religious zeal, fundamentalism and sexism is emanating from the harassment of Aloni."
Abromovitz blamed Rabin for encouraging this harassment, but
he added that despite all her talk and non-kosher eating, Aloni had
granted religious institutions, especially those of the Shas, more
money than had any previous Minister of Education. Abramovitz
concluded: "Aloni may talk blasphemously about God, but she has
been foremost in generosity to those who believe in Him."

The leaders of the Labor Party and their non-traditionalist
sympathizers answered the above expressions of fear, especially after
Oslo, by arguing that concessions to the demands of the Haredim
were necessary to ensure backing for the peace process. This stock
answer did not satisfy many secular Israelis. What Markus concluded
represented broad secular opinion:

> The reason for Rabin's servility to Shas is supposed to be politics.
> Labor experts in skullduggery assure us that the Shas Party may
> leave the coalition if it finds it no longer able to withstand
> pressure from the other Haredi circles ... The conclusion is that
> Labor must do its best to placate them ... Politics is important,
> but freedom of conscience and everyone's right to follow one's
> creed are even more important. Jewish secularism is a creed. The
> crude hypocrisy, with which the ministers fake religious devotions,
> leads nowhere but only damages their government's integrity.
> If Shas wants to leave Rabin's coalition, it will do so by order of
> its rabbis. It will then not help if Rabin puts on an Haredi garb
> and/or if Aloni shaves her head to cover it with a coif. [The
> reference here is to a commandment of traditional Judaism that
> a woman, before marrying, has to shave her head and cover it
> with a coif. The Haredim attempt to enforce this rule strictly.
> Many Jewish, religious women cut only some of their hair and
> cover the remainder with wigs. Many secular, Jewish women are
> enraged by this rule.]

By design, Haredi rabbis and politicians select secular women in
politics as the primary targets of their attacks, even though they
could pinpoint secular men as much, if not more, for transgressions of religious law. The Haredim repeatedly refer to Jewish
women, engaged in politics, as witches, bitches or demons. Although
a bit crude at times in the use of descriptive language, the Haredim
approach mirrors to a great extent traditional Judaism's broadly
based position regarding women. This position not only restricts
the rights of women but in many ways holds women in contempt.
Rule 8 in Chapter 3 of the *Kitzur Shulhan Aruch* (*Abridgment of
Shulhan Aruch*), an elementary textbook for Jews with little talmudic
education, for example, dictates: "A male should not walk between

two females or two dogs or two pigs. In the same manner the males should not allow a woman, dog or pig to walk between them." All Haredi boys between the ages of ten and twelve study and are required to observe this rule. (Few dogs and no pigs can be found in Haredi neighborhoods.) Traditional Judaism also prohibits women from playing even insignificant roles in politics and/or in any public activities in which they may appear to be leading males. Women are forbidden to drive buses or taxis; they can drive private cars only if no males apart from those in their own families or other women are passengers. These and many rules are followed in Haredi neighborhoods. In these neighborhoods women who are "dressed immodestly" are often insulted and/or assaulted. Many traditionally religious Jewish males in other than Haredi neighborhoods, who do not observe inconvenient religious commandments, take the lead of the Haredim in resenting and opposing participation of women in politics. These traditionally religious males regard such participation by women as a threat to their domination of their own families.

The numerous misogynistic statements in the Talmud and in talmudic literature constitute a part of every Haredi male's sacred study. The statement in *Tractate Shabat*, page 152b, defining a woman is exemplary: "A woman is a sack full of excrement." The learned *Talmudic Encyclopedia* (volume 2, pages 255–7), written in modern Hebrew and thus understandable to all educated Israeli Jews, devotes a section to the "nature and behavior of women." In this section the proposition appears that the urge for the sexual act is greater among men than among women. The evidence presented for this is that men tend to hire women prostitutes because their urge for sex is greater than the urge of women. For that reason the Halacha punishes a wife who refuses to have sexual relations with her husband much more severely than it punishes a husband who refuses to have sexual relations with his wife. For the same reason a prospective husband is obliged to see his wife-to-be before marrying her but a prospective wife is not obligated to see her husband-to-be before marriage. After seeing his prospective bride, moreover, the prospective husband can send a messenger and conduct the marriage through the messenger. Jewish folklore contains stories describing the utilization of this procedure.

The halachic prohibition of teaching talmudic literature and/or the Bible to women has been in the past and is currently still of great importance. Studying "Torah Sheba'al Peh" (the oral law) is for the Halacha a supremely important commandment. It is equivalent in importance to all the other commandments put together. (The law, according to belief, was given by God orally to Moses and was handed down orally for many centuries before being written.) This obligation, termed "Talmud Torah" or "learning the Torah" is viewed as independent of time. Every pious male Jew is obligated to devote a portion of all days and nights, including holidays and working days, to this study. A basic talmudic rule frees women from positive obligations that are dependent on special times and obliges women only with positive obligations that are independent of time. Women, for example, are obliged to keep the Sabbath and the holidays that last more than twenty-four hours and are thus considered to be independent of time. Women, on the other hand, are not obliged to hear the shofar (ram's horn) blown on the New Year, which only takes a short time and is thus considered to be dependent on time. (There are a few exceptions to this rule.) A woman is permitted to fulfill what she is not obliged to do; hence she can choose to hear the ram's horn blown on the New Year. This rule underlines the women's religious inferiority to men, since another talmudic dictate is that a person who fulfills a commandment because he is obliged to do so is greater and receives a greater reward from God than a person who fulfills a commandment he is not obliged to fulfill. A Jewish woman that comes to the synagogue on the New Year and hears the ram's horn being blown, according to traditional Judaism, will receive a smaller reward from God than a male who does the same, because she is not obliged to hear whereas he is so obliged. *Tractate Kiddushin* (page 34a) of the Talmud, however, ruled that women are not obliged to fulfill "Talmud Torah," even though it is an obligation independent of time. This ruling is part of Halacha. The rule was later amended to mean that women should learn only the special obligations that they must keep to the extent that they know what to do and what to avoid. The issue, therefore, arose: What parts of sacred studies are women permitted to learn or to be taught? The talmudic answer to this question, based upon many quotations, was given by Maimonides. In his work, *Talmud Torah Laws* (chapter 1, rule 13), Maimonides wrote:

A woman who has studied Torah receives a reward [from God], but it is an inferior one when compared to man's reward. This is because she is not obligated [to do so], and everyone who does what he is not obliged to do gets an inferior reward compared to [the reward given to] one who does what he is commanded to do. The woman nevertheless receives some reward. The sages commanded a father not to teach his daughter Torah, because most woman never intend to learn anything and will, because of the weak understanding, convert the pronouncements of Torah into nonsense. The sages said: "Everyone who teaches his daughter Torah can be compared to one who teaches her insipid matters." This rule, however, applies only to talmudic studies.

Although a woman should not be taught the Bible, she, if taught, would not have been taught insipid matters.

A somewhat shortened version of this is given in the authoritative compendium of the Halacha, *Shulhan Aruch* (Yorah Deah, rule 246, paragraph 6). In modern times the Haredim have attempted to modify those rules to some extent. They have taught and still do teach girls the easier parts of the Talmud, in which arguments between the rabbis, that are considered to be dangerous for the "weak female mind", do not occur. Similarly, the Haredim have taught and do teach girls the Pentateuch but reserve the highest level and most serious commentaries for the boys. The Haredim maintain in their schools a strict separation of girls from boys and do not allow the girls to observe boys playing in the schoolyard.

Many Israeli Jews, who in their youth received thorough talmudic educations, have later in their lives reacted antagonistically against Orthodox Judaism's depiction and treatment of women. Some of these Jews in reaction have written articles that are often published in the Israeli Hebrew press but are almost never translated into English. Kadid Leper, for example, a well-known Israeli journalist who as a youth studied in a yeshiva for years before becoming a secularist, wrote in his April 18, 1997 *Hai'r* article under the title "Woman is a sack full of excrement," the following:

Beatings, sexual brutality, cruelty, deprival of rights, use of a woman as merely a sexual object; you can find all of this there [in the Talmud] ... For two thousand years women had a well-defined place in the Jewish religion [Orthodox Judaism]; this place is different from what the rabbinical establishment describes; according to the Halacha, the place of women is in the garbage heap together with cattle and slaves. According to the Jewish religion [Orthodox Judaism] a man buys for himself a slave woman for her entire life simply by providing food and dress and granting to his wife the sexual act.

This kind of published article, together with the many published reports of rabbinical harassment of women, have not only firmed polarization in Israeli Jewish society but have contributed significantly to the growing secular enmity towards Haredim.

In many areas of Israeli Jewish society, the Haredim continue to maintain their separateness and at the same time assert that other Jews accept Haredi dicta. This is well illustrated by an example from the area of medicine. In his December 25, 1995 *Yediot Ahronot* article, Dov Albaum discussed the request submitted two weeks previously by the Haredim to the Israeli Ministry of Health:

Rabbi Yehoshua Sheinberger, the head of the Medicine by Law Organization, requested what seemed to be an innocent request that, as a concession to the religious Jews, personal blood donations be permitted. Previously, a person who donated a unit of blood for a patient undergoing surgery received a document entitling the recipient of the donation to one unit of blood from the general reserves of the Blood Bank. This new request, if accepted, would create a situation in which blood donors would be able to demand that hospitals or first aid stations give their blood donations only to specific recipients.

Rabbi Sheinberger, supported by two other important rabbis, argued that Haredim usually refuse to donate blood but might change their attitude if this demand were accepted. Albaum in his article discussed the additional motivation behind this request:

Beneath the surface there is a completely different problem that led to the rabbis' approaching the [Israeli] Ministry of Health. Haredi religious law authorities have in recent years dealt with the following issue: "Is it permissible for a pious Jew to receive a blood transfusion from non-Jews or from Jews who do not observe Jewish religious laws?" Haredi rabbis fear that, receiving "tainted," secular blood, or non-Jewish blood might cause a pious Jew to behave badly and even, heaven forbid, harm his observance of the Jewish religious laws.

Several months before the above-mentioned request, Rabbi Ovadia Yoseph addressed this problem at length in his new book, *Questions and Answers – Statements*: "Blood that comes from forbidden [that is, non-kosher] foods may cause a negative effect upon its Jewish recipients. It may produce bad qualities, such as cruelty and/or boldness ... Therefore, a pious Jew, who does urgently need a transfusion and who faces no danger in waiting to receive blood from a strictly religious Jew, should wait." Rabbi Yoseph offered similar advice for those pious Jews needing organ transplants; he advised them only to accept such donations from other pious Jews. This dictate erupted into a serious dispute among rabbis in Israel and astonished many secular Jews. In another published article, Albaum reported that Rabbi Mordechai Eliyahu, a former chief rabbi of Israel, disagreed with Rabbi Yoseph and stated: "When a secular Jew is born, he is born with kosher blood and all the forbidden foods that he later eats are dissolved and made marginal in his blood." In regard to non-Jews, however, Rabbi Eliyahu mostly agreed with Rabbi Yoseph and held that religious Jews should attempt to avoid blood donations from them. Rabbi Eliyahu did not totally forbid blood donations for Jews from non-Jews. He stated:

It is permitted at certain times that Jews receive blood, or in the case of sucklings mother's milk, from non-Jews, in spite of the fact that such blood is detrimental to their Jewish characteristics and spirit. This is because blood is transferred slowly and is made marginal in the cycling of Jewish blood in the body. Nevertheless, when possible, a Jew should avoid receiving such blood.

Rabbi Sheinberger finally admitted that such rulings constituted the primary reason for his request: "The Haredi community has a problem in this area. For the Haredim blood from a Jew who eats only kosher food is preferable to blood from a Jew who does not observe dietary laws." Other Haredi rabbis agreed. Rabbi Levy Yitzhak Halperin, the head of the Scientific Religious Institute for Jewish Law Problems explained: "Blood donations from non-Jews or from Jews who eat forbidden foods are a problem. Jewish religious law holds that a Jewish child should preferably not be breast fed by a non-Jewish woman because her milk consists of forbidden food and contaminates the Jewish child." Such positions and statements antagonized secular Jews and met great opposition from the great majority of members of the Israeli medical profession.

In 1994 Rabbi Sheinberger ignited another controversy and created scandal with a similar request. He met with senior physicians from the Israel Transplants Association and discussed with them the Jewish religious prohibition on organ donations. In Israel Haredi Jews refuse organ transplants from their and/or their relatives' corpses. On this issue the Haredi position influences many people for superstitious as well as religious reasons. Organ transplants in Israel are thus difficult to arrange. Surgeons frequently request Haredi rabbis to appeal to their followers to agree to organ transplants from corpses of their relatives in order to save lives. The surgeons' argument is based upon the Jewish religious law giving priority to saving Jewish lives. In his discussion Rabbi Sheinberger put the condition that only a Haredi rabbi could authorize such transplants. He explained: "Jewish religious law states that it is forbidden to transplant Jewish organs into either non-Jews or Jews who are not pious. It is obvious that it is prohibited under any circumstances to transplant Jewish organs into Arabs, all of whom hate Jews." Rabbi Sheinberger, when asked for his definition of a Jew who is not pious, replied that a rabbi must determine the status of every Jew. Sheinberger's request caused a huge commotion and was rejected.

Many non-Haredi rabbis allow an organ of a non-Jew to be transplanted into a body of a Jew in order to save the life of the Jew. They, however, oppose the transplant of an organ from a Jew into the body of a non-Jew. Some important rabbis go much further in discussing and ruling about differences between Jews and non-Jews on medical matters. Rabbi Yitzhak Ginsburgh, an influential member of the Habad movement and the head of a yeshiva near Nablus, for instance, opined in an April 26, 1996 *Jewish Week* article, reproduced in *Haaretz* that same day: "If every single cell in a Jewish body entails divinity, and is thus part of God, then every strand of DNA is a part of God. Therefore, something is special about Jewish DNA." Rabbi Ginsburgh drew two conclusions from this statement: "If a Jew needs a liver, can he take the liver of an innocent non-Jew to save him? The Torah would probably permit that. Jewish life has an infinite value. There is something more holy and unique about Jewish life than about non-Jewish life." It is noteworthy that Rabbi Ginsburgh is one of the authors of a book lauding Baruch Goldstein, the Patriarchs' Cave murderer. In that book Ginsburgh contributed a chapter in which he wrote that a Jew's killing non-Jews does not constitute murder according to the Jewish religion and that killing of innocent Arabs for reasons of revenge is a Jewish virtue. No influential Israeli rabbi has publicly opposed Ginsburgh's statements; most Israeli politicians have remained silent; some Israeli politicians have openly supported him.

The Haredi demand to establish the Halacha as the law of the state of Israel has in recent years received increased support from the more pious members of the NRP. Briefly summarized, the specifics of this demand are:

- God's political authority must be formally and juridically recognized. Ordained rabbis, God's certified agents, must be the decision makers.
- Rabbis must oversee all social institutions, adjudicate all issues that arise, make final judgements about all social services and censor all printed, pictorial and sound matter.
- Sabbath, other religious laws, physical separation of women from men in public places and "modesty" in female conduct and dress must be enforced by law.
- Individuals must be obligated legally to report all noticed offenses of others to rabbinical authorities.

The theocratic, totalitarian nature of the Haredi demand for the Halacha to be the binding law of the State of Israel is obvious.

⤷ political system based on religious ideas.

3

The Two Main Haredi Groups

A brief consideration of the historical background should provide a basis for understanding the differences between the two major Haredi groups: the Ashkenazi and the Oriental, formerly called Sephardi. Throughout most of their history, Jews lived scattered in different countries. Not surprisingly, separate Jewish communities emerged, comprised of Jewish residents of a single country, of a cluster of countries or sometimes of different parts of a single country. Until about AD 1050 one particular community existed as a Jewish center, recognized by other communities as the authority for dictating rules and issuing instructions binding upon Jews throughout the world. The last such center was the Jewish community of Iraq. After the collapse of the last center in Iraq, the differences between Jewish communities deepened considerably. Different communities, for example, although keeping and using some of the ancient prayers common to all Jews, composed new prayers, used only in their own services. Even the chanting of prayers in different communities changed and thus varied. Religious rules of conduct in almost every conceivable area of life, to which pious Jews adhered, also changed to some extent and varied from one community to another.

The Ashkenazi community that emerged in northern France and western Germany between the tenth and twelfth centuries became more innovative and began to deviate more from previously established patterns than any other community with the possible exceptions of small communities in remote countries, such as Georgia. The Ashkenazi divergences became embedded and persisted. Until this day, for example, most pious Ashkenazi Jews refuse to eat meat or any foods containing meat that are prepared under supervision of non-Ashkenazi rabbis; pious members of other Jewish communities are content with dietary supervision of rabbis not belonging to their community. Thus, a pious Sephardi Jew, visiting a pious Ashkenazi Jew will eat food prepared by the latter, but a pious Ashkenazi Jew visiting a Sephardi Jew will refuse to eat any foods containing meat or often any food whatsoever. Ashkenazi exclusiveness is evident in many other aspects of their religious conduct. Sephardi Jews, on the other hand, developed as early as the twelfth century an exclusiveness of their own, based

3

upon the consideration that they were superior in some ways to other Jews. The Spanish and Portuguese Jews, a part of Sephardi Jewry, especially developed a pride in the supposed "purity of descent." (In Hebrew Sephardi means Spanish.) Most of them not only refused to marry but also often despised being together with Ashkenazi Jews. Moses Maimonides, who lived until 1204 and was both a rabbi and the greatest medieval Jewish philosopher, moralized in a testament addressed to his son:

> Guard your soul by not looking into books composed by Ashkenazi rabbis, who believe in the blessed Lord only when they eat beef seasoned with vinegar and garlic. They believe that the vapor of vinegar and the smoke of garlic will ascend to their nostrils and thus make them understand that the blessed Lord is near to them ... You, my son, should stay only in the pleasant company of our Sephardi brothers, who are called the men of Andalusia [or southern Spain, then ruled by the Muslims] because only they have brains and are clever.

Similar statements, in which members of a Jewish community express feelings of their superiority over other Jews, abound in Jewish literature and are common. Even as late as the 1960s older Sephardi rabbis and other Jewish men in Jerusalem, when signing their names, would invariably add the Hebrew initials meaning "pure Spanish." Ashkenazi exclusiveness, as it developed and deepened over centuries, however, became more all-encompassing and extreme than Sephardi exclusiveness.

The developing exclusiveness had geographical, social and political causes. Prior to the formation of the Ashkenazi community, almost all Jews lived in the Mediterranean basin or in countries, such as Iraq, connected with the basin by trade routes. In the tenth century most Mediterranean countries were under either Muslim or Byzantine rule. The communications between this region and the emerging feudal Europe were tenuous largely because of the language barriers: Greek and Arabic, spoken on the one side, were largely unknown in Western Christian areas, while Latin was largely unknown in the Orient. Jews, who almost always spoke the language(s) of the people among whom they lived, encountered the same communication obstacle as did other people. The Ashkenazi community, therefore, framed its own life style without knowledge about or guidance from the older, Jewish communities. The Ashkenazi Jewish life style developed within the context of the emerging feudalism in Europe, which differed in many crucial respects from other regimes in other areas in that time period. In spreading eastward into the emerging states in central and eastern Europe, the Ashkenazi community solidified its cohesiveness and its identity: these have persisted to date but in more pronounced forms among religious rather than secular Ashkenazi Jews.

Expelled from Spain in 1492 and from Portugal in 1498, Sephardi Jews not only settled in but also transformed other Jewish communities. In these communities the new Sephardi immigrants tended to maintain an exclusiveness and to remain aloof from other Jews. Having come from the relatively developed society of the Spain of the Renaissance and having settled in less developed countries, they soon became the wealthiest, best educated and most politically connected Jews in Mediterranean countries. The Sephardi Jews that settled in Saloniki (now in Greece but then part of the Ottoman Empire) received privileges from the Ottoman Sultan, because they manufactured the best cloth and provided textiles for the uniforms worn by members of elite units of the Ottoman army. The Saloniki Sephardi Jews kept this monopoly for 130 years, losing it only when more modern textiles were imported from England and the Netherlands. Spanish Jews mostly and Italian Jews to a lesser extent actually did most of the creative work in all areas of medieval Jewish culture. Largely because of their wealth and education, Sephardi Jews imposed their customs, language and name upon Jewish communities in all the countries to which they emigrated. One good illustration of this occurred in Jewish communities in the Balkans and what is now Turkey. The Jews in these communities called themselves "Romaniole," taken from the popular name of the Byzantine Empire "Romania." They spoke Greek until about 1550 at which time, influenced by the effects of the Sephardi immigration, began to call themselves "Sephardi" and to speak Ladino, an ancient form of Spanish. The fact is that no Sephardi communities existed other than those made up of the immigrants from the Iberian Peninsula, their descendents or those who assimilated themselves into Sephardi communities. European travelers and some Ashkenazi Jews have referred, and still refer, mistakenly to all non-Ashkenazi Jews as Sephardi. This is because the real Sephardi Jews established a lasting hegemony over other Jewish communities. Many other than Sephardi, non-Ashkenazi members of Jewish communities have more correctly defined themselves not only as Jews but also as Iraqis, Moroccans, Italians or another nationality.

Until the end of the seventeenth century, Ashkenazi Jews constituted a small minority of world Jewry. Their cultural advancement trailed far behind other Jewish communities, especially the Sephardi and Italian. Since the eighteenth century, the populations of Mediterranean countries, especially those in the Ottoman Empire, steadily declined economically and demographically. This trend greatly affected Jewish communities of those countries. Between 1700 and 1850, Jewish populations in these countries steeply declined and became increasingly impoverished. The modest increase in Jewish population between 1850 and 1914 did not to a significant extent offset the decline. From the beginning of the eighteenth century the political and technological advancements in Europe affected the Ashkenazi community. From the mid-eighteenth century the Ashkenazi population began to increase rapidly; by 1800 Ashkenazi Jews had become the majority of world Jewry; this increase and the majority percentage accelerated in the nineteenth century. Jews living in the European part of the Russian Empire, nearly all of them Ashkenazi, proliferated sevenfold between 1795 and 1914. Ashkenazi Jews developed a variety of innovations in Judaism, some of them secularist. By the first half of the twentieth century, Ashkenazi Jews had surpassed the relatively small, non-Ashkenazi minority in every major respect, including Talmudic studies. The current split between religious Ashkenazi Jews and non-Ashkenazi Jews stems from the fact that during the past two centuries, in contrast to what had previously been the case, almost all rabbis of distinction have been Ashkenazi. In non-Ashkenazi communities during this time period the quality of talmudic study, of books published and even of older books being reprinted has disastrously declined.

Until 1948, Zionism and the emigration of Jews to Palestine were predominantly Ashkenazi inventions. Most religious Jews viewed Zionism as being in opposition to Judaism; hence, only Jews emancipated from their religious past could become Zionists. Even so, few Ashkenazi Jews immigrated to Palestine because of Zionist convictions. The great majority of those who immigrated did so only because their lives were so difficult in their own countries of origin. The great majority of Jews in Israel in 1948 were those who had immigrated to Palestine after the increase in anti-Semitism in Europe after 1932 and especially after Hitler came to power in Germany. The number of non-Ashkenazi Jews in Israel at the time of the state's creation was relatively small. For most Jews in non-Ashkenazi communities, the religious influence, especially the messianic strain, was in the 1950s and early 1960s still potent. Living standards in Israel in the 1950s, although below those throughout Europe, were superior to those in most of the Arab Middle East. The Israeli government, therefore, could easily persuade Jews from many countries, for example, Morocco, Yemen and Bulgaria, to immigrate to Israel. The Israeli government induced Jewish immigration from Iraq by bribing the government of Iraq to strip most Iraqi Jews of their citizenship and to confiscate their property. By contrast, few Jews immigrated to Israel from the more advanced countries of the eastern Mediterranean, such as Greece or Egypt.

The majority of the Israeli Jewish population shifted to the non-Ashkenazi. During the period from 1949 to 1965, Ashkenazi Jews in Israel declined to a minority that stabilized at about 40 per cent of Israel's population. The substantial immigration of Jews from the former Soviet Union thereafter increased the Ashkenazi population to about 55 per cent. By virtue of their having come from more advanced countries, the bulk of Ashkenazi Jews were relatively modern in outlook and secular.

The non-Ashkenazi Jews, increasingly referred to as "Orientals" instead of "Sephardis," remained predominantly religious. Upon their arrival in Israel many Oriental Jews and their children were put through a cultural socialization directed by veteran Ashkenazi residents and advocated by members of the Zionist Labor Party then in power. This socialization included a considerable amount of coercive modernization and attempts to secularize the young. The results of this coercion were mixed during most of the first two decades of Israel's existence. The majority of Oriental Jews remained traditionalists, meaning that these people ignored the more exacting commandments of Judaism, such as the ban of Sabbath travel, but followed other commandments, especially those dealing with synagogue attendance. Even more importantly, it meant that they retained belief in the magical powers of rabbis and "holy men." To date, only a few Oriental politicians dare criticize a rabbi in public, even when the rabbi strongly opposes or curses them. Ashkenazi Jews of all political views in contrast criticize rabbis freely. Most Ashkenazi politicians despise any kowtowing to rabbis. Almost all Oriental politicians, including the Black Panthers of the early 1970s and the members of tiny Oriental peace movements, commonly bow to and kiss the hands of rabbis in public.

The Ashkenazi religious minority, particularly its Haredi segment, has resisted secularization of Oriental Jews. They have succeeded to some extent, most particularly in persuading a minority to retain the strict observance of Judaism's commandments. They have established separate religious schools and yeshivot for the Orientals and have admitted, although in strictly controlled numbers, some of the most qualified Oriental youngsters to their own schools and yeshivas. After the passage of time, an Oriental Haredi elite group of rabbis and talmudic scholars emerged in Israel. Almost without exception, Ashkenazi Haredi rabbis trained members of this elite group.

By the beginning of the 1990s, the confrontation between the unbending Haredi version of Ashkenazi exclusiveness and Oriental traditionalism, which previously was potentially explosive, erupted. The Ashkenazi Haredi movement insisted upon completely freezing the situation that existed in central and eastern Europe around 1860. The Oriental Jews, trained by Ashkenazi Haredi Jews, were forced to discard their traditional garb, wear the black Ashkenazi clothing and learn and speak Yiddish. Yiddish was the language of oral instruction in the Haredi yeshivot; Hebrew was reserved for writing. The Oriental traditionalists were also forced to adopt the Ashkenazi manner of praying, which differed in numerous ways from their former method. Revered rabbis, who commanded authority and encountered almost no opposition, imposed those radical changes. By contrast, the various attempts by the Labor movement to impose modernizing constraints upon the Orientals in the 1950s sparked furious opposition among the Oriental masses, who would often criticize politicians but hardly ever criticize rabbis.

The Oriental students in Ashkenazi Haredi yeshivot, after years of docile submission to demands and after being ordained as rabbis, were not granted status equal to that of their fellow students and rabbis. They have continued to accept and even today seem to be content with their inferior treatment. An excellent illustration of this is the inequality in intermarriage with their Ashkenazi peers. All Jewish communities share the time-honored custom that the head of the yeshiva arranges all marriages of yeshiva students. He carefully picks the daughters of rich and pious Jews as wives for students. The better students are matched with the daughters of the wealthiest parents. (The head of the yeshiva also matches daughters of rabbis with sons of the wealthiest parents.) Yeshiva students have selflessly complied with this matchmaking; resisting has been – and still is – considered to be a grave sin. This practice was instituted so that yeshiva students, who had no marketable skills, and their families would be supported. Students could continue their sacred studies, and the entire supporting family would supposedly then be able to enter paradise. More recently, yeshiva heads, when unable to find wealthy, prospective fathers-in-law for students, find prospective wives that are previously trained in skilled professions suitable for Haredi women and are willing to support husbands engaged in "sacred studies." (Such support will supposedly bring the wives to paradise.) By being matchmakers, yeshiva heads have most often been able to control the livelihoods and thus the lives of yeshiva students and their families.

Ashkenazi Haredi Jews have never formally prohibited marriages with pious Jews from other communities. Such marriages, nevertheless, often have been – and still are – considered disgraces. Because of this, the heads of Ashkenazi Haredi yeshivot adopted the custom, still followed, of matching Oriental students, however distinguished in their studies, with either physically handicapped Ashkenazi brides or ones from poor families.

Not surprisingly, an unwritten rule developed whereby Oriental students, however distinguished, would not be appointed to any responsible teaching positions even in lower-rank yeshivot, attended solely by Oriental students. These teaching jobs were reserved for Ashkenazi rabbis, the underlying assumption being that Oriental Jews were not yet sufficiently mature to hold responsible religious positions. When Rabbi Shach, one of the foremost Haredi leaders, explicitly reiterated this assumption shortly before the 1992 elections, he was denounced as being racist by many Ashkenazi secular Jews; neither Oriental rabbis nor Oriental political activists uttered one word of public criticism.

No Oriental initiative was responsible for the creation of the Haredi political party, Shas. Rabbi Shach formed Shas before the 1988 elections, because he, in his rivalry with other prominent Ashkenazi Haredi rabbis, needed to have Knesset members that would be subservient only to him. He, therefore, ordered those rabbis that were his students and retained personal allegiance to him to form two new, separate, Haredi political parties: Degel Ha'Tora (Banner of the Law) would be purely Ashkenazi; Shas (an acronym for Sephardi List for Tradition) would be purely Oriental. After the formation of both parties, the party leaders publicly regarded Rabbi Shach as their highest spiritual authority and vowed to obey him unconditionally. In order to make Shas also attractive to non-Haredi Orientals, Shach handpicked a non-Haredi Oriental rabbi upon whom he could rely – Rabbi Ovadia Yoseph, the former chief rabbi of Israel – to act as the nominal party head. Shach, of course, retained authority. For Shach, Yoseph's greatest virtue was that, after failing to win re-election as chief rabbi due to the NRP's refusal to exert influence on his behalf, Yoseph hated the NRP as fiercely as did Shach himself. As is well known in Israel, hatred between secular Jews cannot match in intensity the mutual hatred between diverse groups of religious Jews, especially in the quarrels between rabbis representing those diverse groups. Shach had good reason to expect that, because of his wish to retaliate against NRP rabbis, Yoseph would remain loyal to him and be content with his subordinate role.

For a while everything worked as Shach had planned. The two parties, controlled by Shach, obtained eight Knesset seats altogether in the 1988 elections; Degal Ha'Tora had two seats; Shas, six seats. The Haredi party, Agudat Israel, against which Shach formed his parties, obtained only five seats. Degel Ha'Tora and Shas preferred a Likud government and after the 1988 elections supported Yitzhak Shamir as the prime minister. Their support may have been decisive. After 1990 Shamir would not have had a Knesset majority without their support. The self-demeaning attempts by the Labor Party leader, Shimon Peres, to reverse this situation failed. Peres spent months attending lessons of Talmud, given in his home by Rabbi Yoseph. Peres attempted unsuccessfully to be received by Rabbi Shach; Shach received many petty

secular politicians but not Peres. Peres made repeated, public pronouncements about how deeply he respected Judaism in general
and the Haredi rabbis in particular. Everything Peres attempted
was in vain. Shach and his rival Haredi rabbis did not bend in their
support for Shamir. Yitzhak Rabin's victory over Peres for the
leadership position in the Labor Party primaries preceding the
1992 elections was largely due to Labor's rank-and-file disillu-
sionment with Peres' attempts to ingratiate himself with Haredi Jews
and to win their support. In spite of this experience, Peres repeated
the same attempts that resulted in the same results in the 1996
elections.

The Haredi parties wielded political power after 1988, most
especially in the 1988–90 period. Peres, still in the government after
1988, supported their demands; Shamir, while Prime Minister, was
even more resolute with support. Haredi political success can best
be measured by the amounts of money the two Haredi parties were
able to obtain from the state through so-called "special money"
grants, not subject to fiscal controls of the state. These special money
grants were made through a voluntary association, formed to
remain under the real control of a Haredi Knesset member or his
friends. The ministry of finance made grants from the state budget
to such associations, most often on the basis of flimsy purpose
statements and with no control exerted over expenditures. The
resultant corruption was enormous, reaching a scale unprece-
dented in the entire history of the State of Israel and finally causing
the withdrawal of such special money grants.

The extensive corruption involved in the obtaining of this special
money did not necessarily mean that the money itself was used
illicitly. Shas spent most of this money to establish a network of
institutions designed to exert a lasting influence and to train cohorts
of militants that in the future could enable the party to maximize
its control over its public. This network consisted of a chain of
educational institutions designed to revive traditional Jewish
education for boys with only sacred and not secular subjects taught.
(Shas largely ignored the education of girls.) Adult males between
the ages of 40 and 50 were encouraged to leave their professions
or give up their businesses in order to enroll in institutions and study
sacred subjects with guaranteed remuneration. The remuneration,
that is, salaries for studying, were admittedly low, but numerous
individuals considered the life of study preferable to their persisting
to do menial work or to maintain decaying businesses. The recruits
did more than study Talmud. They were required to do political
work for Shas. These recruits soon constituted Shas' political
cadre, which has been and remains instrumental in turning Haredi
neighborhoods into electoral constituencies under almost any
conceivable circumstances.

Informed Israeli political commentators have recognized the public and political impact of such Haredi political activity. In his June 26, 1992 article in *Al-Hamishmar*, Professor Gideon Doron, Rabin's major advisor on strategy during the 1992 elections, explained after Rabin's victory why the Labor Party refrained from canvassing votes in Shas-dominated neighborhoods:

> This is a party that keeps its public under continuous influence during election and other times ... Shas' method is to turn electoral outcomes into sources of monetary revenues and spend the money obtained during the four years [between one election and another]. The method succeeds. True, they also use magic spells, amulets and vows that greatly influence their public, but their role is secondary.

According to Doron, the best way to appeal to the Shas constituency is to do so through those of the salaried elite whose role anyway is to keep the constituency under control. Doron pointed out that, with the exception of the previously mentioned elite, Shas' followers are essentially the same as the "Oriental tradition-minded segment of Likud supporters." By acquiring political power, Shas leaders, particularly Rabbi Yoseph, gained self-confidence and began to seek emancipation from the tutelage of Ashkenazi Haredi rabbis. In each Shas-dominated neighborhood, Rabbi Yoseph rather than Rabbi Shach was acclaimed to be the greatest rabbi in the world. After some years of continual adulation by the masses, Rabbi Yoseph almost certainly came to believe that he no longer needed to be subordinate to Rabbi Shach.

The split between Shas and Rabbi Shach came after the 1992 elections and was sparked by a triviality. The split in reality was over the rival claims by Shach and Yoseph to be regarded as the spiritual head of Shas. Rabin, when forming his coalition, approached and accepted the demands of Shas. Before signing an agreement, Shas asked Rabbi Shach for approval. Shach refused, because, as discussed in another chapter, Shulamit Aloni was to be named Minister of Education. Shach's newspaper, *Yated Ne'eman*, editorialized that this appointment was worse than the killing of one million children during the Holocaust. The reasoning employed here was that the Nazis killed the children but did not prevent their souls from going to paradise, whereas the appointment of Aloni could corrupt Jewish souls and deprive them of paradise. Rabbi Yoseph and the Shas Party, nevertheless, decided to risk the souls of Jewish children and joined Rabin's government. Rabbi Shach and his followers reacted negatively in a furious manner that persisted thereafter.

The confrontation between the two Haredi movements has been waged in the magical area over the contest of spiritual authority. In keeping with commonly held and magical Haredi beliefs, the Shas leaders' sin of resisting Rabbi Shach's will could be punished by a few curses resulting in either the deaths or sicknesses of those leaders and/or their family members. The result would allegedly restore heavenly equilibrium. In order to further this magical result, Rabbi Shach's supporters resorted to conduct previously employed in similar situations. They published fake announcements of deaths, hospitalizations and/or traffic accidents of Shas leaders and then either notified the families accordingly by telephone or sent ambulances to their homes. As noted above, internecine hatred between religious Jews, and especially between Haredi rabbis, is often virulent. The existence of such hatred has continually resulted in disunity within ranks that limits Haredi political power. The methods of internecine infighting have been so customarily employed within Haredi culture that, unfortunately for Rabbi Shach's followers, the impact is severely limited. In the domain of magic, moreover, Shas has on its side the great authority and renowned miracle worker, Rabbi Kaduri, who announced that he would shield all Shas leaders by casting cabbalistic spells. Rabbi Kaduri also claimed that God revealed to him that harassment by other Haredi Jews would qualify Shas leaders for the greatest Jewish virtue, sanctification of the Lord's name through martyrdom.

In the contest of spiritual authorities, debate ensued over whether Rabbi Yoseph's spirituality was sufficiently great to validate his challenge to Shach's rabbinical authority, especially in light of Yoseph's former allegiance to Shach. Following the debate all the Shas rabbis decided to obey Rabbi Yoseph. Shas rabbis and followers then began to extol Rabbi Yoseph as "the greatest rabbi of his generation," greater even than any Ashkenazi rabbi. This honor had previously been awarded to Rabbi Shach. Shas had won its independence. The Ashkenazi Haredi Jews thus could not defeat but did sever all connections with Shas. No Ashkenazi rabbi distanced himself from Shach's pronouncements; some added even more venom. The leader of the largest Hassidic sect, the Gur Hassids, reiterated his previously expressed view that Israel lost the Yom Kippur War (of October 1973) because a woman, Golda Meir, was prime minister. He implied that Israel would lose its next war because of Shulamit Aloni. Ashkenazi rabbis and their followers used weapons more hurtful than their curses and pronouncements. They desecrated Shas synagogues, usually just before the beginning of the Sabbath, thus making it difficult to clean in time without desecrating the Sabbath. Many Shas leaders, who had been educated in Ashkenazi institutions and who continued to pray in Ashkenazi synagogues, were harassed or beaten during the reciting of prayers.

One Shas leader, Rabbi Pinhassi, was spat upon and beaten in an Ashkenazi synagogue in the Haredi town of Bnei Brak during a Sabbath prayer session. Some children of Shas leaders were terribly abused. The then Minister of the Interior, Yitzhak Der'i, had to remove his sons from an Ashkenazi yeshiva after they were publicly humiliated. Der'i was repeatedly harassed, often when attempting to pray in synagogues, by Shach's followers and by religious settlers. Shas followers fought back. On several occasions they beat up those who had harassed Der'i; they also desecrated Ashkenazi synagogues in retaliation. Shas retaliations ultimately served their opponent's cause by escalating the conflict.

The split and conflict within Haredi ranks illustrate the religious transformation of Oriental Jews. For over two decades many secular Oriental groups were founded; they all failed to obtain the support of the populations they claimed to represent and, as a result, collapsed ignominiously. Their failure can be attributed to their obstinate refusal to recognize that the Oriental Jewish communities define themselves primarily in religious terms. The Haredi Shas Party will in the foreseeable future likely remain the sole Oriental political party in Israel. This particular case study may help illustrate the nature of religious transformation of a not fully modernized population.

4

The National Religious Party and the Religious Settlers

The ideology of the NRP and Gush Emunim, the group of religious settlers in the territories occupied by Israel since 1967, is more innovative than the ideology of Haredi Jews. Rabbi Abraham Yitzhak Kook, who was the chief rabbi of Palestine and a most prominent rabbinical supporter of Zionism, devised this ideology in the early 1920s and developed it thereafter. Rabbi Kook the elder, as he was called, was a prolific author. His followers considered him to be divinely inspired. After his death in 1935 he achieved the status of a saint in NRP circles. His son and successor as NRP leader, Rabbi Tzvi Yehuda Kook the younger, who died in 1981 at the age of 91, also achieved saintly status. Rabbi Kook the younger wrote no books and did not achieve the talmudic competency of his father, but he possessed a strongly charismatic personality and exerted great influence upon his students. He elaborated orally the political and social consequences of his father's teachings. The rabbis who graduated from his yeshiva in Jerusalem, Merkaz Harav, or Center of the Rabbi, and remained devoted followers of his teaching established a Jewish sect with a well-defined political plan. In early 1974, almost immediately after the shock of the October 1973 war and a short time before the cease-fire agreement with Syria was signed, Rabbi Kook's followers with their leader's blessing and spiritual guidance founded Gush Emunim (Block of the Faithful). The Gush Emunim aims were to initiate new and to expand already existent Jewish settlements in the Occupied Territories. With the help of Shimon Peres, who in the summer of 1974 became the Israeli defense minister and thus the person in charge of the Occupied Territories, Gush Emunim in the remarkably short time of a few years succeeded in changing Israeli settlement policy. The Jewish settlements, which continue to spread throughout the West Bank and to occupy a large chunk of the Gaza Strip, provide testimony of and documentation for Gush Emunim's influence within Israeli society and upon Israeli governmental policies.

Gush Emunim's success in changing Israeli settlement policy in the 1970s is politically explicable. Defense Minister Moshe Dayan determined Israeli settlement policy from the end of the 1967 war until 1974. He did not allow the establishment of Jewish settlements in the bulk of the territories. The only exception he made was to allow a tiny group of Jewish settlers to live near Hebron. Dayan wanted to envelop the densely inhabited parts of these areas by creating a settlement zone in the almost uninhabited Jordan Valley and northern Sinai (the Yamit area). In order to preserve the Israeli alliance with the feudal notables who were in firm control of the villages (although not of the larger towns), Dayan promised not to confiscate village lands; he mostly kept his promise. Gush Emunim demonstrated its strength by organizing enormous demonstrations in 1974 and 1975 opposing the Dayan promise. These demonstrations were also directed against United States Secretary of State Henry Kissinger for backing the Dayan policy. Peres, who became defense minister after Dayan in 1974 in the first Rabin government (1974–77), initiated a new policy which he called "functional compromise" and for which he acquired Gush Emunim support. According to this policy all the land inside the West Bank and the Gaza Strip that was not being used by the inhabitants could be confiscated for the exclusive use of the Jews. Palestinian political leaders who accepted this new policy arrangement would be offered absolute rule over Palestinians. The government of the State of Israel would control only certain essential functions in Palestinian areas.

Prime Minister Rabin at first opposed this policy. In 1975, Peres conspired with Gush Emunim and planned strategy to combat Rabin's opposition. Gush Emunim organized a mass rally in Sebastia, a disused railway station near Nablus. Rabin forbade the demonstration, but Gush Emunim demonstrators succeeded in circumventing the army roadblocks and assembled in Sebastia. During the period of the ensuing lengthy negotiations Peres lent some support to Gush Emunim. More demonstrators arrived on the scene. Finally, a compromise settlement that favored Gush Emunim was reached. Gush Emunim members were allowed to settle in what is now the flourishing settlement of Kedumim. Operating in much the same manner, Gush Emunim in 1976 with the help of Peres founded the settlement Ofra as a temporary work camp and the settlement Shilo as a temporary archaeological camp. Gush Emunim also pursued similar policies and initiated settlement beginnings in the Gaza Strip. The Gush Emunim settlements, agreed to by Peres in 1975 and 1976, still exist and are flourishing. Following the 1977 election of Menachem Begin as prime minister, a "holy alliance" of the religious Gush Emunim and successive secular Israeli governments occurred and has remained in place to date.

Having achieved settlement policy successes, Gush Emunim rabbis cleverly conducted a number of political intrigues and were able to achieve domination of the NRP. From the mid-1980s the

NRP has followed the ideological lead of Gush Emunim. After the death of Rabbi Kook the younger, the spiritual leadership of Gush Emunim became centered in a semi-secret rabbinical council, selected by mysterious criteria from among the most outstanding disciples of Rabbi Kook. These rabbis have continued to make policy decisions based upon their belief in certain innovative elements of ideology not openly advocated or detailed but derived from their distinct interpretation of Jewish mysticism, popularly known as Cabbala. The writings of Rabbi Kook the elder serve as the sacred texts and are perhaps intentionally even more obscure than other cabbalistic writings. In-depth knowledge of talmudic and cabbalistic literature, including modern interpretations of both, and special training are prerequisites for understanding Kook's writings. The implications of Kook's writings are theologically too innovative to allow for a popularized presentation to an otherwise educated Jewish public. This is probably the reason why so few analyses of the Gush Emunim ideology have appeared. The one significant and learned analysis is an essay by Professor Uriel Tal, published originally in Hebrew in *Haaretz* on September 26, 1984, and published in English in *The Jerusalem Quarterly* (No. 35, Spring 1985) under the title: "Foundations of a Political Messianic Trend in Israel." The Tal essay, although marred to some extent by sociological jargon and by some analogies not well adapted to its theme, is the most valuable analysis to date. Several relatively good studies in Hebrew of the more mundane aspects of Gush Emunim have appeared as books. The one study in English is Ian Lustick's book, *For the Land and the Lord: Jewish Fundamentalism in Israel* (1988). The initiative for the Lustick book was apparently connected to Lustick's personal reaction to the Jonathan Pollard espionage affair[1] and began as a paper written for the United States Department of Defense. This may explain the book's excessive concentration on the changing political stances of Gush Emunim and its relative neglect of important parts of ideology. Contrary to what the title suggests, the book contains little description or explanation of Jewish fundamentalism. To some extent, moreover, this book is apologetic; the more extreme aspects of Gush Emunim dogmas and beliefs are not accurately revealed. Some of what is missing in the Lustick book can fortunately be found in the chapter titled "Nationalistic Judaism," in Yehoshafat Harkabi's book, *Israel's Fateful Hour* (1988). The ensuing discussion of Gush Emunim ideas and politics will take cognizance of the Lustick and Harkabi analyses but will rely more upon Tal's study and other Hebrew writings.

The status of non-Jews in the Cabbala as compared to that in talmudic literature is a good beginning point for discussion. Most of the many Jewish authors that have written about the Cabbala in English, German and French have either avoided this subject or have hidden its essence under clouds of misleading generalizations. These authors, Gershon Scholem being one of the most significant, have employed the trick of using words such as "men," "human beings" and "cosmic" in order to imply incorrectly that the Cabbala presents a path leading towards salvation for all human beings. The actual fact is that cabbalistic texts, as opposed to talmudic literature, emphasize salvation for only Jews. Many books dealing with the Cabbala that are written in Hebrew, other than those written by Scholem, present an honest description of salvation and other sensitive Jewish issues. This point is well illustrated in studies of the latest and most influential school of Cabbala, the Lurianic School, founded in the late sixteenth century and named after its founding rabbi, Yitzhak Luria. The ideas of Rabbi Luria greatly influenced the theology of Rabbi Kook the elder and still underlie the ideologies of Gush Emunim and Hassidism. Yesaiah Tishbi, an authority on the Cabbala who wrote in Hebrew, explained in his scholarly work, *The Theory of Evil and the (Satanic) Sphere in Lurianic Cabbala* (1942, reprinted in 1982): "It is plain that those prospects and the scheme [of salvation] are intended only for Jews." Tishbi cited Rabbi Hayim Vital, the chief interpreter of Rabbi Luria, who wrote in his book, *Gates of Holiness*: "The Emanating Power, blessed be his name, wanted there to be some people on this low earth that would embody the four divine emanations. These people are the Jews, chosen to join together the four divine worlds here below." Tishbi further cited Vital's writings in emphasizing the Lurianic doctrine that non-Jews have satanic souls: "Souls of non-Jews come entirely from the female part of the satanic sphere. For this reason souls of non-Jews are called evil, not good, and are created without [divine] knowledge." In his illuminating Hebrew-language book, *Rabbinate, Hassidism, Enlightenment: The History of Jewish Culture Between the End of the Sixteenth and the Beginning of the Nineteenth Century* (1956), Ben-Zion Katz explained convincingly that the above doctrines became part of Hassidism. Accurate descriptions of Lurianic doctrines and their wide influence upon religious Jews can be found in numerous other studies, written in Hebrew. In books and articles written in other languages, and thus read by most interested non-Israeli Jews and non-Jews, such descriptions and analyses are most often absent. The role of Satan, whose earthly embodiment according to the Cabbala is every non-Jew, has been minimized or not mentioned by authors who have not written about the Cabbala in Hebrew. Such authors, therefore, have not conveyed to readers accurate accounts of general NRP or its hard-core, Gush Emunim politics.

A modern and influential expression of the attitudes derived above is evident in the teachings and writings of the late "Lubovitcher

Rebbe," Rabbi Menachem Mendel Schneerson, who headed the Chabad movement and wielded great influence among many religious Jews in Israel as well as in the United States. Schneerson and his Lubovitch followers are Haredim; nevertheless, they involved themselves in Israel's political life and shared many concepts with Gush Emunim and the NRP. The ideas of Rabbi Schneerson that appear below are taken from a book of his recorded messages to followers in Israel, titled *Gatherings of Conversations* and published in the Holy Land in 1965. During the subsequent three decades of his life until his death, Rabbi Schneerson remained consistent; he did not change any of the opinions. What Rabbi Scheerson taught either was or immediately became official, Lubovitch, Hassidic belief.

Regarding the non-Jew the Lubovitcher Rebbe's views were clear even if a bit disorderly: "In such a manner the Halacha, stipulated by the Talmud, showed that a non-Jew should be punished by death if he kills an embryo, even if the embryo is non-Jewish, while the Jew should not be, even if the embryo is Jewish. As we [the talmudic sages] learn from Exodus 22:21, beginning with the words 'and if any mischief will follow.'" This quoted verse is a part of a passage beginning in verse 21, describing what should be done "if men strive and hurt a woman with child," thus damaging the embryo. Verse 22, whose beginning is quoted by the Lubovitcher Rebbe, says in full: "And if any mischief will follow, then you shall give soul for soul." (Some English translations use the wording "life for life" instead of "soul for soul.") The above stated difference in the punishment of a Jew and a non-Jew for the same crime is common in the Talmud and Halacha.

The Lubovitcher Rebbe continued:

The difference between a Jewish and a non-Jewish person stems from the common expression: "Let us differentiate." Thus, we do not have a case of profound change in which a person is merely on a superior level. Rather, we have a case of "let us differentiate" between totally different species. This is what needs to be said about the body: the body of a Jewish person is of a totally different quality from the body of [members] of all nations of the world ... The Old Rabbi [a pseudonym for one of the holy Lubovitch rabbis] explained that the passage in Chapter 49 of *Hatanya* [the basic book of Chabad]: "And you have chosen us" [the Jews] means specifically that the Jewish body was chosen [by God], because a choice is thus made between outwardly similar things. The Jewish body "looks as if it were in substance similar to bodies of non-Jews," but the meaning ... is that the bodies only seem to be similar in material substance, outward look and superficial quality. The difference of the inner quality, however, is so great that the bodies should be considered as completely different species. This is the reason why the Talmud states that there is an halachic difference in attitude about the bodies of non-Jews [as opposed to the bodies of Jews]" "their bodies are in vain." ... An even greater difference exists in regard to the soul. Two contrary types of soul exist, a non-Jewish soul comes from three satanic spheres, while the Jewish soul stems from holiness.

As has been explained, an embryo is called a human being, because it has both body and soul. Thus, the difference between a Jewish and a non-Jewish embryo can be understood. There is also a difference in bodies. The body of a Jewish embryo is on a higher level than is the body of a non-Jew. This is expressed in the phrase "let us differentiate" about the body of a non-Jew, which is a totally different kind. The same difference exists in regard to the soul: the soul of a Jewish embryo is different than the soul of a non-Jewish embryo. We therefore ask: Why should a non-Jew be punished if he kills even a non-Jewish embryo while a Jew should not be punished even if he kills a Jewish embryo? The answer can be understood by [considering] the general difference between Jews and non-Jews: A Jew was not created as a means for some [other] purpose; he himself is the purpose, since the substance of all [divine] emanations was created only to serve the Jews. "In the beginning God created the heavens and the earth" [Genesis 1:1] means that [the heavens and the earth] were created for the sake of the Jews, who are called the "beginning." This means everything, all developments, all discoveries, the creation, including the "heavens and the earth – are vanity compared to the Jews. The important things are the Jews, because they do not exist for any [other] aim; they themselves are [the divine] aim."

After some additional cabbalistic explanation the Lubovitcher Rebbe concluded:

Following from what has already been said, it can be understood why a non-Jew should be punished by death if he kills an embryo and why a Jew should not be punished by death. The difference between the embryo and a [baby that was] born is that the embryo is not a self-contained reality but rather is subsidiary; either it is subsidiary to its mother or to the reality created after birth when the [divine] purpose of its creation is then fulfilled. In its present state the purpose is still absent. A non-Jew's entire reality is only vanity. It is written, "And the strangers shall stand and feed your flocks" [Isaiah 61:5]. The entire creation [of a non-Jew] exists only for the sake of the Jews. Because of this a non-Jew should be punished with death if he kills an embryo, while a Jew, whose existence is most important, should not be punished with death because of something subsidiary. We should not destroy an important thing for the sake of something subsidiary. It is true that there is a prohibition against [hurting] an embryo, because it is something that will be born in the future and in a hidden form already exists. The death penalty should be implicated only when visible matters are affected; as previously noted, the embryo is merely of subsidiary importance.

Comments concerning and partial summaries of the above opinions have appeared, but with insufficient emphasis in the Israeli Hebrew press. In 1965, when the above was published, the Lubovitcher Rebbe was allied in Israel to the Labor Party; his movement had already acquired many important benefits from the government then in power as well as previous Israeli governments. The Lubovitchers, for example, had obtained autonomy for their own education system within the context of religious state education. In the mid-1970s the Lubovitcher Rebbe decided that the Labor Party was too moderate and thereafter shifted his movement's political support sometimes to Likud and sometimes to a religious party. Ariel Sharon was the Rebbe's favorite Israeli senior politician. Sharon in turn praised the Rebbe publicly and delivered a moving speech about him in the Knesset after the Rebbe's death. From the June 1967 war until his death the Lubovitcher Rebbe always supported Israeli wars and opposed any retreat. In 1974 he strongly opposed the Israeli withdrawal from the Suez area, conquered in the October 1973 war; he promised Israel divine favors if it persisted in occupying that land. After his death thousands of his Israeli followers, who continued to hold the views expressed in the above quoted passage, played an important role in Netanyahu's election victory by demonstrating at many cross-road junctions before election day; they chanted the slogan: "Netanyahu is good for the Jews." Although subsequently strongly criticizing Netanyahu for meeting with Arafat, signing the Hebron agreement and agreeing to a second withdrawal, the Rebbe's followers continued their overall preference for the Netanyahu government.

Among the religious settlers in the Occupied Territories the Chabad Hassids constitute one of the most extreme groups. Baruch Goldstein, the mass murderer of Palestinians, was one of them (Goldstein will be discussed in Chapter 6.) Rabbi Yitzhak Ginsburgh, who wrote a chapter of a book in praise of Goldstein and what he did, is another member of their group. Ginsburgh is the former head of the Yoseph Tomb Yeshiva, located on the outskirts of Nablus. Rabbi Ginsburgh, who originally came to Israel from the United States and has good connection to the

Lubovitcher community in the United States, has often expressed his views in English in American Jewish publications. The following appeared in an April 26,1996 *Jewish Week* (New York) article that contained an interview with Rabbi Ginsburgh:

> Regarded as one of the Lubovitcher sect's leading authorities on Jewish mysticism, the St. Louis born rabbi, who also has a graduate degree in mathematics, speaks freely of Jews' genetic-based, spiritual superiority over non-Jews. It is a superiority that he asserts invests Jewish life with greater value in the eyes of the Torah. "If you saw two people drowning, a Jew and a non-Jew, the Torah says you save the Jewish life first," Rabbi Ginsburgh told the *Jewish Week* "If every simple cell in a Jewish body entails divinity, is a part of God, then every strand of DNA is part of God. Therefore, something is special about Jewish DNA." Later, Rabbi Ginsburgh asked rhetorically: "If a Jew needs a liver, can you take the liver of an innocent non-Jew passing by to save him? The Torah would probably permit that. Jewish life has an infinite value," he explained. "There is something infinitely more holy and unique about Jewish life than non-Jewish life."

Changing the words "Jewish" to "German" or "Aryan" and "non-Jewish" to "Jewish" turns the Ginsburgh position into the doctrine that made Auschwitz possible in the past. To a considerable extent the German Nazi success depended upon that ideology and upon its implications not being widely known early. Disregarding even on a limited scale the potential effects of messianic, Lubovitch and other ideologies could prove to be calamitous.

The difference in the attitudes about non-Jews in the Halacha and the Cabbala is well illustrated by the difference expressed specifically in regard to non-Jews who have converted to Judaism. The Halacha, although discriminating against them in some ways, treats converts as new Jews. The Cabbala is unable to adopt this approach because of its emphasis upon the cosmic difference between Jews and non-Jews. The Cabbala explains that converts are really Jewish souls consigned firstly to non-Jewish bodies as punishments and later redeemed by conversion to Judaism either because the punishment ended or because a holy man interceded. This explanation is part of cabbalistic belief in metempsychosis, which is absent in the Halacha. According to the Cabbala, a satanic soul cannot be transformed into a divine soul by mere persuasion.

The ensuing discussion of Gush Emunim ideas and politics takes cognizance of the Lustick and Harkabi studies but relies primarily upon primary source material and upon analyses by Tal and other Hebrew-language writers. Tal described and analyzed Gush Emunim principles by quoting extensively from writings of

Rabbi Yehuda Amital, an outstanding Gush leader who was appointed minister without portfolio in the Israeli government in November 1995, by then Prime Minister Peres and who served in that capacity until June 1996. Peres described Amital as a moderate. In explaining Amital's views, Tal relied heavily upon Amital's published article, "On the significance of the Yom Kippur War [1973]." To illustrate Amital's emphasis upon spiritual yearning and the political-messianic stream of thought, Tal quoted the following:

> The war broke out against the background of the revival of the kingdom of Israel, which in its metaphysical (not only symbolic) status is evidence of the decline of the spirit of defilement in the Western world ... The Gentiles are fighting for their mere survival as Gentiles, as the ritually unclean. Iniquity is fighting its battle for survival. It knows that in the wars of God there will not be a place for Satan, for the spirit of defilement, or for the remains of Western culture, the proponents of which are, as it were, secular Jews.

Tal further interpreted Amital's and thus Gush Emunim's basic views:

> The modern secular world, according to this approach, "is struggling for survival, and thus our war is directed against the impurity of Western culture and against rationality as such." It follows that the alien culture has to be eradicated because "all foreignness draws us closer to the alien, and the alien causes alienation, as is the position of those who still adhere to Western culture and who attempt to fuse Judaism with rationalist empiricist and democratic culture." According to Amital's approach, the Yom Kippur War has to be comprehended in its messianic dimension: a struggle against civilization in its entirety.

Tal proceeded in his discussion to ask Amital a multi-faceted, serious question: "What is the point of all the affliction? Why do wars continue, if the Messiah has already come and if the Kingdom of Israel has already been established?" Amital replied: "The war initiates the process of purification, of refinement, the purifying and cleaning of the congregation of Israel." Tal continued to discuss: "We thus learn that there is only one explanation of the wars: they refine and purify the soul. As impurity is removed, the soul of Israel – by virtue of the war – will be refined. We have already conquered the lands; all that now remains is to conquer impurity."

The followers of the two Rabbi Kooks have applied the above concepts to all other Israeli wars. Rabbi Shmaryahu Arieli, for example, explained, according to Tal, that the 1967 war was a "metaphysical transformation" and that the Israeli conquests transferred land from the power of Satan to the divine sphere. This supposedly proved that the "messianic era" had arrived. Tal also quoted the teachings of Rabbi E. Hadaya: "[The conquests of 1967] liberated the land from the other side [a polite name for Satan], from a mystical force that embodies evil, defilement and moral corruption. We [the Jews] are thus entering an era in which absolute sovereignty rules over corporeality." Tal emphasized that these statements constituted a warning that any Israeli withdrawal from conquered areas would have metaphysical consequences that could result in restoring to Satan sovereignty over that land. Other Gush Emunim leaders directly and indirectly expressed the same ideas in their public statements and writings.

There can be little doubt that Gush Emunim has seriously affected Israeli Jewish religious leaders and lay people. During the time of the Israeli invasion of Lebanon, for example, the military rabbinate in Israel, clearly influenced by the ideas of the two Rabbi Kooks, exhorted all Israeli soldiers to follow in the footsteps of Joshua and to re-establish his divinely ordained conquest of the land of Israel. This exhortation of conquest included extermination of non-Jewish inhabitants. The military rabbinate published a map of Lebanon in which the names of Lebanese towns had been changed to the names of cities found in the Book of Joshua. Beirut, for example, was changed to Be'erot. The map designated Lebanon as land belonging to the ancient northern tribes of Israel, Asher and Naphtali. As Tal wrote: "Israel's military presence in Lebanon confirmed the validity of the Biblical promise in Deuteronomy 11:24: 'Every place on which the sole of your foot treads shall be yours; our border shall be from the wilderness, from the river Euphrates, to the western sea.'" The followers of the two Rabbis Kook viewed Lebanon as being delivered from the power of Satan with its inhabitants being killed in the process." Such a view is not exceptional; it has numerous ancient and modern parallels, both religious and secular. The idea of a murderous purification of land from the evil and defilement that provoke God is common. In her chapter, "The Rites of Violence," in the book, *Society and Culture in Early Modern France*, Natalie Z. Davis, for example, presented the same idea as being the rationalization for the massacres perpetrated by France in the second half of the sixteenth century. In his excellent book, *The Pursuit of the Millennium*, to cite another example, Norman Cohn discussed Christian religious movements that sought to bring about the millennium by the use of force resulting in the deaths of many people.

Three interpretative and interrelated comments about Tal's analysis of Gush Emunim should be made. First, the rabbis, cited as authorities by both Tal and the authors of this book, are not obscure or fringe rabbis but are important Israeli figures. As previously noted, Shimon Peres, when prime minister, regarded one of them, Rabbi Amital, as a moderate and appointed him minister without portfolio. Second, Tal was able to comprehend the real essence of what he termed the "political messianic trend." His expertise in German Nazism, particularly in Nazi ideology and its sources, almost certainly helped him in his study of Gush Emunim. (See Tal's book in Hebrew, *Political Theology and the Third Reich*, Tel-Aviv University Press, 1989.) The similarities between the Jewish political messianic trend and German Nazism are glaring. The Gentiles are for the messianists what the Jews were for the Nazis. The hatred for Western culture with its rational and democratic elements is common to both movements. Finally, the extreme chauvinism of the messianists is directed towards all non-Jews. The 1973 Yom Kippur War, for instance, was in Amital's view not directed against Egyptians, Syrians and/or all Arabs but against all non-Jews. The war was thus directed against the great majority of citizens of the United States, even though the United States aided Israel in that war. This hatred of non-Jews is not new but, as already discussed, is derived from a continuous Jewish cabbalistic tradition. Those Jewish scholars who have attempted to hide this fact from non-Jews and even from many Jews have not only done a disservice to scholarship; they have aided the growth of this Jewish analogue to German Nazism.

The ideology of the Rabbis Kook is both eschatological and messianic. It resembles in this respect prior Jewish religious doctrines as well as similar trends in Christianity and Islam. This ideology assumes the imminent coming of the Messiah and asserts that the Jews, aided by God, will thereafter triumph over the non-Jews and rule over them forever. (This, it is alleged, will be good for the non-Jews.) All current political developments will either help bring this about sooner or will postpone it. Jewish sins, most particularly lack of faith, can postpone the coming of the Messiah. The delay, however, will not be of long duration, because even the worst sins of the Jews cannot alter the course of redemption. Sins can nevertheless increase the sufferings of Jews prior to the redemption. The two world wars, the Holocaust and other calamitous events of modern history are examples of punishment. The elder Rabbi Kook did not disguise his joy over the loss of lives in World War I; he explained that loss of lives was necessary "in order to begin to break Satan's Power." The followers of the elder Rabbi Kook's pronouncements often have detailed in depth such explanations. Rabbi Dov Lior, one of the best-known rabbis of the aforementioned Gush Emunim rabbinical council and the rabbi of Kiryat Arba, for instance, argued that Israel's failure in its 1982 invasion of Lebanon was due to the lack of faith manifested in the signing of the peace treaty with Egypt and the returning of "the inheritance of our ancestors [Sinai] to strangers." Lior also explained in an article about him, published in the *Hadashot Supplement* of December 20, 1991, that the capture by the Syrians of two Israeli diplomats stationed in Junieh, Lebanon, in May 1984, was "a just punishment for the maltreatment in detention of our boys from the Jewish underground." In the *Hadashot* article Lior added "I do not know what sufferings can yet befall all the Jews" for this crime.

Explanations that may appear to the uninitiated to be outlandish and bizarre are sometimes the most readily acceptable to Gush Emunim followers. This is especially the case when these followers believe redemption is near at hand. They believe that Satan, as described in the Cabbala, is rational and well-versed in logic; they believe further that the power of Satan and of his earthly manifestation, the non-Jews, can at times only be broken by irrational action. Gush Emunim thus founded settlements on the exact days of United States Secretary of States James Baker's recurrent arrivals in Israel not merely to demonstrate Gush Emunim power but also as part of a mystical design to break the power of Satan and its American incarnation. In the past, different Jewish religious movements, for example, the movement of the false Messiah Shabtai Zvi in 1665 and 1666 and early Hassidism, had employed similar logic. Certain Christian and Islamic movements also employed analogous logic at certain times.

Gush Emunim ideologues, especially Rabbi Kook the elder, not only derived their ideas largely from Jewish tradition but were also innovative. How they developed the Messiah concept is illustrative. The Bible anticipated only a single Messiah. Jewish mysticism anticipated two Messiahs. According to the Cabbala the two Messiahs will differ in character. The first Messiah, a militant figure called "son of Joseph," will prepare the material preconditions for redemption. The second Messiah will be a spiritual "son of David" who will redeem the world by spectacular miracle-making. (Gush Emunim followers believe that miracles occur at various times.) The cabbalistic conception is that the two Messiahs will be individuals. Rabbi Kook the elder altered this idea by anticipating and advocating that the first Messiah will be a collective being. Kook identified his group of followers as the collective "son of Joseph." Gush Emunim leaders, following the teaching of Rabbi Kook the elder, continue to perceive their rabbis, and perhaps all followers as well, as the collective incarnation of at least one and perhaps two divinely ordained Messiahs. Gush Emunim members believe that this idea should not be revealed to the uninitiated until the right time. They believe further that their sect cannot err because of its infallible divine guidance.

Rabbi Kook's second innovation concerned the relationship of the first Messiah to ignorant non-believing Jews, both secular and religious. Rabbi Kook derived this concept from the biblical prophecy that the Messiah "bringing salvation" will be "riding upon an ass and upon a colt, the foal of an ass" [Zechariah 9:9]. The Cabbala regarded this verse as evidence for two Messiahs: one riding upon an ass and the other upon a colt. The question here was: How could a collective Messiah ride upon a single ass? Kook answered the question by identifying the ass with Jews who lacked wisdom and correct faith. Kook postulated that the collective Messiah would ride upon these Jews. This meant that the Messiah would exploit them for material gains and would redeem them to the extent that they could be redeemed. The idea of redemption through contact with a spiritually potent personality has been a major theme common to all strands of Jewish mysticism. It has been applied not only to humans and their sins but also to animals and inanimate objects. In Israel this idea is still a part of religious education. Popular books for religious children contain many stories that allegedly illustrate this point. One of the most repeated stories is about a virtuous wild duck that is caught, killed and made into a succulent dish for a holy rabbi. This duck is considered to be redeemed by its being eaten by the holy man. The Gush Emunim innovation here has been to apply this not only to non-believing Jews who are redeemed by following the collective Messiah but also to all conceivable material objects, ranging from tanks to money. Everything can be redeemed if touched or possessed by Jews, especially messianic Jews. Gush Emunim members apply this doctrine to the conflict in the Holy Land. They argue that what appears to be confiscation of Arab-owned land for subsequent settlement by Jews is in reality not an act of stealing but one of sanctification. From their perspective the land is redeemed by being transferred from the satanic to the divine sphere. Gush Emunim, so its followers believe, is by virtue of exclusive access to the total and only truth more important than the remainder of the Jewish people. Gush Emunim rabbis utilize the following analogy of the messianic ass: given its lowly status in the hierarchy of beings, the ass must remain ignorant of the noble purpose of its divinely inspired rider. This is the case in spite of the fact that the ass surpasses the rider in size and sheer power. The divine rider in this analogy leads the ass toward its own salvation. Because of his noble purpose the rider may have to kick the ass during the course of the journey in order to make sure that the ass does not stray from the ordained path. In the same way, the Gush Emunim rabbis assert, this one messianic sect has to handle and lead the ass-like Jews, who have been corrupted by satanic Western culture with its rationality and democracy and who refuse to renounce their beastly habits and embrace the true faith. To further the process, the use of force is permitted whenever necessary.

The final innovation of Rabbi Kook the elder contributed most decisively to the popularity and political influence of his early followers and subsequently of Gush Emunim. During the period of redemption this innovation affected the conduct of the elect in relation to worldly concerns and contacts with other Jews and non-Jews. Rabbi Kook taught that the elect should not stand aloof from the rest of the world, as Jews had often done in the past. Realizing that other people were sinful and even satanic in nature, the elect had to attempt to bridge the gap between themselves and the others by actively involving themselves in society. Only by so doing would the elect have any chance to sanctify others. The elect should provide an example, exert influence politically and increasingly make contact with other people. Since the 1920s this doctrine has greatly influenced the behavior of those affiliated with the NRP. After being established in 1974, Gush Emunim vigorously reasserted this doctrine in spite of great resentment of the public. Unlike Orthodox Jews previously, Rabbi Kook's followers began to dress like secular Jews and only distinguished themselves outwardly by wearing skullcaps. To date they have followed the Israeli secular clothing fashions of the 1950s. In their schools they introduced portions of secular teaching into their curricula. They permitted their people to enroll in Israeli secular universities. They additionally established the religiously oriented Bar-Ilan University. Although restricting the Bar-Ilan teaching staff to religious Jews, Gush Emunim sought to expand the university's scope of instruction to include all the usual academic disciplines. The Haredim have consistently resented and viewed with abhorrence these pursuits of what they regard as secularization. Rabbi Kook insisted that each Jew had a religious duty to fight and to train to fight. NRP members have faithfully followed this teaching. Many Gush Emunim members have been and still are officers of the Israeli army's select units; their proportion in such units has continually increased. Gush Emunim religious school students have gained renown for their excellent combat qualities, their high motivation to fight, their relatively high casualty rate during the Lebanon war and their willingness to beat up Palestinians during the Intifada.

Gush Emunim has won broad public sympathy in Israeli Jewish society because of its attitude towards army service. This contrasts sharply with the societal antagonism directed against the Haredim for their dodging of military service. The doctrine of sanctity, attributed by the two Rabbi Kooks to almost every Zionist enterprise, contributed even more to the widespread public sympathy for and support of Gush Emunim. Tal contrasted the religious Zionist outlook of Rabbi Kook the younger and Gush

Emunim with that of the secular left. Tal defined the secular left's Zionist outlook as a "poetic, lyrical notion, according to which the return to the soil, life within nature, the agricultural achievements, the secular creativity [are essential parts]." The two Rabbi Kooks, while acknowledging that the secular left's notion unwillingly served the coming of messianic redemption, emphasized "the military victories upon holy soil and the Jewish blood spilled on this soil." Rabbi Kook the younger, together with other Gush Emunim leaders, went further, according to Tal, by defining "the State of Israel as the kingdom of Israel and the kingdom of Israel as the kingdom of heaven on earth." Followers of Rabbi Kook still refer to Israel as the "earthly support of the Lord's throne." Israel Harel, one of the most important Gush Emunim leaders, used this expression to make a political point in his weekly column in *Haaretz* on September 12,1996. Quoting an early essay by Rabbi Kook the elder, Harel wrote that the State of Israel was "the base of the Lord's throne in this world" and thus is and should be completely different from states "considered by Locke, Rosseau and others." For such people as Harel, total holiness envelops and justifies everything Israel does within the context of divinely inspired guidance. Tal wrote that from this vantage point "every action, every phenomenon, including secularism, will one day be engulfed by sacredness, by redemption." It is not inconceivable that this type of sacredness could lead to the exploding of nuclear bombs in order to end the power of Satan and to establish "the base of the Lord's throne in this world."

In many respects Gush Emunim members and the majority of NRP supporters have continued to resemble the early Zionist pioneers. This fact has boosted their public image. They have helped to promote this image by presenting themselves to the uninitiated as successors of the pioneers of the 1920s and 1930s who are still cherished in the Jewish national memory and lauded in Israeli education. As previously indicated, Gush Emunim members, except for their miniscule skullcaps, continue consciously to emulate the dress and mannerisms of the early pioneers. The almost exclusively Ashhenazi background of both the early pioneers and the Gush Emunim settlers help this emulation. All Gush Emunim rabbis are Ashkenazi. The accepted Israeli standards of religious education, discussed in Chapter 3, are largely responsible for the absence of Oriental Jews among Gush Emunim rabbis. Although unwillingly to join, many Oriental Jews have supported and continue to support Gush Emunim. The Likud constituency has to date consistently supported Gush Emunim. By contrast, most members of the Labor Party supported Gush Emunim until the end of the 1970s but changed after Gush Emunim opposed the peace treaty with Egypt and demanded that Lebanon be annexed "as a part of the heritage of our ancestors, the tribes of Asher, Naphtali and Zebulun." Gush Emunim infuriated many Labor supporters by continuing to advocate other extreme hawkish policies and by fiercely opposing Sharon's 1982 alliance with the Lebanese Falangists, who were Christians and therefore considered to be idolaters. Gush Emunim's position in 1982 was that Jews in their battles and conquests should only rely upon God's help. Any alliances with non-Jews could incur God's wrath and lead to His withholding help. Such ideas were, even for extreme Labor Party hawks, unacceptable.

Gush Emunim and NRP politics must be understood within the context of ideology. The ideology makes clear what members of these groups wish to accomplish. Books written in English have unfortunately failed to discuss adequately this ideology. Lustick's book, *For the Land and the Lord*, which discusses Gush Emunim's outward political behavior, is the prime example. Lustick relied to a great extent upon the writings of Harold Fisch for his analysis of Gush Emunim's political ideology. Fisch, a professor of English literature who seemingly has only limited competence in the Talmud and Cabbala, has mostly written for English-speaking readers and has primarily concentrated upon Christian fundamentalists in the United States. Lustick also relied somewhat upon the writings of Rabbi Menachem Kasher. Kasher was a highly respected talmudic scholar who wrote in Hebrew and influenced potential Gush Emunim initiates. His messianic tracts are well-known to many Gush Emunim and Yeshiva students. Lustick only briefly quoted Kasher twice and then obfuscated what he did quote. In our book we have relied more upon what Kasher wrote and have additionally utilized other Gush Emunim literature.

Gush Emunim activists live in a homogeneous West Bank society that they control. This society is mostly protected against "contamination" by rival detested ideologies, especially those that stem from Western culture and have been to some extent influenced the secular part of Israeli Jewish society. The possibility clearly exists that the Gush Emunim homogeneous society and its NRP supporters can increase their political power and influence within Israeli society. The ideology of the two Rabbis Kook is the determining force of NRP and Gush Emunim political action. The fundamental political tenet of Gush Emunim is that the Jewish people are unique. Gush Emunim members share this tenet with all Orthodox Jews, but they interpret it somewhat differently. Lustick discussed this tenet by focusing upon the Gush Emunim denial of one classical secular Zionist theme. Lustick correctly pinpointed the two assumptions of this theme, the first being that "Jewish life had been distorted on both the individual and the collective levels by the abnormality of diaspora existence." Second, only by undergoing a "process of normalization," by emigrating to Palestine and by forming a Jewish state can Jews become a normal nation. Quoting Fisch, Lustick stated that for Gush Emunim this classical idea "is the original delusion of the secular Zionists." The Gush Emunim argument is that secular Zionists measured that "normality" by applying non-Jewish standards that are satanic. The secular Zionists focused upon certain nations that they considered "normal" and asserted that the non-Jews in these normal nations were more advanced than were most diaspora Jews. Because of this, so argued the secular Zionists, Jews should try to emulate those non-Jews by becoming a "normal" people in a "normal" nation state. The Gush Emunim counter argument is: "Jews are not and cannot be a normal people. Their eternal uniqueness ... [is] the result of the covenant God made with them at Mount Sinai." Lustick further explained this Gush Emunim position by quoting one of the group's leaders, Rabbi Aviner: "'While God requires other normal nations to abide by abstract codes of justice and right-eousness, such laws do not apply to Jews.'" Haredi rabbis often cited this idea in their writings, but they strictly reserved its glaring consequences for the yet-to-come messianic age. The Halacha supports this reservation by carefully distinguishing between two situations in discussing codes of justice and righteousness. The Halacha permits Jews to rob non-Jews in those locales wherein Jews are stronger than non-Jews. The Halacha prohibits Jews from robbing non-Jews in those locales wherein the non-Jews are stronger. Gush Emunim dispenses with such traditional precautions by claiming that Jews, at least those in Israel and the Occupied Territories, are already living in the beginning of the messianic age.

Lustick failed to explain adequately the messianic age consid-erations and the distinctions between Jews and non-Jews. Harkabi's treatment was better. In discussing the halachic teaching and the Gush Emunim position regarding murders, Harkabi explained that the murder of a Jew, particularly when committed by a non-Jews, is in Jewish law the worst possible crime. He then quoted the Gush Emunim leader, Rabbi Israel Ariel. Relying upon the Code of Maimonides and the Halacha, Rabbi Ariel stated: "A Jew who killed a non-Jew is exempt from human judgment and has not violated the [religious] prohibition of murder." Harkabi noted further that this should be remembered when "the demand is voiced that all non-Jewish residents of the Jewish state be dealt with according to halachic regulations." Gush Emunim rabbis have continually reiterated that Jews who killed Arabs should not be punished. Gush Emunim members not only help such Jews who are punished by Israel's secular courts but also refuse to call those Jews "murderers." It logically follows that the religious settlers and their followers emphasize the "shedding of Jewish blood" but show little concern about the "shedding of non-Jewish blood." The Gush Emunim influence on Israeli policies can be measured by the fact that the Israeli government's policy on this matter has clearly reflected the Gush Emunim position. The Israeli government under both Labor and Likud leadership has refused to free Palestinian prisoners "with Jewish blood on their hands" but has not hesitated to free prisoners "with non-Jewish blood on their hands."

Another practical consequence of such attitudes is Gush Emunim's impact upon the conduct of the Israeli government in all matters concerning the territories. Gush Emunim continues to encourage Israeli authorities to deal cruelly with Palestinians in the West Bank and the Gaza Strip. The refusals of Prime Ministers Rabin, Peres and Netanyahu to advocate the evacuation of even a single Jewish settlement is attributable primarily to the influence of Gush Emunim. Gush Emunim's influence upon all Israeli governments and political leaders of varying political persuasions has been significant.

The Gush Emunim attitude towards Palestinians, always referred to as "Arabs living in Israel," is important. Lustick mostly avoided this subject. Harkabi dealt with it honestly by extensively quoting the statements of Rabbis Tzvi Yehuda Kook, Shlomo Aviner and Israel Ariel. Kook, Aviner and Ariel viewed the Arabs living in Israel as thieves; they based their view upon the premise that all land in Israel was and remained Jewish and that all property found thereon thus belonged to Jews. Harkabi, who learned this when doing the research for his book, expressed his shock: "I never imagined that Israelis would so interpret the concept of historical right." Harkabi listed in sub-chapters of his book the numerous applications and extensions of this doctrine. He pointed out that for Gush Emunim the Sinai and present-day Lebanon are parts of this Jewish land and must be liberated by Israel. Rabbi Ariel published an atlas that designated all lands that were Jewish and needed to be liberated. This included all areas west and south of the Euphrates River extending through present-day Kuwait. Harkabi quoted Rabbi Aviner: "We must live in this land even at the price of war. Moreover, even if there is peace, we must instigate wars of liberation in order to conquer it [the land]." It is not unreasonable to assume that Gush Emunim, if it possessed the power and control, would use nuclear weapons in warfare to attempt to achieve its purpose.

For Gush Emunim, as Harkabi made clear and Lustick indirectly confirmed, the God-ordained inferiority of non-Jews living in the state of Israel extends to categories other than life and property. Gush Emunim has developed a foreign policy for the state of Israel to adopt. This policy stipulates that Arab hostility towards the Jews is theological in nature and is inherent. The conclusion drawn is that the Arab–Israeli conflict cannot be resolved politically. This conclusion is supported by Lustick's quoting the prominent Gush Emunim leader and former Knesset member, Eliezer Waldman: "'Arab hostility springs, like all anti-Semitism, from the world's recalcitrance to be saved [by the Jews]'" (pp. 77–9). Lustick also quoted other Gush Emunim leaders who left no doubt about their refusal to enter into political agreements with "present-day Jewish inhabitants of the land who resist the establishment of Jewish sovereignty over its entirety." Lustick quoted Fisch who argued that Arab resistance could be attributed to Arabs' seeking "to fulfill their collective death-wish." Gush Emunim rabbis, politicians and ideological popularizers have routinely compared Palestinians to the ancient Canaanites, whose extermination or expulsion by the ancient Israelites was, according to the Bible, predestined by a divine design. This genocidal theme of the Bible creates great sympathy for Gush Emunim among many Christian fundamentalists who anticipate that the end of the world will be marked by slaughters and devastation. Gush Emunim has from its inception wanted to expel as many Palestinians as possible. Palestinian terrorist acts allow Gush Emunim spokespeople to disguise their real demand for total expulsion by arguing that expulsion is warranted by "security needs."

Harkabi quoted the views of Mordechai Nisan, a lecturer at the Hebrew University in Jerusalem, that were published in the August 1984 issue of *Kivunim*, an official publication of the World Zionist Organization (pp. 151–6). According to Nisan, who relied upon Maimonides, a non-Jew permitted to reside in the land of Israel "must accept paying a tax and suffering the humiliation of servitude." In keeping with a religious text of Maimonides, Nisan, according to Harkabi, demanded that a non-Jew "be held down and not [be allowed to] raise his head against Jews." Paraphrasing Nisan further, Harkabi wrote: "Non-Jews must not be appointed to any office or position of power over Jews. If they refuse to live a life of inferiority, then this signals their rebellion and the unavoidable necessity of Jewish warfare against their very presence in the land of Israel." Such views about non-Jews, published in an official publication of the World Zionist Organization, resemble Nazi arguments about Jews. Harkabi commented: "I do not know how many Jews share his [Nisan's] belief, but the publication of the article in a leading Zionist periodical is a cause for grave concern."

The three following examples of other articles that appeared in Hebrew-language newspapers provide additional analyses of NRP and Gush Emunim attitudes. One of these articles deals with the most extreme group within Gush Emunim, named Emunim (Being Faithful). Established after the formation of the Rabin government in 1992, Emunim is led by Rabbi Benny Alon, the son of retired

Deputy President of the Israeli Supreme Court Menahem Alon. Rabbi Alon, quoted by Nadav Shraggai in his September 18,1992 *Haaretz* article, stated:

> The method of the mid-1970s will no longer work under a government whose moral profile is defined by the Meretz Party and whose members' hearts and minds are filled with scorn for the entire land of Israel and for Judaism. They not only want a Palestinian state without any Jews to be established in the very midst of the land of Israel. They also want a secular democratic state to replace the Jewish state of Israel. This government is spiritually rotten.

Rabbi Alon then contrasted the 1992 government leaders with the Labor leaders of the mid-1980s and before, who "felt like warm-hearted Jews feel" and were thus responsive to Gush Emunim's pressures. Alon continued, "But you cannot apply the same methods with the likes of [Meretz MK] Dedi Tzuker or [Meretz member] Moshe Amirav who coordinate their deeds with our enemies." In preparing his September 18, 1992 *Maariv* article, journalist Avi Raz questioned Alon further and discovered Emunim's tactics: "Emunim wants to discredit Rabin [the then prime minister] by forcing him to rely [for a Knesset majority] on the MKs from the Arab parties and thus to destroy the legitimacy of his government." Rabin and Peres made concessions but nevertheless insisted upon expanding Jewish settlements. In his article Raz quoted Alon further:

> From the spiritual point of view Rafael Eitan is wrong and should be criticized when he justifies Jewish settlements on the basis of helping Israeli's security. Security considerations in favor of the settlements are not the point. As I see it, politics rest upon spirituality. A body politic needs a soul. Israel's security and even the survival of the Jewish nation are no more than material dimensions of the spiritual Jewish depth. When we say that we must prevent the formation of a Palestinian state in order to save the Jewish state from extinction, we are not talking about spiritual things.

As Raz observed: "Blessed with profound spirituality, Alon and his associates go to the United States for five days in order to request Christian fundamentalists to support financially their activities." Alon and his associates succeeded in acquiring some of this requested funding. As Jewish fundamentalists who abominate non-Jews, they forged a spiritual alliance with Christians who believe that supporting Jewish fundamentalism is necessary to support the second coming of Jesus. This alliance has become a significant factor in both US and Middle Eastern politics.

The second example concerns the policies of Gush Emunim itself under the Labor and Meretz government of the 1990s. In his October 5, 1992 *Haaretz* article, Danny Rubinstein quoted Gush Emunim leaders who believed the goal of Rabin's policies was "to destroy root and branch the [Jewish] settlements in the territories and all accomplishments of Zionism." Rubinstein carefully distinguished between the secular Golan Heights settlers and Gush Emunim. The Golan Heights settlers claimed that Rabin's policies were mistaken, because peace with Syria could be reached on Israeli terms. Gush Emunim claimed that "the Washington negotiations [with the PLO] amount to nothing else than a dialogue of human beings with a herd of ravenous wolves, aiming solely at turning the entire land of Israel into the entire land of the Arabs." This does not mean that Gush Emunim declined to take money for its own purposes from the government that negotiated "with a herd of ravenous wolves."

In his October 14, 1992 *Haaretz* article, Nadav Shraggai discussed a symposium, organized and underwritten by the ministry of religion in conjunction with the ministry of education, headed by Shulamit Aloni. The symposium's theme was: "Is autonomy for resident aliens in the Holy Land feasible?" Rabbi Shlomo Goren, the symposium's major speaker, explained: "'Autonomy is tantamount to a denial of the Jewish religion.'" According to Goren, the Halacha considers the denial of Judaism to be the gravest Jewish sin and enjoins pious Jews to kill those infidels who deny Judaism. Rabbi Goren likened such infidels to those people who advocated autonomy. This indicated that an attempt to assassinate Rabin would occur for religious reasons. Goren argued further that Judaism prohibits "granting any national rights to any group of foreigners in the land of Israel." Goren also denied that a Palestinian nation existed. He asserted: "Palestinians disappeared in the second century BC, and I have not heard of their being resurrected." Goren reassured his audience that, undeterred by widespread infidelities, "the process of redemption, already underway for one hundred years, cannot be reversed when Divine Providence awaits us all the time." Another symposium participant, Rabbi Aviner, concurred with Goren that Judaism forbade granting even a small amount of autonomy to the Palestinians. Rabbi Zalman Melamed, chairman of the Committee of the Rabbis of Judea, Samaria and Gaza, made the same point even more clearly: "No rabbinual authority disputes that it would be ideal if the land of Israel were inhabited by only Jews." Rabbi Shlomo Min-Hahar extended the argument to Muslims and Christians specifically by claiming: "The entire Muslim world is money-grubbing, despicable and capable of anything. All Christians without exception hate the Jews and look forward to their deaths."

Israeli taxpayers, including Muslim and Christian Arabs, paid for this symposium, during which rabbinical leaders delivered such arguments. Prime Minister Rabin and the ministers of religion and education approved and did not utter publicly negative criticism of any of the views expressed. Rabin's approval might be understood as a part of his deliberate encouragement of political programs at variance with what he claimed to favor. Minister of Education Aloni's approval can be understood rationally only as another manifestation of her weakness, carelessness and foolishness. Both Rabin and Aloni visited Germany shortly before this symposium and fiercely condemned publicly the "German hatred of foreigners." They carefully avoided mentioning racist statements and recommendations made by rabbis in Israel about how foreigners should be treated. They did not mention, let alone condemn, Rabbi Melamed's advocacy of transfer, that is, the total expulsion of all non-Jews from the land of Israel. Such mention might have complemented their denunciation of German xenophobia.

The third example, also taken from the Hebrew press, stems from a book of responsa, published in 1990. The book, *Intifada Responses*, written by the important Gush Emunim rabbi, Shlomo Aviner, provides in plain Hebrew halachic answers to the questions of what pious Jews should do to Palestinians during situations that arise at times similar to the Intifada. The book is divided into brief chapters that contain answers to questions. The answers do not relate to Israeli law. Quotations from the first two chapters (pp. 19–22) illustrate the essence of the questions and answers contained in this book. The first exemplary question in Chapter 1 is: "Is there a difference between punishing an Arab child and an Arab adult for a disturbance of our peace?" The answer begins by cautioning people not conversant with the Halacha that comparisons should not be made between Jewish and Gentile underage minors; "As is known, no Halachic punishments can be inflicted upon Jewish boys below the age of thirteen and Jewish girls below the age of twelve ... Maimonides wrote that this rule applied to Jews alone ... not to any non-Jews. Therefore, any non-Jews, no matter what age, will have to pay for any crime committed." In providing his answer, Rabbi Aviner proceeded to quote another ruling by Maimonides that warned Jews not to punish a non-Jewish child who can be presumed to be "short of wisdom." Aviner concluded that determining whether a non-Jewish child is to be regarded as an adult depends upon whether that child, even if younger than thirteen, has sufficient understanding. According to what Aviner wrote in his book, any Jew is capable of judging whether a non-Jewish child should in this sense be considered and punished as an adult. The second exemplary question is: "What shall we do if an Arab child intends to threaten a [Jewish] life?" Rabbi Aviner explained that all prior responsa dealt only with the actual commissions of crimes by non-Jewish children. He explained in this answer that if a non-Jewish child intended to commit murder, for example, by throwing a stone at a passing car, that the non-Jewish child should be considered a "persecutor of the Jews" and should be killed. Citing Maimonides as his authority, Aviner maintained that killing the non-Jewish child in this instance is necessary to save Jewish life.

In the second chapter of his book Rabbi Aviner posed and answered a single question: "Does the Halacha permit inflicting the death penalty upon Arabs who throw stones?" His answer was that inflicting such a punishment is not only permitted but is mandatory. This punishment, moreover, is not reserved for stone throwers but can be invoked for other reasons. Aviner asserted that a rabbinical court or a king of Israel "has the power to punish anyone by death if it is believed that the world will thereby be improved." The rabbinical court or king of Israel can alternatively punish non-Jews and wicked Jews by beating them mercilessly, by imprisoning them under the most severe conditions and/or by inflicting upon them other extreme suffering. Gush Emunim spokespeople have argued that this power of the rabbinical court and king of Israel can devolve to the Israeli government, provided that government abides by the correct religious rulings. The punishments, mentioned here, should be invoked if the authorities believe that such punishment will deter other wicked people. Aviner made clear his preference was to invoke the death penalty and /or severe flogging upon any non-Jew found guilty of intending to throw stones at Jews.

The discussion in this chapter should distinguish qualitatively the Gush Emunim-NRP form from the Haredi form of Jewish fundamentalism. The greater potential danger clearly rests with the Gush Emunim and the NRP, because their members have involved themselves in the state in order to sanctify Israel.

The Nature of Gush Emunim Settlements

Media coverage of Israeli settlements in the Occupied Territories has primarily focused upon effects on Palestinians and the threat posed to peaceful resolution of conflict. From the prospective of Jewish fundamentalism the religious settlements should be viewed from three standpoints: their standing as citadels of messianic ideology, their present and potential influence upon Israeli society and their potential role as the nuclei of the new society that messianic leaders want to build.

Such discussion must be preceded by two comments concerning the settlements, as viewed by Israeli society. The first comment is that a great majority of Israeli citizens, represented by Knesset members, favor Israel's retaining all settlements. In early 1999, at least 100 of the 120 Knesset members, including all the Labor Party members, almost certainly support this position even though minor differences exist about the form of retention. All Arab Knesset members oppose retaining the settlements; hence the percentage of Jewish Knesset members in favor is still even greater than a mere counting might indicate. In Israeli Jewish society, nevertheless, a sharp popular difference in point of view about settlements still exists. Some small groups on the left oppose all settlements. More importantly, most Israeli Jews consider it normal that Jews live in some settlements but abnormal that Jews live in other settlements. This distinction is usually ignored outside Israel, especially in the Arab world.

The majority of Israeli Jews regard living in settlements in the "greater Jerusalem" area as normal. "Greater Jerusalem" is an Israeli urban and social term, not limited in meaning to the Green Line or to the municipal borders of Jerusalem, as established during the 1967 annexation. Living in "greater Jerusalem" means living in a place with bus connections adequate for Jews to travel by public transportation to Jerusalem for shopping or evening entertainment and to return home by midnight. In early 1999, more than 250,000 Israeli Jews, about 5 per cent of the total Israeli population, lived in "greater Jerusalem." The total population of all other West Bank, Gaza Strip and Golan Heights settlements is about 100,000.

These 100,000 are not solidly grouped in a small area, closely connected with a big city, but are divided into many small settlements. Ariel, the largest West Bank settlement outside of "greater Jerusalem," for example, has about 15,000 inhabitants; Kiryat Arba has less than 6000; many settlements have about 100 inhabitants. These numbers show that the majority of Israeli Jews regard living in those settlements as abnormal and refuse to settle there. In spite of the money expended and the other forms of support by Israeli governments for so long a time period, only a small number of Jews have opted to live in settlements in the occupied territories outside of "greater Jerusalem."

In the settlements outside of "greater Jerusalem" another distinction, constantly made by the Israeli Jewish public, must be noted. Those settlements whose inhabitants are similar socially and politically to the majority secular segment of Israeli Jewish society have been and still are viewed differently than are those settlements whose inhabitants are mostly or totally religious Jews. (As previously stated only 20 per cent of all Israeli Jews are religious.) This is seen in Israeli election results, reported by the media about every four years for each locality, including each settlement. In the "greater Jerusalem" settlements, the voting pattern does not differ from the Jewish average behind the Green Line; in other secular settlements the pattern is almost the same with only a small tilt to the right. The Labor and Meretz parties regularly receive good percentages of the total vote. In the religious settlements, on the other hand, the inhabitants rarely even vote for Likud or other right-wing secular parties; they vote instead for religious parties and quite often only for the NRP. In Kiryat Arba in the 1992 elections, for example, the four largest secular parties – Labor, Likud, Meretz and Tsomet – received altogether less than 5 per cent of the vote. Nationally, those parties together received about 80 per cent of the national vote. In the 1996 election the Likud vote in Kiryat Arba rose to 24.4 per cent because of Netanyahu's promises; in the separate vote for prime minister that year Netanyahu received 96.3 per cent and Peres only 3.6 per cent. (In the national vote for prime minister that year Netanyahu received 50.1 per cent and Peres 49.3 per cent.) Beit El B is a typical smaller religious settlement in which Netanyahu received 99.6 per cent of the prime minister's vote in 1996 to only 0.3 per cent for Peres. In the Knesset election that same year in Beit El B, the NRP received 76.4 per cent and Moledet, the most right-wing party represented in the Knesset, with strong religious tendencies, received 14.5 per cent. Thus, NRP and Moledet, the two parties that garnered together 11 of the 120 Knesset seats or 9.1 per cent in 1996, received 90 per cent of the Beit El B vote. In contrast, in the secular settlement, Alfey Menashe, Netanyahu received 71.5 per cent and Peres 28.4 per cent of the vote.

The most exposed and isolated settlements are those inhabited by religious settlers. Although largely ignored by the media outside of Israel, this is a significant fact. In these exposed and isolated settlements, only religious messianic Jews are prepared to settle. To a greater extent, this has been the major reason why all Israeli governments have supported the religious messianic settlements regardless of how the inhabitants there have voted. Netzarim, situated in the middle of the Gaza Strip, is a good example of these settlements. To the north of Netzarim is Gaza City, to the south, some of the largest refugee camps. Each conglomeration has about 200,000 inhabitants. In mid 1998, Netzarim had about 120 religious messianic Jewish settler families. (At the time that the Oslo agreement was signed, Netzarim had almost 60 families.) Some of the adult males living in Netzarim spend most of their time studying Talmud. Near Netzarim is an army base that guards a military road crossing the Gaza Strip from east to west. This road, which according to the Oslo agreement is under exclusive Israeli control, cuts the Gaza Strip into two parts. The army base is strategic in controlling Gaza but is represented to the Israeli Jewish public and to the outside world as necessary to protect the settlement of Netzarim. Secular, traditional and/or Haredi Jews have not opted to settle in Netzarim and have given no indications of settling there in the future. Thus, the Israeli government, wishing to maintain the control of the road, must depend upon the messianic settlers who are ideologically dedicated to settle in such a place.

Settlements in the Occupied Territories can be correctly understood only within the context of overall Israeli strategy. The basic concept, held since 1967 by both Labor and Likud with different degrees of hypocrisy, has been to oppress Palestinians with maximum efficiency. Maximum efficiency includes minimal number of Jewish forces to achieve the specific purpose. The major idea is that well-trained Jewish soldiers should to the greatest extent possible be reserved for any major war with one or more of the Arab states. Soon after acquiring the Occupied Territories in June, 1967, the Israeli government seriously considered the "Jordanian option." This idea was that Jordanian forces would come to the West Bank to do the necessary job for Israel. The government of Jordan, however, refused to agree to this plan. Hence, the government of Israel then devised and instituted the "village leagues," composed of local Palestinians who effectively ruled the West Bank for some years with only slight support of the Israeli army. The Intifada broke the "village leagues." Both the "Jordanian option" and the "village leagues" concepts were devised for the same purpose as was the Oslo process in the 1990s. Prime Minister Rabin clearly explained that this purpose was to have Palestinians ruled on Israelis' behalf by their own people. This was to be accomplished without interference from human right organizations and without Israeli legal hindrances to the arbitrary will of the conquest regime. The Israeli army, according to this thinking, would be free to concentrate upon its grand military strategy.

Israeli strategy regarding the Gaza Strip and the West Bank in the period after Oslo was and still is based upon settlements being the foci of Israeli military power. This strategy can best be described by considering the Gaza Strip, where the geography is much clearer than in the West Bank. The Gaza Strip, as clearly seen on published maps, is criss-crossed by military roads. In keeping with the Cairo Accords, these military roads remain under exclusive Israeli jurisdiction and are patrolled by the army, either jointly with Palestinian police or separately. The Israeli army has the legal right to close any section of these roads to Palestinian traffic, even if the section is within an area ruled by the Palestinian Authority. The Israeli army uses this right routinely either when a convoy on route to a settlement is passing or when a decision is made to embarrass the Palestinian Authority. One of these roads, the Gaza City bypassing road, traverses the length of the Strip, carefully bypassing the main cities and refugee camps. Another military road, joined to a strip of land, cuts off the Gaza Strip from Egypt. Other roads traverse the Gaza Strip from the Israeli border on its east side to the sea or to the Jewish settlement block (Qatif) on the west. One such road, the Netzarim road, meets the Gaza City bypassing road at Netzarim, thus rendering Netzarim a strategi- cally important crossroad. Shortly after the signing of the Oslo Accord, the Israeli Hebrew press reported that large forces of the border guards and the army were stationed near Netzarim where a new base had been constructed for them. The official status of Netzarim allowed Israel to do this legally and to acquire the support of that part of the Israeli Jewish public that is more devoted to settlements than to army bases. As the well-known commentator Nahum Barnea quipped: "Had a Netzarim not existed, it would have been invented."

The overall effect of all these roads is that the Gaza Strip is sliced into enclaves controlled by the bypassing roads. The role of the Jewish settlements in the Gaza Strip is to serve as pivots of the road grid. This is devised to ensure more effectual perpetual Israel control. This new form of control, labelled "control from the outside" by Rabin and other Labor politicians, allows the army to dominate the Gaza Strip with only a minor expenditure of forces. This is far preferable to the former situation in which huge control presence had to be expended for direct patrolling of cities and refugee camps of the Gaza Strip. The Hebrew press has continually referred to the earlier form of control as the "control from the inside" and has emphasized that it was less effective and required more forces than the "control from the outside." Changing from inside to outside control continues to depend upon the grid of roads which in turn depends upon settlements such as Netzarim. As already stated but worth repeating, only religious Jews who believe in messianic ideology have been willing to establish and live in such settlements.

The situation in the West Bank, outside the greater Jerusalem, is geographically more complicated than the Gaza Strip but is essentially based upon the same principles of "control from the outside." This control is centered upon a grid of roads whose foci are the settlements. A few settlements were founded for sentimental reasons. Ariel Sharon, wanting to provoke the United States Secretary of State James Baker during his visits to Israel in 1991 and 1992, helped establish these few settlements. Small groups of fundamentalist Jews, even more extreme than Gush Emunim, also helped establish these small settlements. Although given prominent media coverage, these settlements remained relatively insignificant, representing only a small proportion of all the settlements. Settlements, such as Kiryat Arba and the separate Jewish settlement in Hebron, have been supported by all Israeli governments primarily for strategic reasons. Although at times creating smokescreens by making insulting comments about settlers, Prime Minister Rabin from the time of the Oslo agreement until his death strengthened most of the settlements, especially those in the West Bank. Yossi Beilin, one of the chief architects of the Oslo agreement, repeatedly reassured the Israeli public that the Labor government had not abandoned the settlers. Beilin, as reported in *Maariv* on September 27, 1995, rebutted accusations made by Likud members of Knesset:

> Their most ridiculous accusation is that we have abandoned the settlers. The Oslo Accord was delayed for months to guarantee that all the settlers would remain intact and that the settlers would have maximum security. This entailed making an immense financial investment in them. The situation in the settlements has never been better than that created following the Oslo Accord.

Even more important is that the Labor government had an opportunity to remove the Hebron settlers, or at least a part of them, in the period of shock after Goldstein's massacre. The Labor government refrained from doing so. In his August 18, 1995 *Davar* article, Daniel Ben-Simon revealed the following about discussion of the issue in Prime Minister Rabin's office: "The heads of all Israeli security services opposed the evacuation of Hebron's settlers." Such opposition underlined the settlements' strategic importance and the dependence of both the Israeli government and army upon the messianic settlers.

The messianic ideology, described in the prior chapter, and the many pronouncements of messianic rabbis and lay leaders show that the aim of Gush Emunim, unlike the aim of Israeli governments, is not limited to the strategic value of utilizing settlements to keep control of the Occupied Territories. The more important aim of Gush Emunim leaders is to create in their homogeneous settlements models of a new society. They hope this new society will spread until it finally absorbs the secular, traditional and Haredi Jewish population of the state of Israel into the collective Jewish identity that they envision. This identity will, they believe, be the religious, ethnocentric, anti-liberal and anti-universalist society ordered by God. In attempting to conceptualize their plan, Gush Emunim leaders can tolerate democracy only so long as it helps to create the divine Jewish kingdom. They believe that any values not consistent with Jewish values, as established by the Halacha and Cabbala, should be suppressed. Human and civil rights, as well as the concept of statehood, should be established by a specified divinely inspired group of rabbis. These views became more widely acceptable in Israeli society, especially among NRP members, after the October 1973 war. In that war secular Israeli militarism suffered a defeat. The widely perceived failure of generals led to the formation of an esoteric elite that supposedly derived its knowledge from a higher source than mere strategic considerations. Some of the leading generals in that war were regarded as hedonists who were careless with the military affairs entrusted to them; Gush Emunim rabbis and lay leaders appeared to many Israeli Jews to be endowed with dedication, a sense of mission, moral superiority, strict honesty in financial affairs and a sense of their own certitude. This characterization, similar to that of Hamas leaders in Palestinian society, continued thereafter. Gush Emunim leaders have remained dedicated to their principles and are financially honest. In a society pervaded by many kinds of corruption, this is most important. Gush Emunim has been and still is endowed, moreover, with a territorial base of its own, replete with dedicated followers who can expertly handle weapons and execute military operations.

The power of Gush Emunim increased significantly between 1974 and 1992. In addition to its own members it acquired a periphery of supporters with varying degrees of commitment. Perhaps its greatest achievement after 1974 was its ability to influence Israeli Jewish culture and collective identity during a period when ethnocentric ideas rose to the fore in Israeli society. Most of the political right wing, as well as many Labor Party supporters, remained sympathetic to Gush Emunim so long as Palestinians in the territories remained relatively docile. This situation lasted until the outbreak of the Intifada in December 1987. Before the Intifada, many Israeli Jews felt that the control of Palestinians from the inside was not too costly and was bearable. Hence, many secular Israeli Jews felt that they could afford to support the Gush Emunim version of the conquest rather than the Moshe Dayan version, which prevailed until 1974 and was based upon cooperation with conservative Palestinian notables. Cooperation with the traditional Palestinian notables made it unnecessary to keep large Israeli forces inside the areas densely inhabited by Palestinians. Because the notables were alienated by the settling and by the resultant confiscation of land in those areas, "village leagues" were invented as a substitute for the traditional forces. The Intifada showed that this prop was only of temporary value. The settling of the Gaza Strip and the remainder of the West Bank began in 1975 when Rabin for the first time was prime minister and Peres was the defense minister in charge of the territories. These two architects of the so-called peace process of the 1990s were largely responsible for one of the major factors preventing peace.

The onslaught of the Intifada changed sentiment within Israeli Jewish society. The Israeli government deployed more Israeli soldiers in the territories. This caused many secular Israeli Jews to reconsider the costs involved in occupying the territories. Many of these Jews concluded that the cost was unwarranted. A new situation in Israeli society then developed and continued thereafter. The coalition of messianists and their various supporters, all ethnocentric to some extent, joined together and formed one camp. The other camp consisted of a politically and socially heterogeneous group of people, united in opposition to the type of Jewish theocracy that they saw as the inevitable consequence of the continued support of Gush Emunim and its settlements. The continuing Israeli domination of the Occupied Territories, dictated to some extent by Gush Emunim, developed into a major issue in the struggle between these two Israeli Jewish camps.

The rapid organization of Gush Emunim settlers boosted the expansion and power of religious settlements after 1974. The rabbis who became and remained the dominant leaders of the Gush Emunim settlers in 1991, organized themselves into the Association of Judea and Samaria Rabbis. The group was founded after President Bush of the United States pressured the Shamir government to participate in the Madrid Conference. Lay settler leaders were afraid of what might develop at the Madrid Conference. As Dov Albaum wrote in the January 7, 1994 issue of *Yerushalaim*: "The rabbis, trusting in the divine promise, took advantage of that situation by filling the leadership vacuum." The power of the rabbinical association increased after the Oslo agreement. Albaum continued his analysis by quoting Daniel Shilo, the rabbi of the Kedunim messianic settlement:

> The Judea and Samaria rabbis are now solving the gravest problems the religious settlers face when they begin to lose faith in the Jewish settlement of Judea and Samaria, as ordered by God, to be an instrument of the Jewish redemption. Jews who lack faith even begin to ponder whether the whole idea of settlement in the territories might not be fundamentally wrong or whether the process of divine redemption is not in its retrogression stage or whether the Almighty is not trying to signal to us to halt the settling. In such a time rabbis have the obligation to provide the answers. This is why we rabbis have more power than any conceivable lay Gush Emunim authority.

The rabbis used this power to emphasize that their followers were obligated to have faith in them. This is often disguised as having faith in God.

Albaum further observed:

> The Judea and Samaria rabbis are not satisfied with being vested only with spiritual power. They began developing their own intelligence network, which quickly became extensive, using information gathered from religious or otherwise sympathetic officers of the Israeli army's high command. General Moshe Bar-Kochba, a member of the General Staff who recently died after retiring from the army, was named by the Judea and Samaria rabbis as one of their major informants. Bar-Kochba allegedly informed the rabbis regularly and in advance about the plans for army operations in the territories. Upon learning about his actions, other officers followed in his footsteps. Thereupon, the army command, in order to gain access to the real leadership of the religious settlers, decided to regularize those relations and to inform the rabbis officially about its operations. A battalion commander, for example, did not hesitate to dress a local settlement rabbi in army uniform, take him to a look-out post and identify to him the undercover soldiers operating in local Arab villages. [The commander hoped] that he would thus convince the Judea and Samaria rabbis to stop blocking the major highways and thereby obstructing the unit's movements. This was not an isolated instance. The heads of the Judea and Samaria Settlement Council, comprised of religious laymen, now confront a rabbinical council of what is effectively a kingdom of Judea, which arose before their eyes. The council of laymen derives some consolation from its solid connections with government agencies. Rabin, whose top priority interest is to reach a dialogue with religious

settlers, keeps summoning the Judea and Samaria Council members for intimate talks. He cannot have the same contact with the kingdom of Judea rabbis, because they consider it demeaning to address a sinner like him. They also know that the lay council members would not dare to make a major decision without first obtaining their blessing.

The Oslo process shocked Gush Emunim rabbis and lay settlers. This occurred in spite of the great material support for settlements that Gush Emunim received in the 1990s from Prime Ministers Rabin, Peres and Netanyahu. A few messianic rabbis offered explanations for the occurrence of Oslo and attempted to console their flock about the process, but they met with almost no success. Religious symbolism, especially appearing in apocalyptic forms, blocked acceptance. The sight of Palestinians waving their flags, the appearance of armed Palestinian police and the proliferating symbols of the Palestinian Authority constituted visible evidence for the failure of the messianic vision of quick redemption. This in turn deepened the hatred of "Jewish traitors," whose treason allegedly spoiled God's plan and influenced the majority of Jews to disregard the divine command and to follow the traitors. This hatred, directed mostly at Rabin and his ministers, was consistent with the Cabbala, which held that the redemption of the Jews had almost occurred at various times only to be prevented each time because a majority of the nation opted to follow a heretic or a traitor. In Jewish history those who have most strongly believed in the coming victory of redemption have also most strongly harbored feelings of betrayal. After Oslo such people were mostly concentrated in the religious settlements.

Hatred of Arabs and secular Jews has not been solely limited to members of religious settlements. In his March 11, 1994 article, published in *Shishi*, Nerri Horowitz focused upon another group of extremists, called Hardelim.[1] Horowitz analysed Hardelim's "twofold hatred of Arabs and secular Jews" and presented documentation in the form of quotations from their copious and abstruse literature, filled with cabbalistic references. Although esoteric, the literature of the Hardelim has influenced a majority of religious Jews. (A minority of religious Jews have opposed the Hardelim advocacy.)

Nadav Shraggai presented a more popular description of this "twofold hatred" ideology in his February 18, 1994 *Haaretz* article. Shraggai pointed to the renunciation by some religious settlers and other religious Jews of the traditional prayer for the State of Israel, which was never accepted by the Haredim but said by NRP followers on every sabbath and religious holiday since 1948. Shraggai noted that some religious Jews who had previously recognized the State of Israel as holy renounced this prayer and the holiness of the state; they became convinced that the government and therefore the state, in accepting Oslo, had "betrayed its sacred mission." After concluding that Rabin and his ministers were traitors, the messianists viewed as particularly offensive the following words of the prayer: "O, God, radiate your light and truth upon Israel's leaders, ministers and advisers." Shraggai correctly insisted that his analysis focused upon the relatively moderate antagonists. These moderates contented themselves with intense ideological debate but did not, as did the extremists, plan and engage in murder and other violent acts. Shraggai wrote:

> The personal, ideological and religious crisis in which the national-religious Jewish community in Israel has found itself, generated doubts about the very foundations of religious Zionism: namely its historic alliance with secular Zionism and its wholehearted acceptance of the State of Israel. In the past that alliance revolved around the perception that the secular State of Israel was the first stage in the process of redemption. At present, even the moderates question this assumption. These doubters do not have much in common with radicals like the admittedly marginal Yehuda Etzion of the Jewish Underground who opposes any Jewish state that is not a monarchy ruled by the Davidic dynasty, or Mordechai Karpel, the founder of the Jewish Nation Exists for Eternity movement, which also wants to turn Israel into a theocratic monarchy.

Shraggai noted that several influential rabbis, including Azri'el Ariel who eulogized the assassin Goldstein, led the "moderates." Shraggai quoted Rabbi Ariel:

> The religious settlements were established not only to create facts on the ground but also to affect the hearts and minds of the Jewish people. We believed that, by encountering the holy parts of the land as if they were alive, the hearts of the Jewish masses would be united with the heart of the land. We envisaged the process as reconnecting the national Jewish consciousness with its spiritual roots.

Rabbi Ariel further opined:

> For a majority of Jews the settlements have failed to restore that sacred linkage. The majority of Jews have renounced the Jewish roots present in their souls, profaning themselves by [committing the] sin of choosing the so-called "morality" of Western culture instead of their own moral values. In the state of that grave sin their hearts have remained unaffected by the land of Israel …

We now have to build the sacred and observant community from within. Let us stop looking out. Let us stop to seek paths [that lead] to the hearts of our sinning Jewish brethren. One day, those who have effectively abandoned the Jewish religion will find their dreams shattered. They will become afflicted by a sense of emptiness. After having faltered on every path, they will come to seek us. Until then our role will consist of raising a generation of the truly chosen and holy ones, a generation capable of receiving Jewish repentant sinners with open arms.

In presenting his argument, Rabbi Ariel did not mention Palestinians. Although presumably realizing that Palestinians on all sides surround their sacred and observant communities, Rabbi Ariel and others like him have consistently considered irrelevant the existence of Palestinians; they have concerned themselves with secular Jewish Zionists. Shraggai quoted Ariel: "Historic Zionism has reached its end in bankruptcy ... The real Zionism, the holy one with profound roots, exists only where the really religious Jews are living; in the mountains of Judea and the valleys of Samaria."

In his article Shraggai additionally quoted the articulate settlement rabbi, Yair Dreyfus. Maintaining that Israel was committing spiritual apostasy by making an agreement with the PLO, Rabbi Dreyfus argued further that the finalization of that agreement would "mark the end of the Jewish-Zionist era in the sacred history of the land of Israel." Dreyfus, as quoted by Shraggai, continued:

Historians will record that the Jewish-Zionist era lasted from 1948 to 1993. It ended when most Jews had turned into Canaanites. Hence, 1993 marks the beginning of the new Canaanite era ... in that era of sin Jewish political thought, cultural-educational thought included, will be polluted by a speedy Arabization. The Jewish left will continue its treacherous practices of dismissing Jews from key posts and replacing them with Arabs. This will be done in the government, broadcasting authority, land authority, editorial boards of newspapers and boards of university directors. Every important position will be filled by an Arab.

Although his predictions were not fulfilled after 1993, Rabbi Dreyfus has remained steadfast in his belief about the new Canaanite era. For him pollution apparently often resulted when Jews had contact with Gentiles. Rabbi Dreyfus accused secular Jews of "wanting to create a new Israeli-Canaanite personality and thus destroying authentic Judaism by blending it with alien elements." He feared that this new personality would eliminate Jewish-Zionist motivation. He accused the Meretz Party of blending Communism into it and by this process polluting Zionism. This blend, Dreyfus contended, "has begotten the seed for growth of a new Middle Eastern ethnicity: the Canaanite-Palestinian pseudo-Jews." He concluded:

> The true Jews, desirous to live as Jews, will have no choice but to separate themselves in ghettos. The new, sinful Canaanite-Palestinian state [Israel after Oslo] will soon be established upon the ruins of the genuine Jewish-Zionist state. It will not be, as Israel was expected to become by being true to the word of God, a foundation of God's throne on earth. God may even make war against this polluted throne of his. The Jews who lead us into that sin no longer deserve any divine protection. We must fight those who separated themselves from the true Israel. They have declared a war against us, the bearers of the word of God. Our leadership will walk a Via Dolorosa before it understands that we are commanded to resist the state of Israel, not just its present government. Our cooperation with its agencies can only be based upon a new covenant. Without it, we are going to surrender supinely to a government of sin. Instead of doing so, we shall pursue a merciless struggle against the Canaanite-Palestinian entity.

By expressing his opinions openly and forcefully, Rabbi Dreyfus both represented and influenced the thinking of most religious settlers before and after the Rabin assassination. Notwithstanding the hostility to Christianity existent in historical Judaism and religious Zionism, the parallels here to specific Christian theological formulations are conspicuous.

For secular Israeli Jews, the most important NRP and religious settler issue has revolved around the penetration of young NRP followers into the combat and elite units of the army and its officer corps. For nearly twenty-five years after the June 1967 war, this penetration on balance enhanced the image and importance of the NRP in Israeli society; a kind of partnership between the NRP and the secular majority emerged. The initiation of the Oslo process, however, provoked some rethinking by many secular Jews and raised some tough issues. The Rabin assassination heightened apprehension of and aroused fears about the NRP's penetration into the military. All of this occurred because of the strong military character of Israeli Jewish society. This character developed not only because Jewish males serve in the military for at least three years,[2] but also because they, after finishing their time of duty, continue serving as reservists for one month each year until the age of fifty-four. The fact that about one-half of all Israeli Jewish females serve in the military for at least two years additionally contributes to the shaping of this character. Those who serve in the combat and/or elite units or as pilots enjoy tremendous social prestige when they leave the service and often are able to exert political influence. The political weakness of religious parties, especially the NRP, before 1967 was directly related to the relative absence of religious soldiers in combat and elite units of the army. This situation changed slowly after 1967. When Gush Emunim appeared in 1975, its lay leaders and especially its rabbis began educating and inspiring young NRP followers to adopt the military profession as a religious duty, to join the combat and elite units of the army and to become officers. Young NRP followers became dedicated, disciplined and efficient soldiers, ready, if necessary, to sacrifice their lives for their country. The army high command and a large segment of the Israeli Jewish population welcomed this development with positive enthusiasm. The NRP thus earned public appreciation, just as the kibbutz movement had done previously, because of the excellent military performances of its young members.

The Oslo process initiated a change in the almost unqualified admiration of Gush Emunim and the NRP. Fears arose that NRP followers in the army might refuse to carry out government orders for Israeli withdrawals from parts of the occupied territories and/or for the removal of one or more Jewish settlements. The fears expanded following the Rabin assassination. Even before the assassination, Baruch Kimmerling, in his April 6, 1994 *Haaretz* article, reflected a bit of the early apprehension and fear. He discussed the increasing penetration of the Israeli army by religious zealots and the powerful influence of the religious settlers upon units stationed in the territories. Kimmerling concluded: "Now it is all important that the army's command sees to it that every army unit is supervised. Perhaps those officers and even entire units, which were for too long involved in negotiations with the religious settlers and in protecting them and which have in the process developed too much affinity with them, should be instantly disbanded." Kimmerling regarded his recommendation as only a stop-gap solution. The army high command did not accept and most of the attentive public ridiculed the recommendation at that time. Kimmerling recognized that "in the long range" the problem that had arisen would be insoluble without a deep change in society. He wrote: "On the one hand, it is difficult to see how the army, having a significant number of officers adhering to ideology of religious settlers, could evacuate a Jewish settlement. On the other hand, I find it difficult to imagine how the Israeli army could be ideologically purified."

Worth noting here are the two unique schemes devised for young NRP followers in an organized fashion to serve in and penetrate the combat and elite units. The first scheme was formulated as an arrangement, not governed by law, between two independent parties: the Israeli defense ministry and the rabbinical heads of the NRP's Hesder Yeshivot religious schools. According to this arrangement, Hesder Yeshivot students receive a special kind of draft service. They are not inducted into the army in the normal way and thus do not serve continuously for three years in units assigned by the army according to its needs. The regular army units almost always consist of soldiers holding differing religious and secular views. The Hesder Yeshivot students instead are inducted into the army as a group and serve in their own homogeneous companies, accompanied by their rabbis who are responsible for and watch over the students' "religious purity." They serve for eighteen months rather than for the full three years. The eighteen-month period is not continuous but is rather divided into three six-month periods. After each period of army service, the Hesder Yeshivot students leave the army for a six-month period of talmudic study in a yeshiva wherein the presumably negative influences of having met secular Jewish soldiers are supposedly countered. The Hesder Yeshivot soldiers continue to serve in reserve units under the usual conditions. The political pressure exerted by Gush Emunim and the sympathy for its members felt by army generals in the 1970s were partly responsible for this special arrangement. The major reason for its continuation, however, is the excellent military quality and record of Hesder Yeshivot students. Their performance is far above the average of those in the Israeli army and their dedication is even greater. Not only the generals but also other soldiers hold this view. During the three years of the Lebanon War (1982–85) and in the aftermath of fighting in the "security zone," for example, Hesder Yeshivot students continued fighting and winning even after a high proportion of Israeli soldiers had been wounded and killed. Soldiers in Hesder Yeshivot units also distinguished themselves during the suppression of the Intifada; they were noted for their cruelty to Palestinians, which was from many perspectives much more severe than the Israeli army average. The homogeneous composition of Hesder Yeshivot companies of soldiers is another reason for the continuation of the special arrangement. When the army commanding officers have wanted to inflict especially cruel punishment upon Palestinians or others, they have most often relied upon and used religious soldiers. In more ordinary companies, consisting of soldiers holding varying political views, some members might object to illegal cruelty and even inform media people of its use. In Hesder Yeshivot units the religious soldiers, who are anyway more cruel than most secular Jews, will not object to the orders.[3]

From 1996, when indications appeared that membership in the Hesder Yeshivot had stopped increasing and may have begun to decrease, the religious pre-military academy scheme became the chief means of organized penetration by NRP supporters into the Israeli army. By this arrangement the young men, usually eighteen years of age, who enter religious pre-military academies are given draft deferments for one or one and one-half years of study. Afterwards, they serve for three years in ordinary combat or elite units. This is in contrast to serving, as do Hesder Yeshivot students, in homogeneous companies or units. The teachers in these academies are for the most part not rabbis but rather ex-officers who possess some talmudic knowledge. Only a small amount of the teaching is devoted to military subjects and training in hiking and endurance. Most of the teaching and study time is devoted to those parts of the Talmud and other religious literature that inculcate dedication to the land of Israel and to other values favored by Gush Emunim. The ascetic pre-military academy life is attractive to religious youth who are often in reaction against the hedonistic life style of secular Israeli youth. Since their inception the pre-military academies have been situated in settlements in the Occupied Territories. The army has from the beginning subsidized these academies to some extent, but the major part of the support money has come from private donors. Most graduates of these pre-military academies are well prepared and advance to the officer corps. Persuaded that the Israeli army is sacred, those who come out of these academies almost always serve their full three-year terms. Some serve for a much longer time and become career officers.

After the Rabin assassination, many Israelis began to view the increasing number of NRP followers in the army as a threat to the government and to the Israeli regime as a whole. Ran Edelist summarized this concern well in his September 13, 1996 article in the Hebrew-language newspaper *Yerushalaim*, titled "First We Shall Conquer the Supreme Court and Then the General Staff." The title of this article suggests the desire to penetrate and conquer the most important institutions of the State of Israel. In discussing the general aims of the messianic religious right, of which the religious settlers are the advance guard, Edelist wrote:

> Their institutions have the stamina of a long-distance runner since they believe in the eternal survival of the Jewish nation; in this framework they prepared four approaches for the battle of the land of Israel: settlements, financial support, education and promotion of their men in the army to achieve domination of a future General Staff. This is not a conspiracy but a cool estimate of a national situation in their struggle for a future image of Israeli society and a sophisticated use of an opportunistic government, enabling them to fill their budgets. It is not a case of good and bad but a struggle about the character of the State of Israel. The

religious right wing uses the legitimate approach of conquering positions of power of which the General Staff is central. It may be said that since the inception of Israel the secret slogan of Israeli politicians was "we shall conquer first the security apparatus and then the Knesset and government." Ben-Gurion did this when he pushed out Sharett and Lavon. Golda Meir's slogan was "the party is everything," and since her time the Labor party has ruled in the General Staff. This rule was so absolute that Begin and Shamir, during the time that they were prime ministers, did not succeed in shaking this and forming another General Staff that would be influenced by their ideology.

Understanding Israeli politics, the religious settlers devised and evolved their plan of penetrating the army, its officer corps and ultimately the General Staff. As Edelist wrote:

> The religious settlers understood that with the help of only party politics and their ideology they would not get far and would not achieve a State of Israel in the borders promised by God. If they therefore want to be represented in every place in which the important decisions are made, especially in the army as a whole and particularly in the General Staff, they must be represented in such places. First the aim and then the means to achieve that end were decided.

The Hesder Yeshivot and the religious pre-military academies became those means.

Other Israeli political observers and commentators seconded Edelist's analysis. In his January 24, 1997 *Haaretz* article, titled "The Army of the Lord," Yidan Miller, for example, described the views of Dr Reuven Gal, who served as the chief psychologist of the Israeli army between 1976 and 1982 and then became the director of the highly respected Karmel Institute for Military and Social Research. Dr Gal, according to Miller, summarized the data about volunteering to serve in combat units from 1994 through 1996 and compared them with corresponding data of 1989. Dr Gal reported that whereas 60 per cent of secular youth in 1989 wanted to serve in combat units, the average for the 1993 to 1996 period dropped to 48 per cent. Most of that decline occurred in 1995 and 1996. The decline was greatest in the secular kibbutzim, localities with large leftist majorities. The drop was from 83 per cent in 1989 to 58 per cent in the 1993 to 1996 period. In comparison, among the religious youth the wish to volunteer to combat units remained constant at about 80 per cent during the same time. In religious kibbutzim, the figure went to 90 per cent. Before the Oslo agreement a large majority of religious youth entering the army considered a commander's order to be superior to any instruction from a rabbi. This had changed by 1996. Citing Dr Gal's summary, Miller wrote: "For a significant part of them [the religious youth] instruction by a rabbi had an equal and sometimes superior value than did an order from a commander."

Publication of such findings disturbed many secular Jews. They attempted to acquire for their youth opportunities for army careers similar to those afforded religious youth. They advocated the establishment of secular pre-military academies. During the first two years of the Netanyahu government, however, when the Oslo process stagnated, the numbers of secular youth who volunteered to serve in combat units increased to a point unparalleled since the 1970s. This adversely affected the attempted penetration into the army of the messianic religious right. Comprising only 6 to 7 per cent of the Israeli Jewish population,[4] the messianic religious right depended for its penetration upon the absence of motivation of other Jews to serve in combat units.

Following Netanyahu's election in 1996, two factors motivated more Israeli Jewish youth to volunteer for combat units. The rising level of Arab hostility to Israel and to its elected government constituted the first factor. Some Arab leaders issued war threats. Most of Israel's Jewish youth considered all of this unjustified and responded in the traditional Israeli manner by advocating increased militarism. The second factor arose from the perception that Netanyahu's government was a new coalition of Jewish minorities, which as never before in the history of the state has allowed those previously excluded from important social opportunities and advancements to succeed. For the first time in Israeli history the defense minister and the chief of staff were Oriental Jews. The older, Labor-sympathizing elite members of the army opposed those appointments. This most likely encouraged young Israeli Jewish males who were not from Ashkenazi Labor-supporting families to seek careers as army officers. Most of these and other such young men previously thought that they would not be allowed to become career officers. Among the lower-income class of Israeli Jews an army career with its relatively high salaries is prestigious as well as economically attractive. Except for computer experts, doctors and other highly educated specialists, the way to a good career is to serve in a combat unit.

Ironically, the collapse of the detested Oslo process adversely affected the religious settlers in their attempt to penetrate the Israeli army and in that way to achieve a commanding influence over Israeli policies. During most of the time that the Oslo process continued under the Rabin and Peres governments, the religious settlers' chances of penetrating the army increased. The religious settlers' chances of determining specific Israeli policies decreased after Netanyahu and Likud came to power in 1996. Perhaps, this development provides us with an example of what is sometimes the fate of fanaticism: the fanatic group thrives when it perceives itself to be in danger or threatened by other parts of its own society. Conversely, when faced by a society that has become unified against what is believed to be an outside threat, the fanatic group is less able to penetrate major institutions such as the army and to influence long-range policy.

The Real Significance of Baruch Goldstein

The story of the massacre committed by Baruch Goldstein in the Patriarchs' Cave in Hebron on February 25, 1994, is well known. Goldstein entered the Muslim prayer hall and shot worshippers mostly in their backs, killing 29, including children, and wounding many more. In this chapter we shall not describe that massacre; rather we shall focus upon Goldstein's career prior to the massacre and upon the reactions of the Israeli government and fundamentalist Jews to the massacre a short time after it occurred. This should provide a vivid illustration of Jewish fundamentalism. We shall extend our discussion of some details until the summer of 1998.

One important background fact about Goldstein exemplifies the influence of Jewish fundamentalism in Israel: long before the massacre, Goldstein as an army physician repeatedly breached army discipline by refusing to treat Arabs, even those serving in the Israeli army. He was not punished, either while in active or reserve service, for his refusal because of intervention in his favor. Political commentators discussed this story in the Hebrew press even though not a single Israeli politician referred to it. This story deserves detailed exploration in our analysis of Jewish fundamentalism.

In his March 1, 1994, *Yediot Ahronot* article, Arych Kizel, a regular *Davar* correspondent, wrote that Goldstein, shortly after immigrating to Israel and as a conscript assigned to an artillery battalion in Lebanon as a doctor, refused to treat Gentiles. According to Kizel, Goldstein, after refusing to treat a wounded Arab, declared: "I am not willing to treat any non-Jew. I recognize as legitimate only two [religious] authorities: Maimonides and Kahane." Kizel further reported:

> Three Druze soldiers who served in Goldstein's battalion approached their commander and asked for another doctor to be stationed in their battalion, because they were afraid that Goldstein would refuse to treat them in case they were wounded. Because of their request Goldstein was reassigned to another battalion. He continued to serve as a military doctor both in the

conscript army and in the reserves. After some years he was reassigned to the regional Hebron brigade of the central command where he thereafter served his reserve stint. Immediately after receiving this assignment, he told his commanders that his religious faith would make it impossible for him to treat wounded or ill Arabs; he asked to be reassigned elsewhere. His request was granted, and he was reassigned to a reserve unit serving in South Lebanon.

Amir Oren, who subsequently became the military correspondent of *Haaretz*, provided the most complete story of Goldstein's relations with the Israeli army and the entire Israeli political establishment in his March 4 *Davar* article. According to Oren, after the 1984 elections and the subsequent formation of the national unity government, then Defense Minister Yitzhak Rabin and then Chief of Staff General Moshe Levy learned about Goldstein's refusal to treat non-Jews in Lebanon. Oren wrote:

> When Goldstein's refusal to treat non-Jewish patients became evident to his commanders, both the artillery corps and medical corps commanders quite naturally wanted to court-martial him and thus get rid of him. They took it for granted that this could be easily done, because Goldstein had graduated only from the army's course for medical officers. [Goldstein did not have combat officer training, which is normally a prerequisite for admission to the course for medical officers.] The two corps [commanders] also knew that Goldstein, while attending the army's course for medical officers, had become notorious as an anti-Arab extremist.

According to other Hebrew press reports, some of Goldstein's trainee colleagues demanded that he be dismissed from the course; their demand was refused. Oren related: "[Goldstein] was already then protected by highly placed people in senior ministries. Those patrons requested that Goldstein be allowed to serve in Kiryat Arba rather than in a combat battalion." The situation then developed into "a bone of contention between the commander of the army's medical corps and its chief rabbi." Oren continued:

> In the end the issue of what to do with an officer who openly refused to obey orders by invoking Halacha has never been resolved, even if that officer openly refused to provide medical help both to Israeli soldiers and POWs. Can we avoid being stunned by the army's failure to court-martial Goldstein? Why was no order to court-martial him ever issued by the entire chain of the army command? That chain of command included the

commander of the northern command, Reserve General Orri Or [a Labor MK and later in 1994 the chairman of the Knesset Committee for Foreign and Defense Affairs], and General Amos Yaron, who now is the commander of the manpower department. Why did they refuse to decide without first consulting the chief rabbi? The already embarrassed medical corps [commanders] now [after the massacre] admit that they were scared by publicity that might have propelled the religious parties and religious settlers' lobbies to make things more of a mess than ever before. The fear of publicity time after time prompted the army commanders to give in to all kinds of Goldsteins, rather than to denounce their views and court-martial them.

Many sources corroborated Oren's hinting that this Goldstein situation did not constitute a unique case. The story told by Oren revealed the pervasiveness of the religious parties' influence in the Israeli army. Jewish orthodoxy's stance against non-Jews, as openly advocated by Goldstein's idolized leader, Rabbi Meir Kahane, was – and still is – an essential position held by the major religious parties. As such, this stance has had a strong impact upon the Israeli army. Had Rabin and the army commanders mentioned by Oren, moreover, felt no affinity whatsoever with Kahane's and Goldstein's views, they would not have given in to the religious parties with such abandon and thus sacrificed all consideration of military discipline. Israeli policies, directed towards Palestinians, other Middle East Arabs (perceived by Zionists as non-Jews) and people of other nations, are only explainable by assuming that they are based upon anti-Gentile feeling. The anti-Gentile feeling is strongest among the most religious Jews but exists as well in this secular milieu. This is the reason why support for Goldstein in 1984 and 1985 had a sequel in the excuses by many Israeli leaders for the slaughter. These excuses were thinly disguised by mostly hypocritical expressions of shock.

Goldstein's refusal to give proper medical treatment to non-Jews continued after he was transferred to Kiryat Arba. In his February 27, 1994 *Yediot Ahronot* article, Nahum Barnea wrote:

The senior Israeli army officer in the Hebron area told me about his two encounters with Baruch Goldstein. The second time he saw him was in the company of Kach goons who were abusing President Ezer Weisman during his visit to Kiryat Arba. The first time he encountered Goldstein was after an Israeli soldier had wounded a local Arab in his legs. The Arab was brought to an army clinic for treatment, but Goldstein refused to treat him. Another army physician had to be summoned to substitute for Goldstein. The officer did not explain why Goldstein was thereafter not demoted in rank but was rather allowed to keep performing his duties in the reserves. Incidentally, his misconduct also constituted a violation of the oath he had taken upon becoming a doctor, but for this the Israeli army cannot be blamed.

Barnea made clear that the entire Israeli establishment, not just the army, was responsible for the leniency granted to Goldstein for his misdeeds. The leniency lasted until the massacre. Only after the massacre did the official line change to shock, coupled with assertions that Goldstein had acted alone. Thus, during the first three hours after the slaughter Rabin and his retinue insisted either that Goldstein was a psychopath or that he was a devoted doctor who happened to suffer a momentary derangement. Barnea reported: "Within hours a whole edifice of rationalization was built, according to which Goldstein had allegedly been under unbearable mental pressure, because he had to attend so many wounded and dead [persons], including Arabs." The men who propagated this lie knew that Goldstein had refused to treat Arabs. Barnea continued: "Thus, the Arabs were made guilty for what he could not avoid doing. The implication was that the Arabs assaulted him rather than the other way around and that he really acted for the benefit of the Arabs by letting them finally realize that Jewish blood could not be shed with impunity." This brazen lie was maintained as long as possible before being abandoned without apology. The propagation of such a lie reveals the influence of Jewish fundamentalism upon the secular parts of the Israeli establishment.

Goldstein represented Jewish fundamentalism in the extreme. Some of the Gush Emunim leaders at the time of the massacre were only a bit less extreme. Barnea compared Goldstein's attitude toward non-Jews with that of Rabbi Levinger, the Gush Emunim leader whom he interviewed on the day of the massacre:

> Levinger was in a good mood; after arguing about how religious settlers should respond to the massacre, he shortly before had won the three hour debate at a session of the Kiryat Arba municipality. The secretary of the Council of Judea, Samara and Gaza District, Uri Ariel, [who became director of the prime minister's office in 1998] proposed condemning the massacre. Levinger staked his authority behind the proposal that the [Israeli] government should instead be condemned [for putting Goldstein] under unbearable mental pressure [propelling him to action].

In the discussion the terms "murder," "massacre" or "killing" were avoided; instead the terms used were "deed," "event" or "occurrence." The reason is that according to the Halacha the killing by a Jew of a non-Jew under any circumstances is not regarded as murder. It may be prohibited for other reasons, especially when it causes danger for Jews. In many cases the real feelings about a Jew murdering non-Jews, expressed in Israel with impunity, correspond to the law. Levinger told Barnea that the resolution "expresses in passing" the sorrow about dead Arabs "even though it emphasizes the responsibility of the government." When asked by Barnea whether he felt sorry, Levinger answered: "I am sorry not only about dead Arabs but also about dead flies."

Goldstein on principle had refused to treat non-Jews for many years before the massacre. He worked as the municipal doctor of Kiryat Arba and treated Arabs only when he could not avoid doing so. Barnea quoted one of Goldstein's colleagues from the Kiryat Arba clinic who recalled that "whenever Goldstein arrived at a traffic accident spot and recognized that some of the injured were Arabs, he would attend to them but only until another doctor arrived. Then, he would stop treating them. 'This was his compromise between his doctor's oath and his ideology,' said his colleague."

The Halacha enjoins precisely the behavior of Goldstein's refusing to attend non-Jews. The Halacha dictates that a pious Jewish doctor may treat Gentiles when his refusal to do so might be reported to the authorities and cause him or other Jews unpleasantness. There is reason to believe that whenever doctors as pious as Goldstein were forced to treat Arabs they behaved as did Goldstein. In his previously cited *Yediot Ahronot* article, Arych Kizel added that the Israeli army found that Goldstein's conduct did not require any disciplinary measures. A *Maariv* correspondent wrote in his March 8, 1994 article that Goldstein's military service record was sufficiently distinguished to earn him a ceremonial promotion from the rank of captain to that of major. The president of Israel would have officially awarded this promotion on April 14, 1994, Israel's independence day. Only Goldstein's death, which occurred at the time of the massacre, prevented what would have been a revealing promotion.

An even greater example of Jewish fundamentalism's influence upon the secular part of the Israeli establishment can be detected in the official arrangement of Goldstein's elaborate funeral at a time that the deliberate character of the massacre could not be denied. The establishment was affected by the fact, widely reported in the Hebrew press but given little place in the foreign press, that within two days of the massacre the walls of religious neighborhoods of west Jerusalem (and to a lesser extent of many other religious neighborhoods) were covered by posters extolling Goldstein's virtues and complaining that he did not manage to kill more Arabs. Children of religious settlers who came to Jerusalem to demonstrate sported buttons for months after the massacre that were inscribed:

"Dr Goldstein cured Israel's ills." Numerous concerts of Jewish religious music and other events often developed into demonstrations of tribute to Goldstein. The Hebrew press reported these incidents of public tribute in copious detail. No major politician protested against such celebrations.

President Weizman expressed more extravagantly than others his sorrow for the massacre. Weizman, as reported by Uzi Benziman in his March 4, 1994 *Haaretz* article, was also engaged in lengthy and amiable negotiations with Goldstein's family and Kach comrades concerning a suitably honorable funeral for the murderer. Kiryat Arba settlers, many of whom had already declared themselves in favor of the mass murder in radio and television interviews and had lauded Goldstein as a martyr and holy man, demanded that General Yatom, the commander responsible for the Hebron area, allow the funeral cortege to parade through the city of Hebron, in order to be viewed by the Arabs even though a curfew existed. Yatom did not object outright to the demand but opposed it as something that could cause disorder. Tzvi Katzover, the mayor of Kiryat Arba and one of the most extreme leaders of the religious settlers, telephoned Weizman and threatened that the settlers would make a pogrom of Arabs if their demands were not met. Weizman responded by telephoning the chief of staff and asking why the army opposed the demand of the settlers. According to Benziman, Chief of Staff Barak answered: "The army was afraid that Arabs would desecrate Goldstein's tomb and carry away his corpse." In further negotiations involving Barak, Yatom, Rabin, Kach leaders and Kiryat Arba settlers, Weizman assumed the consistent position, as stated by Benziman, that "the army should pay respect to the desires and sensibilities of the settlers and of the Goldstein family." Ultimately, the negotiated decision was that a massively attended funeral cortege would take place in Jerusalem and that the police would close some of the busiest streets to the traffic in Goldstein's honor. Afterwards, the murderer would be buried in Kiryat Arba along the continuation of Kahane Avenue. According to Benziman, Kach leaders at first rejected this compromise. General Yatom had to approach the Kach leaders in person and beg them abjectly for their agreement, which he finally secured. Yatom also had to obtain consent from the notorious Kiryat Arba rabbi, Dov Lior. As reported in the March 4, 1994, issue of *Yerushalaim* Lior declared: "Since Goldstein did what he did in God's own name, he is to be regarded as a righteous man." Benziman explained the conduct of Weizman and his entourage: "After the fact the officials of the presidential mansion justify those goings on by the need to becalm the settlers' mood." After the funeral the army provided a guard of honor for Goldstein's tomb.

The tomb became a pilgrimage site, not only for the religious settlers but also for delegations of pious Jews from all Israeli cities. The details of Goldstein's funeral as arranged through the office of President Weizman are significant. The facts below were taken mostly from the Ilana Baum and Tzvi Singer report, published in *Yediot Ahronot* on February, 28 1994. The funeral's first installment took place in Jerusalem. Among the estimated thousand mourners only a few were settlers from Kiryat Arba. Baum and Singer noted: "Without having met Goldstein personally, other mourners most of whom were Jerusalemites, were enthusiastic admirers of his deed. Many more were Yeshiva students. A large group represented the Chabad Hassidic movement, another group [consisted of anti-Zionist] Satmar Hassids." Other Hassidic movements were also well represented. (Not mentioned in the English-language press, Goldstein, a follower of Kahane, was also a follower of the Lubovitcher rabbi.) Baum and Singer continued:

> People awaiting the arrival of the corpse could be heard repeating: "What a hero! A righteous person! He did it on behalf of all of us." As usual in such encounters between religious Jews, all the participants tuned into a single, collective personality, united by their burning hatred of the Israeli media, the wicked Israeli government and, above all else, of anyone who dared to speak against the murder.

Before the start of the procession well-known rabbis eulogized Goldstein and commended the murder. Rabbi Israel Ariel, for example, said: "The holy martyr, Baruch Goldstein, is from now on our intercessor in heaven. Goldstein did not act as an individual; he heard the cry of the land of Israel, which is being stolen from us day after day by the Muslims. He acted to relieve that cry of the land!" Toward the end of his eulogy Rabbi Ariel added: "The Jews will inherit the land not by any peace agreement but only by shedding blood." Ben-Shoshan Yeshu'a, a Jewish underground member, sentenced to life imprisonment for murder and amnestied after a few years spent under luxurious hotel conditions, lauded Goldstein and praised his action as an example for other Jews to follow.

Border guards, police and the secret police protected the funeral cortege. Baum and Singer related:

> An entire unit of border guards precede the cortege; they were followed by young Kahane group members from Jerusalem who continuously yelled: "death to the Arabs." While obviously intending to find an Arab to kill, they could not spot one. Suddenly, a border guard noticed an Arab approaching the

cortege behind a low fence. The border guard immediately jumped over the fence, stopped the Arab and, using force, led him away to safety before anyone could notice. He [the border guard] thus saved him [the Arab] from a certain lynching.

Behind the young Kahane group members was a coffin, which was surrounded by leaders of Kahane splinter groups, some of whom were wanted by the police. (The police and the secret police claimed later that they did not recognize these wanted leaders. The press correspondents easily recognized them.) Baum wrote:

Tiran Pollak, a Kahane group leader wanted by the police, granted me an interview near the coffin. "Goldstein was not only righteous and holy," he told me, "but also a martyr. Since he is a martyr, his corpse will be buried without being washed, not in a shroud but in his clothes. The honorable Dr Goldstein has always refused to provide medical help to Arabs. Even during the war for Galilee he refused to treat any Arab, including those serving in the army. General Gad Navon, the chief rabbi of the Israeli army, at that time contacted Meir Kahane to ask him to persuade Baruch Goldstein of blessed memory to treat the Arabs. Kahane, however, refused to do so, because this would be against the Jewish religion." Suddenly the crowd began yelling: "Death to the journalists." I looked around and realized that I was the only journalist inside the crowd of mourners. I clung to Tiran Pollak and begged him to "please protect me." I was scared to death that the crowd might recognize me as a journalist.

Military guards transported Goldstein's coffin to Kiryat Arba through Palestinian villages. A second round of eulogies was delivered in the hall of the Hesder Yeshiva Nir military institution by a motley of religious settlers, including the aforementioned Rabbi Dov Lior. Lior said: "Goldstein was full of love for fellow human beings. He dedicated himself to helping others." The terms "human beings" and "others" in the Halacha refer solely to Jews. Lior continued: "Goldstein could not continue to bear the humiliations and shame nowadays inflicted upon us; this was why he took action for no other reason than to sanctify the holy name of God."

Tohay Hakah reported in *Yerushalaim* on March 4, 1994 upon another Lior eulogy of Goldstein a few days after the funeral. He recalled that Lior several years ago was excoriated in the press for recommending that medical experiments be performed on the live bodies of Arab terrorists. The outcry against this recommendation influenced the attorney general to prevent the otherwise guaranteed election of Lior to the Supreme Rabbinical Council of Israel. The attorney general, however, did not interfere with Lior's current rabbinical duties. The press reported upon other eulogies, delivered not only in religious settlements but in religious neighborhoods of many Israeli towns during the days immediately following the slaughter. The Hebrew press reportage of these eulogies suggests that the most virulent lauding of Goldstein and the calling for further massacres of Arabs occurred in the more homogeneous religious communities.

The approval of Goldstein and his mass murder extended well beyond the perimeters of the religious Jewish community. Secular Israeli Jews, especially many of the youth, praised Goldstein and his deed. That Israeli youth were even more pleased by the massacre than were the adults is well-documented. The concern here nevertheless will be with the adult population, which in many ways is the most significant. According to Yuval Katz, who wrote an article published in the March 4, 1994 issue of *Yerushalaim*, it is not true that "with the exception of a few psychopaths, the entire nation and its politicians included, has resolutely condemned Dr Goldstein, even though, luckily for us, all major television networks in the world were last week still deluded by this untruth." Katz told how a popular television entertainer, Rafi Reshef, who was not controlled as tightly as the moderators in sedate panels, "could this week announce the findings of some reliable polls." Katz continued:

> It is important that according to one poll about 50 per cent of Kiryat Arba inhabitants approve of the massacre. More important is another poll that showed that about 50 per cent of Israeli Jews are more sympathetic toward the settlers after the massacre than they were before the massacre. The most important poll established that at least 50 per cent of Israeli Jews would approve of the massacre, provided that it was not referred to as a massacre but rather as a "Patriarch's Cave operation," a nice-sounding term already being used by religious settlers.

Katz reported that the politicians and academics interviewed by Reshef failed to grasp the significance of those findings. Attributing them to a chance occurrence, they refused to comment upon them. He tended to excuse them:

> I presume that those busy public figures, along with everybody else who this week exerted himself to speak in the name of the entire nation simply did not have time to walk the streets in the last days. Yet, with the exception of the wealthiest neighborhoods, people could be seen smiling merrily when talking about the massacre. The stock popular comment was: "Sure, Goldstein is

to be blamed. He could have escaped with ease and have done the same in four other mosques, but he didn't."

The impression of many other Israelis corresponded to the Reshef findings. People were rather evenly divided into two categories: in one category the people were vociferous in cheering the slaughter; in the other category the people mostly remained silent and condemned the massacre only if encouraged to do so. Katz continued:

> Therefore, this was the right time to draw finally the obvious conclusion that we, the Jews, are not any more sensitive or merciful than are the Gentiles. Many Jews have been programmed by the same racist computer program that is shaping the majority of the world's nations. We have to acknowledge that our supposed advancement in progressive beliefs and democracy have failed to affect the archaic forms of Jewish tribalism. Those who still delude themselves that Jews might be different than [people of] other nations should now know better. The spree of bullets from Goldstein's gun was for them an occasion to learn something.

The wise comments of Katz were not heeded in Israel except by a minority. It may be that had more Israeli Jews paid attention and heeded the words of Katz the murder of Yitzhak Rabin would have been averted. In the view of this book's authors, the important difference between the real shock caused by Rabin's murder and the lack of shock caused by Goldstein's massacre lies in the fact that Goldstein's victims were non-Jews.

Although less direct than Katz, many other commentators in the Israeli Hebrew press have focused upon that part of the Israeli Jewish public who were shocked by the rejoicing over the massacre of innocent people and disturbed by the apologia offered by many politicians and public figures. Some of those people who were shocked described the backers of and apologists for Goldstein as "Nazis" or "Nazi-like." These same people, who can be considered moderate hawks rather than Zionist doves, had before the massacre reacted negatively to the use by a few Israeli Jewish critics of such terminology in describing a part of the Israeli Jewish population. These "moderate hawks" had habitually labelled many Arab organizations, such as the Abu Nidal group and the Popular Front for the Liberation of Palestine, "Nazi" or "Nazi-like." They did not repudiate their views about these Arab organizations; they merely concluded that some Jewish individuals and organizations also merit being so labelled on equal terms with some Arabs. The prestigious journalist, Teddy Preuss, reflected upon all of this in a most severe but substantially representative manner in his March 4, 1994 *Davar* article:

> Compared to the giant-scale mass murderers of Auschwitz, Goldstein was certainly a petty murderer. His recorded statements and those of his comrades, however, prove that they were perfectly willing to exterminate at least two million Palestinians at an opportune moment. This makes Dr Goldstein comparable to Dr Mengele; the same holds true for anyone saying that he [or she] would welcome more of such Purim holiday celebrations. [The massacre occurred on that holiday.] Let us not devalue Goldstein by comparing him with an inquisitor or a Muslim Jihad fighter. Whenever an infidel was ready to convert to either Christianity or Islam, an inquisitor or Muslim Jihad fighter would, as a rule, spare his life. Goldstein and his admirers are not interested in converting Arabs to Judaism. As their statements abundantly testify, they see the Arabs as nothing more than disease-spreading rats, lice or other loathsome creatures; this is exactly how the Nazis believed that the Aryan race alone had laudable qualities that were inheritable but that could become polluted by sheer contact with dirty and morbid Jews. Kahane, who learned nothing from the Nuremberg Laws, had exactly the same notions about the Arabs.

Really, Kahane had the same notions about non-Jews. Although less scathing than Preuss, other Israeli commentators suggested the same consideration.

In contrast to the above criticism were the even more numerous comments about the harm caused to Israeli Jews by the Goldstein massacre. The lament in the February 28, 1994 *Haaretz Economic Supplement*, for example, was headlined: "Goldstein's massacre caused distress on the Tel-Aviv stock market." Other papers voiced similar sentiments. More importantly, Shimon Peres and other senior dovish politicians presented a typical political apologia in their criticism of the massacre, which they delivered in a meeting of the Knesset Committee for Foreign and Defense Affairs. Specific detail of this meeting is included below to illustrate the real opinions of most Israeli politicians and their general disregard of a major massacre of non-Jews except as it affected the interests of Israel and its allies. A March 8, 1994 *Haaretz* article reported the discussion at this meeting. Peres wasted no time expressing heartfelt shock about the murdered Palestinians but spoke instead about the harm to Israel caused by the "pictures of corpses that the entire world could watch." Peres did not condemn the armed religious settlers for their public rejoicing and shooting; he deplored the harm caused to Israel and to themselves by the pictures of them. As quoted in *Haaretz*, Peres added: "The events in Hebron also adversely affected the interests of President Mubarak and King Hussein, and even more of the PLO and its leadership." Peres then went on to say: "We have had Jewish Kibbutzim located in the midst of Arab-inhabited areas for 80 years, and I cannot recall a single instance of such a slaughter nor of firing at Arab buses nor of maiming Arab mayors." At this point in the discussion senior Likud politicians interpolated Peres. As reported in *Haaretz*:

The first to interrupt Peres' speech was Sharon. "Kibbutzim are dear to me no less than to you, but there have been many cases when somebody from a kibbutz would go out to murder Arabs." Peres answered: "The two cases are not comparable, because in the case under discussion the murderer was supported by a whole group of followers." Benny Begin [answered]: "Why are you always talking in generalities?" Peres [responded]: "I am not. I only maintain that in order to pursue the peace process we need the PLO as a partner, and now this partnership is in straits and we need to help the PLO." Sharon [answered]: "You mean that we should help that murderer [Arafat]." Peres, angrily banging the table [responded]: "And what about Egyptians with whom you, Likud, made peace? Didn't Egyptians murder Jews? Really. What's the difference between war and terrorism? Does it make any difference how 16,000 of our soldiers were killed? Everywhere, states are making deals with terror organizations." Netanyahu [spoke]: "No state exists that has made a deal with an organization still committed to its destruction. The PLO has not rescinded the Palestinian Covenant. You are dwelling upon the crime committed in Hebron not in order to reassure people [Jews] living there but in order to advance your plan to establish a Palestinian state." Peres [answered]: "It is you and your plans that will lead to the formation of a Palestinian state, because it is you, the Likud, that created the PLO in Madrid. It is you who conceived the autonomy in the first place, contrary to all our [previously pursued] aims." Netanyahu [stated]: "Autonomy is not the same thing as state." Peres [continued]: "But it is Sharon who is first to say that autonomy is bound to lead to a Palestinian state ... I am not less steadfast than are you; this is why I have elaborated the most restrictive possible interpretation of autonomy in Oslo, in relation to its territory, power and authorities. This is why we are against international observers and consent only to the temporary presence of representatives from the countries contributing money. And regarding the Palestinian Covenant, they have renounced it publicly, but they find it difficult to convene their representative bodies to ratify this renunciation." Begin [answered]: "Let me remind you that the PLO has not undertaken publicly to rescind the Palestinian Covenant." Peres [answered]: "I don't give a damn about you and/or your legalistic verbiage! Arafat said that he renounced the Palestinian Covenant and for me Arafat is the PLO."

The above passage shows, among other things, that knowledge of Israeli politics and more generally Jewish affairs can be best attained by using the original sources of what Jews say among themselves.

The continuing process of Goldstein's elevation to the rank of saint by groups of Israeli Jews and his worship as such began soon after the massacre. In his February 28, 1994 *Haaretz* article, Shmuel Rosner recounted a sermon delivered on the Sabbath after the massacre by Rabbi Goren, the former chief military rabbi and chief rabbi of Israel. Rosner wrote: "Goren's conclusion was that next time an authorization would be needed for a massacre. The authorization should come from the community 'not from the [present] illegal government.'" Rosner observed that the audience liked Goren's sermon but would have preferred, as would numerous other Israeli Jews, that the army rather than Goldstein had committed the massacre.

In the days and weeks after the massacre, appreciation of Goldstein and his deed spread throughout the Israeli religious community and among its supporters in the United States. The initial expressions of that appreciation may be most significant, because they were spontaneous and because they illustrated the influence, even beyond the messianic community, of an ideology that approved indiscriminate killing of Gentiles by Jews. Avirama Golan described in her February 28, 1994 *Haaretz* article how news about Goldstein on the day of the massacre became known in the overwhelmingly Haredi city of Bnei Brak and how the next day a religious Jewish crowd reacted with praise of Goldstein during a mass entertainment event. The massacre occurred on Purim, the festival during which religious Jews are merry and sometimes drink alcoholic beverages to the point of drunkenness. Bnei Brak streets were filled to capacity by joyful celebrants that day; a special security force, comprised of religious veterans of the Israeli army's elite units, had been hired by the mayor to enforce order and modesty. Golan described the response in the streets to the spreading news of the massacre:

A hired security guard, with a huge gun in his belt, a black skullcap on his head, and special insignia of "Bnei Brak Security Team" on his chest, stared at a fundraising stall. Then he noticed his pal across the street. "A Purim miracle, I'm telling you, Purim miracle," he shouted at the top of his voice. "That holy man did something great. 52 Arabs at one stroke." However, the fundraiser, a slim yeshiva student, was skeptical. "That's just impossible," he said. "Those must be just stories." But the people standing around confirmed the news. "It was on the radio," they said. "Where?" "In the Patriarchs' Cave in Hebron." The yeshiva student turned pale. "I don't mind the Arabs, but it is us who will pay the price," he said. "What are you talking about?" the security guard shouted, "It's a Purim miracle. God has helped." People around the stall formed two groups: on the one hand those who said that God Himself ordained a well-deserved punishment of the Arabs; on the other, those who remained silent throughout. The fundraiser went on writing receipts and shaking his head. "Oh," he said, "nothing really happened." The Bnei Brak functionary's wife said that dozens of visitors who, as is customary on Purim, visited their home that morning, were shocked. "By the murder?" somebody asked. "To tell you the truth, not exactly by the murder. About what may now happen to the Jews."

Jumping to the evening of the next day, Golan continued: "Masses of religious Jews were expected to come to Yad Eliahu Stadium [the biggest in Israel] to be entertained by the famous religious jazz singer, Mordechai Ben-David. For months before the massacre, this evening had been planned as a demonstration intended to save the land of Israel from Rabin, Peres and other Jewish infidels." All factions of the religious community were represented in the crowd. Golan again continued:

The first part of the evening passed quietly and even rather dully. Only after the intermission, some minutes before the star of the evening was to appear, the crowd went on a rampage. The master of the ceremony called upon a Kiryat Arba resident to address the crowd. He started by praising that "righteous and holy physician, Dr Goldstein, who rendered us a sacred service and got martyred in the process." The speaker called upon the audience to mourn him. By and large, the audience remained silent. Some applauded. Only a single individual, wearing a small beard and a knitted skullcap, stood up and yelled: "I disagree; that was a cold-blooded murder!" Instantly he was physically assaulted. Many in the crowd yelled: "Kick the infidel out of the hall!" The tempers calmed down only when Ben-David finally appeared on the stage and began singing. Outside after the performance some people reminisced that more Gentiles had been killed by the Jews in Susa during the original Purim [75,000]. They, therefore, reasoned that this was the right time to kill a comparable number of Gentiles in the holy land.

No wonder that Dov Halvertal, a member of the almost defunct faction of the NRP doves, told Golan: "This Purim joy epitomizes the moral collapse of religious Zionism ... If religious Zionism does not undertake soul-searching right now, I doubt if it will ever have another opportunity."

Subsequent developments showed that neither the religious Zionists nor other factions within the Jewish religious community were or are in any mood to engage in soul-searching. On the contrary, the appreciation of Goldstein and the feeling that Jews have a right and duty to kill Gentiles who live in the land of Israel are growing. In his March 23, 1994 *Haaretz* article, Nadav Shraggai discussed the visit of a delegation of all Israeli branches of the Bnei Akiva, the large youth movement affiliated with the NRP, to Kiryat Arba and Hebron, which was then under a curfew selectively applied to its Arab inhabitants. The purpose of this visit was to "encourage Jewish settlers." Yossi Leibowitz, a settler leader from Hebron, as described by Shraggai, "beaming with satisfaction visible in his face asked the delegation: 'Have you already visited the tomb of holy Rabbi Doctor Goldstein?' " The visitors rejected the suggestion but did not utter one word of rebuke to the worshippers of the new saint. They then had to withstand a flurry of abuse from their local Bnei Akiva comrades who argued that their refusal to pay homage to Goldstein amounted to support of the left. Local rabbis affiliated with the NRP seconded the denunciation. Rabbi Shimon Ben-Zion, a senior teacher in the local Hesder Yeshiva and hence a state employee, delivered a eulogy of Goldstein and of what he called "his act." He added: "[If the government] keeps bowing low to Arabs, all of whom are murderers, [and if] the Jews fail to establish a firm rule over the land of Israel [there will be] more Goldsteins." Most visitors made counter-arguments; they were nevertheless influenced by their hosts' arguments; they came to believe that their duty to support the Jewish settlers in Hebron was more important than any minor disagreements about Goldstein's sainthood.

Gabby Baron reported in the March 16, 1994 *Yediot Ahronot*:

Deputy Minister of Education Mikha Goldman was physically assaulted yesterday after delivering a welcoming speech at a meeting of Jerusalem's district teachers in the Binyaney Ha'umah hall in that city. He managed to avoid being hurt. His speech infuriated dozens of religious teachers, because he talked about his visit to Kiryat Arba and the shock he experienced when finding how enthused the religious school children were by the massacre in the Cave of the Patriarchs. A virtual riot erupted in the hall, which was filled by about 5000 Jerusalem district teachers, as soon as he spoke about it. Dozens of religious teachers jumped onto the podium. A female teacher who managed to reach it [the podium] picked up a flowerpot from the speaker's table; she was ready to hurl it at him when at the last moment she balked. All the religious teachers assembled in rage in front of the podium and decried the deputy minister as "a fascist." Goldman insisted upon continuing his speech. When he ended, he had to leave the building under heavy guard, thanks to which the pursuing teachers were unable to injure him.

Neither Education Minister Amnon Rubinstein nor Prime Minister Rabin uttered a single word in condemnation of the incident.

On April 5, 1994, Israeli radio reported that Rabbi Shimon Ben-Zion had distributed a leaflet among the Kiryat Arba and Hebron settlers requesting financial contributions for a book about "Saint Baruch Goldstein." On April 6, *Yediot Ahronot* published the text. The book refers to Goldstein as "Rabbi Doctor Baruch Goldstein of blessed memory, let the Lord avenge his blood." The Kiryat Arba municipal council backed the ideas of Ben-Zion. In his April 5, 1994 *Haaretz* article, Amnon Barzilay reported that two days earlier Gush Emunim leaders, including Mayor Benny Katzover, had an amicable talk with Prime Minister Rabin who apologized to them for his past outbursts against them and promised never to repeat them. (The outbursts anyway were intended for consumption of the Israeli "doves," Arafat and the Western media.) The two sides agreed to cooperate closely in the future. Thus, Rabin understandably found it ill-advised to say anything about Rabbi Ben-Zion's idea.

About one year later the Kiryat Arba municipality obtained a permit from the Civil Administration of the Occupied Territories to build a large and sumptuous memorial on Goldstein's tomb, which has become a place of pilgrimage. Thousands of Jews from all Israeli cities, and even more from the United States and France, have come to light candles and pray for the intercession of "holy saint and martyr," now in a special section of paradise close to God and able to obtain for them various benefits, such as cures for diseases from which they suffer, or to grant them male offspring. The visitors have donated money for Goldstein's comrades. No Orthodox rabbi has criticized this.

The well-publicized worship of the new saint has brought increasing opposition from secular Jews. (The opposition of Palestinians, especially those living in Hebron, to the hero-worship of Goldstein and to the monument to this mass murderer are not within the scope of this book but should be obvious.) After a long campaign in the press, Knesset members passed a piece of legislation in May, 1998, that prohibited the building of monuments for mass murderers and ordering removal of existing ones. The Israeli army should have removed the monument immediately after passage of the law in the Knesset. Instead army spokesmen announced that negotiations over the Goldstein monument were on-going with Goldstein's family and local rabbis.

The book in praise of Goldstein, titled *Blessed the Male*, was published in 1995 and sold in many editions. Most of the readers were from the religious public. The book contained eulogies of Goldstein and halachic justifications for the right of every Jew to kill non-Jews. Rabbi Yitzhak Ginsburgh, the then head of the Kever Yosef (tomb of Joseph) Yeshiva, located on the outskirts of Nablus, wrote one chapter of that book. The essence of Rabbi Ginsburgh's views were presented in Chapter 4. His and other such ideologies, even if expressed more cautiously, explain Goldstein's massacre, the considerable support Goldstein and later his followers have received from religious Jews and the ambiguous attitude of Israeli governments to this crime. Those people, especially Germans, who were silent and did not condemn Nazi ideology before Hitler came to power are also, at least in a moral sense, guilty for the terrible consequences that followed. Similarly, those who are silent and do not condemn Jewish Nazism, as exemplified by the ideologies of Goldstein and Ginsburgh, especially if they are Jews, are guilty of the terrible consequences that may yet develop as a result of their silence.

The Religious Background of Rabin's Assassination

Prime Minister Yitzhak Rabin was murdered for religious reasons. The murderer and his sympathizers were and still are convinced that the killing was dictated by God and was therefore a commandment of Judaism. Comprehensive surveys, published in the Hebrew press, of people in religious neighborhoods and especially religious settlements indicated great sympathy for the murder. The polarization of approval and disapproval in the Israeli Jewish community over the killing of the prime minister of the Jewish state has increased since the time of the murder. Many Israeli Jews, significant numbers of Jews living outside Israel and most non-Jews do not possess sufficient knowledge of Jewish history and religion to put this kind of an assassination into its proper context. In this chapter we shall attempt to provide the historical-religious background necessary for an understanding of the Rabin assassination.

Jewish history has been replete with religious civil wars or rebellions accompanied by civil wars in which horrifying assassinations were committed. The Great Rebellion (AD 66–73) of Jews against the Romans that culminated in the destruction of the Second Temple and in mass suicide in Masada is exemplary. The defenders of Masada were, as many present-day visitors to the Masada site are seemingly unaware, a band of assassins called Sikarikin, a name taken from the word for a short sword that group members hid under their robes and used to kill their Jewish opponents in crowds of people. In the Talmud the word means terrorists or robbers and is applied only to Jews. Neither Masada nor this particular group are mentioned in the Talmud or in any part of the traditional writing preserved by Jews. Actually the Sikarikin were an ancient Jewish analogue to modern-day terrorists. Their suicide activity resembled the terrorist behavior of the suicide bombers who are so abhorred in the state of Israel. The Sikarikin escaped to Masada not from the Romans but from their Jewish brethren. Shortly after the rebellion against the Romans began, the Roman army that was advancing to Jerusalem was initially defeated and had to withdraw. The Sikarikin attempted forcefully to establish their leader, Menahem, as absolute king. The Jews of Jerusalem then attacked and defeated the Sikarikin in the temple itself, killing most of them including Menahem. The remaining Sikarikin escaped to Masada where they stayed during the rebellion; they did not fight the Romans but instead robbed neighboring Jewish villages. Three years after the Sikarikin defeat, the Roman army, commanded by Titus, approached Jerusalem for the final onslaught. (Titus' chief of staff, Tiberius Julius Alexander, was a Jew, the nephew of the great philosopher, Philo.) Jerusalem was divided into three parts; each part was under the command of a different leader; the leaders had already been fighting with one another for two years. The Roman Empire at that time was then concerned about a civil war. One of the leaders, Eliezer the Priest, commanded the Temple and used it as his stronghold. On Passover eve in the year AD 70, another rebel leader, Yohanan of Gush Halav, utilized brilliant strategy to overcome Eliezer. He dressed his soldiers as pious pilgrims who seemed to be coming to the temple for the Passover sacrifice. After being admitted to the temple by the gullible Eliezer without a body search, they, after guessing correctly that Eliezer and his men would not carry arms in a place so holy, pulled out their swords and slaughtered all their opponents. The well-known Masada terrorists became Jewish and Israeli national heroes, as did the Jerusalem Jews who killed most of the Sikarikin. Yohanan of Gush Halav also became a national hero, but Eliezer the Priest, perhaps because he was killed by Jews, was completely forgotten. In these and in many similar incidents in Jewish history, killing was allegedly committed for the greater glory of God. Yigal Amir, Rabin's assassin, made such an allegation.

The violence between Jews did not end with the loss of Jewish independence and the ceasing of Jewish rebellions. (The last Jewish rebellion occurred in AD 614.) From the Middle Ages until the advent of the modern state, Jewish communities enjoyed a great degree of autonomy. The rabbis who headed and had the authority in these communities were most often able to persecute Jews mercilessly. The rabbis persecuted Jews who committed religious sins and even more harshly persecuted Jews who informed upon other Jews to non-Jews or in other ways harmed Jewish interests. The rabbis generally tolerated violence committed by some Jews against other Jews, especially against women, so long as the Jewish religion and their own interests were not harmed. The relevancy of this aspect of Jewish history to the Rabin murder is obvious. The assassin, Yigal Amir, is a talmudic scholar who was trained in a yeshiva that inculcated its students to believe that this violence committed by rabbis over a lengthy time period was in accordance with God's word.

Long before Rabin's assassination, scholarly studies of Jewish history, written in Hebrew, recorded the violence mentioned above. The assassination aroused so much public interest in this topic that the Hebrew press published numerous articles either written by or resulting from interviews with distinguished Israeli scholars. Rami Rosen's November 15, 1996 *Haaretz Magazine* article, titled "History of a Denial," is an excellent and representative example. Although Rosen interviewed several distinguished historians, he relied primarily upon the views of Professor Yisrael Bartal, the head of the department of Jewish history at the Hebrew University in Jerusalem. Bartal began his statement:

> Zionism has described the diaspora Jews as weak people who desire peace and abhor every form of violence. It is astonishing to discover that orthodox Jews are also providing similar descriptions. They describe past Jewish society as one not interested in anything other than the Halacha and the fulfillment of the commandments. The entire Jewish literature produced in eastern Europe, however, teaches us that the reverse is true. Even in the nineteenth century the descriptions of how Jews lived are filled with violent battles that often took place in the synagogues, of Jews beating other Jews in the streets or spitting on them, of the frequent cases of pulling out of beards and of numbers of murders.

Citing the authorities interviewed, Rosen explained that many murders were committed for religious reasons. It was usual in some Hassidic circles until the last quarter of the nineteenth century to attack and often to murder Jews who had reform religious tendencies, even if small ones. These Hassidic Jews also attacked one another because of frequent quarrels between different holy rabbis over spheres of influence, money and prestige. After having learned the opinions of the best Israeli scholars, Rosen asked:

> Were Yigal Amir, Baruch Goldstein, Yonah Avrushmi [who threw a hand grenade into a Peace Now demonstration, killing one and wounding a few people] and Ami Poper [who killed seven innocent Palestinian workers and was adopted as a great hero by extremists] parts of the Jewish tradition? Is it only by chance that Baruch Goldstein massacred his victims on the Purim holiday?

Rosen answered his own question:

> A check of main facts of the [Jewish] historiography of the last 1500 years shows that the picture is different from the one

previously shown to us. It includes massacres of Christians [by Jews]; mock repetitions of the crucifixion of Jesus that usually took place on Purim; cruel murders within the family; liquidation of informers, often done for religious reasons by secret rabbinical courts, which issued a sentence of "pursuer" and appointed secret executioners; assassinations of adulterous women in synagogues and/or the cutting of their [the women's] noses by command of the rabbis.

Rosen included in his long article many well-documented cases of massacres of Christians and mock repetitions of the crucifixion of Jesus on Purim, most of which occurred either in the late ancient period or in the Middle Ages. (Some isolated cases occurred in sixteenth-century Poland.) From the eleventh century until the nineteenth century, Ashkenazi Jews were more violent and fanatical than were the Oriental Jews, although the fanaticism of the Spanish Jews during both Muslim and Christian rule was exceptional. Jewish historians have not yet determined the causes of those differences. The influence of Christian fanaticism on the Jews may have been a cause. The Jews who lived in Spain may have been influenced by the fact that Muslim Spain was more fanatical than the rest of the Muslim world.

The violence perpetrated against women for centuries and other aspects of internal group violence influenced the developing character of traditional Jewish society. This character set the contextual framework for Rabin's assassination. Citing a few case examples here may further understanding of this character. Rabbi Simha Asaf's book, *The Punishments After the Talmud Was Finalized: Materials for the History of Hebrew Law* (Jerusalem, 1922) is a marvelous source of information. Rabbi Asaf, who subsequently became a professor at the Hebrew University and in 1948 was one of the first nine judges of the Israeli Supreme Court, was a distinguished scholar and a religious Jew. Convinced that a Jewish state would be established, he wrote his book in order to show that a sufficient number of legal cases existed in the history of punishments inflicted by Jewish religious courts to provide precedents.

Although some variances in halachic interpretation and in practice existed, violence against women, as defined in any reasonable and modern way, was routinely practiced for centuries in most Jewish communities. Some rabbis allowed the Jewish husband to beat his wife when she disobeyed him. Other rabbis limited this "right" by requiring that, prior to the beating, a rabbinical court, after considering the husband's complaint, had to issue an order. Presumably as an extension of this husband's right, rabbinical courts in Spain ordered the cruellest punishment for Jewish women suspected of fornication, prostitution and adultery and a much lighter punishment for Jewish male fornicators. In the early fourteenth century a local Jewish notable asked the famous Spanish rabbi, Rabenu[1] Asher, whether it was correct punishment to cut the nose of a Jewish widow, made pregnant by a Muslim. The notable added that, although the evidence itself was not conclusive, the pregnancy was well-known in the city. Rabenu Asher answered: "You have decided beautifully to cut her nose in order that those committing adultery with her will find her ugly, but let this be done suddenly so that she will not become an apostate [before her nose is cut]" (Asaf, p. 69). In a case wherein a male fornicated with Muslim women, Rabbi Yehuda, the son of Rabenu Asher, ordered only excommunication or imprisonment (Asaf, p. 78). This same punishment was prescribed when male Jews owned a Muslim female slave with whom other male Jews fornicated. The rabbis regarded the commission of adultery of Jewish women with Jewish men as less serious. In such a case one rabbi ordered that the woman's hair be shorn and that she be officially excommunicated in the synagogue in the presence of other women (Asaf, p. 87). The Sephardic Jews of Jerusalem sheared women's hair as punishment for such sexual sins still in the nineteenth century. In some recorded cases the punishment was based upon the belief that the sexual sins of Jews, especially those committed by women, prevented rain from falling. The rabbis supposed that the rain would fall if Jewish women sinners were punished. Enlightened Hebrew press commentators at the time humorously noted that the rain did not fall even after women had been punished. In places where more modern attitudes prevailed, however, Spanish and Portuguese Jews desisted from these ancestral customs. Asaf quotes the elders of the Portuguese Jewish community in Hamburg in the late seventeenth century who, although having publicly accused members of their community of having intimate relations with non-Jewish women, expressed their regret that they could not punish them. Asaf pointed to the reason: "In every such case they must get permission from the town judges" (p. 95). The Jewish community, Asaf wrote, could only inflict religious sanctions, such as telling two brothers that they could not enter the synagogue until they had dismissed a notorious servant from their home (p. 97).

The Jewish rabbinical authorities in some eastern parts of Europe could inflict somewhat tougher punishments. These punishments, however, were less severe than those that had been imposed in Spain. The heads of the Jewish community in Prague decided in 1612 that all Jewish prostitutes had to leave the town by a certain date or be branded after that date with a hot iron (Asaf, p. 114). The prostitutes' main offence was that they were seen drinking non-kosher wine with some unnamed notables of the community. The most tolerant communities were those in Italy who, as Asaf recorded, gave full encouragement to the prostitutes, because they saved "bachelors and fools from the worse sins of adultery or of cohabitation with non-Jewish women."

In his previously mentioned article, Rosen recorded research of new Jewish historians showing that Italian Jews copied the Renaissance custom according to which a husband or brother can kill his wife or sister with impunity if he suspects her of adultery. To remove the resultant blemish upon the honor of an insulted husband, Jews committed many of these murders in the synagogue during prayer in order to obtain publicity. A Jew, named Ovadia, from Spoleto, for instance, murdered his wife in the synagogue and, after explaining his reasons, received no punishment. The Italian authorities put Ovadia on trial and fined him, but the Jews did not believe he had done anything wrong. Soon thereafter, he remarried another Jewish woman. Brothers in other cases murdered suspected women. Referring to his research, Rosen cited one such case in Ferrara in the mid-sixteenth century. The murderer brother worked for a charity organization that was affiliated with the congregation; he was able to continue in his job after the murder. Rosen determined and reported that in such cases the rabbis usually did not react.

Jewish autonomy before the rise of the modern nation state allowed rabbis to engage in a wide spectrum of persecution, of which violence against women was but one category. The rabbis employed various types of violence against Jews who committed religious or other sins. Jewish fundamentalists, wanting to revive a situation that existed before the hated modern influences allegedly corrupted the Jews, emphasized this violence. The centrality of violence in the Halacha played an important role in the development of Orthodox Judaism. Orthodox Judaism historically had a double system of law. There was, on the one side, a more normal system of law, but there was, on the other side, been a more arbitrary system of law employed in emergencies. These emergency situations most often occurred when rabbis had great communal power. The rabbis, alleging that heresy and infidelity were at dangerously high levels, often suspended the normal system of laws, at least in the area of guarding the beliefs of the community, and used emergency powers to avert God's wrath. A relevant example for our study concerns the death penalty. In the normal system of law, the halachic application of the death punishment against a Jew was almost impossible to carry out, as opposed to its much easier application against a non-Jew. Even inflicting less severe punishment against Jews, such as thirty-nine lashes, was difficult. The normal talmudic alternative to the death penalty for Jews who killed other Jews was release of the Jewish murderer without further punishment. The Talmud posits another alternative. This alternative, as described by Maimonides in his commentary, *Laws of the Murderer and of Taking Precautions*, chapter 4, rule 8, is that Jewish murderers, absolved of the death punishment by a rabbinical court, could be "put into a small cell and given first only a small amount of bread and water until their intestines narrowed and then [fed] barley so that their bellies would burst because of the illness."

Rabbinical judges experienced difficulty in inflicting punishment when Jewish autonomy was limited by secular authorities. Only those rabbinical judges who were appointed by what was called "laying of hands,"[2] for example, could at first inflict flogging limited to thirty-nine lashes. Rabbis later devised a new more arbitrary way of inflicting punishment called "stripes of rebellion." The new method, which could be used by any rabbi, included harsher punishments. The number of lashes, for example, was unlimited. The cutting of limbs and unlimited imprisonment time were added. After the talmudic period and following the declines of the Roman and Sassanid Empires and of the Muslim caliphates, Jewish communities in many places became more autonomous and thus the opportunities for rabbis to impose more severe punishments increased.

The Jewish religious authorities perpetrated most of the violence against Jews who were considered to be heretics or religious dissenters. The punishments imposed had to be warranted by the Talmud, or at least by interpretation of the Talmud. The Talmud was composed under the rule and authority of two strong empires, the Roman and the Sassanid; both of these empires limited the powers of Jewish autonomy much more than did subsequent medieval regimes. Talmudic sages frequently complained that under the rule of these two empires, they did not have the power to punish Jewish criminals with death but rather only with flogging. The few cases in which talmudic sages attempted to execute a Jewish criminal prompted strict official investigations. One of these few cases, mentioned in the Palestinian Talmud, concerned a Jewish prostitute in the third century who was finally executed. Apparently because execution was so difficult to enforce, the Talmud does not order a death punishment for Jewish heretics but does enjoin pious Jews to kill them by employing subterfuges. The major halachic codes, although emphasizing that the death punishment should be inflicted only if execution was possible, contain such prescription. The paradigmatic expression of this command in the codes comes ironically under the section devoted to saving life. The question is posed: What is a pious Jew to do when he sees a human being drowning in the sea or having fallen into a well? The talmudic answer, still accepted by traditional Judaism, is that the answer is dependent upon the category to which the human being belongs. If the person is either a pious Jew or one guilty of no more than ordinary offences, he should be saved. If the person is a non-Jew or a Jew who is a "shepherd of sheep and goats," a category that lapsed after talmudic times, he should neither be saved nor pushed into the sea or well. If, however, the person is a Jewish heretic, he should either be pushed down into the well or into the sea or; if the person is already in the well or sea, he should not be rescued. This legal stipulation, although mutilated by censorship in certain editions of the Talmud and even more in most translations, appears in *Tractate Avoda Zara* (pp. 26a–b). Maimonides also explained this stipulation in three places: In the *Laws of Murderer and Preservation of Life*, Maimonides contrasted the fate of non-Jews with that of Jewish heretics. In the passages from *Laws of of Idolatry* Maimonides only discussed Jewish heretics. In *Laws of Murderer and Preservation of Life* (chapter 4, rules 10–11), he wrote:

The [Jewish] heretics are those [Jews] who commit sins on purpose; even one who eats meat not ritually slaughtered or who dresses in a sha'atnez clothes (made of linen and wool woven together) on purpose is called a heretic [as are] those [Jews] who deny the Torah and prophecy. They should be killed. If he [a Jew] has the power to kill them by the sword, he should do so. But if he has not [the power to do so], he should behave so deceitfully to them that death would ensue. How? If he [a Jew] sees one of them who has fallen into a well and there is a ladder into the well, he [should] take it away and say: "I need it [the ladder] to take my son down from the roof," or [he should say] similar things. Deaths of non-Jews with whom we are not at war and Jewish shepherds of sheep and goats and similar people should not be caused, although it is forbidden to save them if they are at the point of death. If, for example, one of them is seen falling into the sea, he should not be rescued. As it is written: "Neither shall you stand against the blood of your fellow" (Leviticus 19:16) but he [the non-Jew] is not your fellow.

In *Laws of Idolatry*, chapter 2, rule 5 Maimonides stated:

Jews who worship idolatrously are considered as non-Jews, in contrast to Jews who have committed [another] sin punishable by stoning; if he [a Jew] converted to idolatry he is considered to be a denier of the entire Torah. [Jewish] heretics are also not considered to be Jews in any respect. Their repentance should never be accepted. As it is written: "None that go into her return again, neither [do] they hold the paths of life" (*Proverbs* 2:19). [This verse is actually a reference to men who frequent "a strange woman," that is, a prostitute.] In regard to the heretics who follow their own thoughts and speak foolishly, it is forbidden to talk with or to answer them, as we have said above [in the first section of the work] so that they may ultimately contravene maliciously and proudly the most important parts of the Jewish religion and say there is no sin [in doing this]. As it is written: "Remove your way far from her and come not near the door of her house." (Proverbs 5:8).

The last verse refers again to men who "frequent a strange woman", that is, a prostitute. The commentators explained that this passage meant that a truly repentant idolatrous Jew is accepted by the Jewish community, but a heretic is not accepted. A heretic who wants to repent, however, may do it alone. The main reason for this difference is seemingly that an idolatrous Jew, including one who converts to Christianity, accepts another religious discipline, while a heretic follows his own views and is thereby considered to be more dangerous. In chapter 10, rule 1 of *Laws of Idolatry*, Maimonides, after explaining the extermination of the ancient Canaanites and again asserting that no Jews should be killed, said: "All this applies to the seven [Canaanite] nations, but Jewish informers and heretics should be exterminated by one's own hand and put into hell, because they cause trouble to Jews by removing their hearts from being true to the Lord, like Tzadok, and Beitos [the alleged founders of the Sadducean sect] and their pupils. Let the name of the wicked perish." In his next rule Maimonides asserted that non-Jews should not be healed by Jews except when danger of non-Jewish enmity exists. In his *Fundamental Laws of Torah*, the first treatise of his codex, chapter 6, rule 8, Maimonides, after explaining that Jews are forbidden to burn or otherwise to destroy the holy script and that they may not even damage any Hebrew writing in which one of the seven sacred names of God is written, ruled:

If a Torah scroll was written by a Jewish heretic, it should be burned, together with all its sacred names [of God], because the heretic does not believe in the holiness of God and could not write it for God but must have thought that it is like other books. Therefore, given this view, God is not sanctified [by it] and it is a commandment to burn it [the scroll] so that no memory is left of the heretics or to their deeds. But, a Torah scroll written by a non-Jew should be put away with the other holy books that deteriorated or were written by non-Jews.[3]

Although he did not instruct Jews to burn heretical books, Maimonides probably based the above passage upon many directives issued by talmudic sages since about AD 100. These directives called for the burning of books by heretics. Indeed, talmudic sages even boasted at times about burning such books themselves. Halachic codes did not so instruct, but rabbinical responsa frequently called for and Jewish history is replete with examples of Jews burning Jewish books. Together with burial of books in cemeteries, this reached a high point in the eighteenth century. Although minimized in many apologetic histories of Jews, especially in works written in English, the burning and the burial in cemeteries of books in the history of Judaism was far more intense than in the histories of either Christianity or Islam.

Traditional Judaism also forbade independent thoughts. In his *Laws of Idolatry*, chapter 2, rule 3, Maimonides, after explaining that a Jew should not think about idolatry, continued:

And it is not only forbidden to think about idolatry but [about] any thought that may cause a Jew to doubt one principle of the Jewish religion. [The Jew] is warned not to bring it to his consciousness. We shall not think in that direction, and we shall not allow ourselves to be drawn into meditations of the heart, because human understanding is limited, and not every opinion is directed to the real truth. If a Jew, therefore, allows himself to follow his [independent] thoughts, he will surely destroy the world because of insufficient understanding. How? He may sometimes be seduced to idolatry and sometimes think about the uniqueness of the Lord, sometimes that he exists and other times that he does not; [he may] investigate what is above [in the sky] and what is below [under earth], what is before [the world was created] and what is after [the end of the world]. He may think about whether or not prophecy is true; he may think about whether or not the Torah was given by God. Because such people do not know the [true] logic to be used in order to reach the real truth, they become heretics. It is about that issue that the Torah warned us. As it is written: "And that you seek not after your own heart and after your own eyes that you are using to prostitute yourselves" (Numbers 16:39). [This verse is included in the third passage of "Kry'at Sh'ma," one of the most sacred Jewish prayers that is said daily in the morning and in the evening.] This means that every Jew is forbidden to allow himself to follow his own insufficient knowledge and to imagine that his own thoughts are capable of reaching the truth. The sages have said: "after your own heart" means heresy; "after your own eyes" means prostitution. This prohibition, even though the sin causes a Jew to lose paradise, does not carry the penalty of flogging [because flogging is inflicted only in cases of deeds].

Such prohibitions of any independent thinking (which some Haredim apply to some of Maimonides' own writings) were common in post-talmudic Judaism and have persisted to date in part of Orthodox Judaism. Orthodox Judaism totally prohibited independent thinking about issues discussed freely by St Augustine regardless of whatever answers he put forward. Indeed, such issues are almost never mentioned today by Orthodox Jewish scholars.[4] Many theological problems freely discussed by Thomas Aquinas[5] were and remain unthinkable in traditional Judaism. (Traditional Judaism today includes not only Orthodox but much of Conservative Judaism as well.) Amazingly, many people, especially in English-speaking countries, still attribute to post-talmudic Judaism the intellectual distinction achieved in numerous countries by many Jews in the past 150 years. This delusion has contributed to the spread of fundamentalist Judaism. In reality, the contrary has been the case. Most of the Jews who attained intellectual distinction were influenced by rebellion against this type of totalitarian system; they negated some of its major tenets.

In addition to advocating that heretics be killed, whenever possible, by employing one method or another, traditional Judaism directed that heretics while still alive should under all possible circumstances be treated in a worse manner than non-Jews or Jews who converted to another religion. One socially important example of such directed treatment is the burial of the heretic's corpse, together with the ceremonies to be observed by the family after the burial. Whereas traditional Judaism permits and sometimes even obliges Jews to bury most Jewish sinners, it strictly prohibits Jews to bury Jewish heretics and/or a few types of Jewish sinners. *Tractate Trumot* of the *Palestinian Talmud*, chapter 8, halacha 3, discusses a Jewish butcher in the town of Tzipori in Galilee who sold non-kosher meat. This butcher fell from a roof and was killed. Rabbi Hanina Bar Hama, a sage in the early third century AD, encouraged the Jews of the town to let their dogs eat the corpse. Such behavior was usually not feasible; hence, later authorities were more moderate. Maimonides and later rabbis were content with prohibiting the family of the heretic to mourn his death and ordering the family to rejoice. Maimonides clearly put this in his *Laws of Mourning*, chapter 1, rule 10:

All who separate themselves from public custom [of the Jews], such as those who do not fulfil commandments and do not honor the holidays or do not frequent synagogues or houses of study but rather regard themselves free and [behave] like other nations, and heretics, converts and informers should not be mourned; when they die, their brothers and all other relatives should put on white garments, make banquets and rejoice, since those who hate the Lord, blessed be he, have perished.

Most Jews rigorously followed this rule of Maimonides until the beginning of Jewish modernization; some orthodox Jews follow this rule to date.[6] In the small towns of eastern Europe in the nineteenth century, Jews devised another custom of humiliating burial of heretics and other Jewish sinners. This custom, often mentioned in the contemporary Hebrew and Yiddish literature, was called "ass burial." It was derived from the biblical verse, Jeremiah 22:19, where the prophet predicts that King Yohoiakim of Judah "will be buried as an ass." This custom had three general components. First, members of the Jewish burial society, called the Holy Society and consisting of the fiercest zealots of the town, would first beat the heretic's corpse. Then the corpse would thereafter be put on a cart filled with dung and was in that condition paraded through the town. Finally, the corpse would be buried beyond the fence of the graveyard without religious rites. The two expressions, "ass burial" and "beyond the fence" became proverbial terms in Hebrew and Yiddish and are still used to denote social ostracism. The famous Jewish writer, Peretz Smolenskin (1840–85), wrote a Hebrew novel, titled *Ass Burial*, which is still read. In his novel Smolenskin told the story of a young Jew in a Russian small town who, because of a petty quarrel with the chief of the Jewish burial society, was declared a heretic. The Jewish congregation hired an assassin who murdered the heretic. The heretic was buried in an ass burial. Smolenskin was the father of the naturalistic style in Hebrew literature. His novels were based upon a close observation of Jewish life as it was in his time.

Learned authorities often disagreed on the definition of heretic. Talmudic sages enumerated several kinds of heretics who were called by different names. The Talmud emphasized one type of heretic, called "apikoros" apparently named after followers of the Greek philosopher, Epicurus. In *Tractate Sanhedrin*, page 99b of the Talmud, the Apikoros were designated as all Jews who were disrespectful to rabbis. One talmudic sage asserted that a Jew who was disrespectful to another Jew in the presence of a rabbi was a heretic. Rabbi Menahem Ha'Meiri, in commenting upon the above passage, said that a Jew who called a rabbi by his name without using the honorific title was a heretic. The prevalent opinion until the twentieth century was that Jews who were disrespectful to rabbis were not heretics but were only "like heretics." Real heretics were those who denied the validity of the Talmud as religious authority. This definition did not lessen the punishment of heretics and other sinners, when feasible to employ under emergency laws. This definition lessened the duty, imposed by the Talmud, of separating many Jews who paid taxes from the congregation. In the first half of the twentieth century, two famous rabbis, Rabbi Hazon Ish and Rabbi Kook the elder both ruled that laws regarding

heretics "do not apply because visible miracles do not occur." To
what extent the Hazon Ish–Kook opinion is followed today is
difficult to determine. At this point in our discussion, nevertheless,
the focus is upon pre-modern times.

Our survey of punishments, inflicted under emergency Jewish
laws upon Jewish heretics and other sinners, begins with pronouncements by the last Jewish rabbis whose authority was and still
is universally acknowledged. These rabbis were the heads of yeshivot
in Iraq until about 1050; they were named "Ge'onim." (In the
singular each of them bore the name "Ga'on," which in Hebrew
means "genius.") The Ge'onim left many responses to questions
addressed to them from all parts of the Jewish world. These
questions were concerned with how Jews, especially Jewish
communities, should behave. In his previously mentioned book
(1922), Rabbi Simha Asaf quoted a collection of such responses
ordering that a Jew who violates the sabbath should be flogged and
should have his hair shaved (p. 45). Rabbi Paltoi Ga'on, as noted
by Asaf, in AD 858 answered the more difficult question: Should
a Jew who sinned on either the Sabbath or a holiday be flogged on
that sacred day if the danger exists that he may escape before the
Sabbath or the holiday ended? Rabbi Paltoi answered by reminding
his questioners that the congregation had a prison and that the sinner
could be imprisoned on the Sabbath or on the holiday and then
flogged afterwards. Rabbi Paltoi, nevertheless, after acknowledging that the act of flogging violated the Sabbath in certain ways,
concluded that the concern about the Sabbath or holiday violations
should not prevent the flogging of Jewish sinners on the sacred day
(Asaf, p. 48). Rabbi Tzemach Ga'on, who lived after Rabbi Paltoi,
was asked what to do with a Jewish priest who married a divorced
woman, which as noted by Asaf is forbidden to priests (p. 52). Rabbi
Tzemach Ga'on expressed the fear that such a sinner, if only
flogged, would go to another place and during synagogue services
would participate in the priest's blessing by stretching out over the
heads of congregation members his hands with his fingers separated.
Rabbi Tzemach Ga'on, therefore, ordered that the last joints of the
priestly sinner's fingers should be cut off, thus identifying and
making it impossible for the sinner to participate in the blessing.
The last and most famous Ga'on, Rabbi Ha'i, who died in 1042,
devoted a long response, cited by Asaf, to an explanation of how
Jewish sinners were flogged during his time; he detailed, moreover,
how they were specifically flogged by his court. He emphasized that
the whip was made of hemp and for the worst sinners was especially
thick. The sinner was bound "right hand to the right foot and left
hand to the left foot." The one who flogged him stood near his head.
The ceremony began with a reading of the appropriate biblical
verses. After the flogging, the sinner stood naked with his dress in

his hand and acknowledged the justice of his sentence. Finally, the court asked God to have mercy on him. In other responsa, cited by Asaf on pages 56 and 57, Rabbi Ha'i specified the sins for which Jews should be flogged. Cutting one's hair on the minor holidays, putting on shoes during the mourning periods and violating the Sabbath were three examples. Asaf pointed out further on pages 58 and 59 that other responsa in the eleventh century provided proofs that the Jews of Egypt flogged sinners in front of the doors of synagogues and that the rabbis of Italy, because of the general political chaos and much greater Jewish autonomy, could and did execute sinners. Asaf specifically recorded the numerous death sentences inflicted by the Babylonian rabbi, Abu Aharon, who immigrated to Italy; for example, Rabbi Abu Aharon sentenced an adulterer to be strangled and a man who committed incest with his mother-in-law to be burned. Asaf illustrated the wide parameters of flogging by reporting that another unnamed Italian rabbi stipulated that if a Jew living in a courtyard area with other Jews sold his flat to a non-Jew, he should be flogged.

In Spain, whether under Muslim or Christian rule, Jewish autonomy and the consequent punishment of Jewish sinners were most developed and punishments were recorded in the largest number of cases. On page 62, Asaf quoted Rabbi Samuel the Prince,[7] who died in 1046: "Spanish Jews were always free of heresy, except in a few villages near the Christian land where suspicion exists of some heretics being harbored in secret. Our predecessors have flogged a part of [those] Jews who deserved to be flogged, and they have died from flogging." Rabbi Ha'i, as previously mentioned, insisted that the Jew being flogged must acknowledge the justice of his sentence and repent. Refusal to repent, Ha'i and many other rabbinical authorities made clear, compelled more flogging even until death. Spain may have become "free of heresy" at least partially because previous heretics were flogged to death. Rabbi Samuel's boast was confirmed to some extent, according to Asaf on page 63, by the story of the Jewish philosopher and historian, Rabbi Avraham Ibn Daud who, in his book *Shalshelet Ha'kabalah (Chain of Tradition)*, told how the Karaites, when they began to spread, were humiliated and expelled from all the towns of Castile except for one.[8] Somewhat later, after Rabbi Daud's death, Maimonides moderated the flogging punishment. In his commentary on the Mishnah, *Tractate Khulin*, quoted by Asaf on page 64, Maimonides maintained that Jews who committed sins which would normally result in the death penalty should "now only be flogged and excommunicated but their excommunication should never be removed."

The Jewish sins punished with the greatest cruelty, apart from informing which will be separately discussed below, were acts of disobedience to the will of and/or physical attacks upon rabbis. Such acts were not rare occurrences. Asaf on page 67 quoted the late thirteenth-century responsa of Rabbi Shlomo ben Aderet, the famous rabbi of Barcelona. Rabbi ben Aderet endeavored to show that any rabbi can "together with the elders" sentence Jews who oppose the rabbi's authority and are "notorious for their wickedness", not only to flogging but to the more severe punishments of having their hands or feet cut off or of being killed. Many other rabbinic responsa dealt in detail with such severe punishments. Asaf reported on page 72 that the previously mentioned Rabenu Asher was angry with Rabbi Moshe of Valencia for ruling against a usual custom and thus Asher's own authority in a matter of sabbath observance. From Toledo, Asher wrote to Rabbi Yitzhak of Valencia and ordered him to condemn the offending Rabbi Moshe to death unless he (Rabbi Moshe) did not repent after being fined and excommunicated. Rabenu Asher also dealt with the financial aspect of inflicting the death penalty. In his responsa to "the holy community of Avila," as reported by Asaf on page 74, the execution of the wicked was compared to the building of city walls; executions supposedly defended the purity of Judaism just as the walls defended their physical safety. Thus, just as every Jew could be compelled to pay taxes for the upkeep of the walls, every Jew could be compelled to pay for the execution of the wicked Jews.

Our final example from Spain is a summary of the responsa of Rabbi Yehuda, the son of Rabenu Asher. This responsa, quoted by Asaf on page 77, is important not only because it documents the use of violence but also because it describes the normal procedure in emergency cases of halachic decision making in cases brought before the rabbinical court. The elaborate display of reasoning in Jewish emergency law, differing totally from Halacha, is well illustrated in this responsa.

A cornerstone of the normal halachic procedure, based upon the Bible and employed in all cases brought before the rabbinical court, is that, in the absence of written documents that are used only in civil cases, every judgment must be based upon the testimony of two or more male Jewish witnesses. The testimony of each of the two witnesses must be exactly the same as determined in direct interrogation. In the illustrative example presented in his responsa, Rabbi Yehuda cited a case of a Jew who beat another Jew so severely that, as a consequence of this, the latter died. Two witnesses, Moshe and Avraham (family names not given), saw the beating. Two other witnesses, Yoseph and Yitzhak, saw only the beginning of the beating; they then left and thereafter returned to see the beaten man lying on the ground with blood pouring from his head. After giving thanks to God for "inspiring the kings of the earth to give Jews the power to judge [their offenders] as we are judging now," Rabbi Yehuda explained how the principles of current Jewish law that are not all according to Halacha have to be applied in the case under consideration. Rabbi Yehuda, as quoted by Asaf, decided:

> If only the testimony of Moshe and Avraham is found to be valid, the offender should be executed. If only one of their testimonies is found to be valid together with finding the testimony of either Yoseph or Yitzhak to be valid, the offender's hands should be cut off. If the testimony of either Moshe or Avraham is found to be valid but the testimony of both Yoseph and Yitzhak is found to be invalid, the offender's right hand should be cut off. If the testimony of both Moshe and Avraham is found to be invalid but the testimony of both Yoseph and Yitzhak is found to be valid, the offender's left hand should be cut off. If all the testimonies are found to be invalid, the offender should be exiled from the city because the fact that he killed [the victim] became notorious.

In other European countries, Jewish autonomy and thus its consequences were less powerful than in Spain. Perhaps this was because the other states, in spite of their feudal nature, were stronger than the Spanish kingdoms before the latter part of the fifteenth century. In England, where royal power was especially strong and where Jews settled only after England's conquest by William I, there were, so far as we know, no cases of rabbis' flogging or otherwise punishing Jews for religious offenses. In continental Europe, where Jewish autonomy depended more on the feudal lords than on the king or emperor, however, there were significant numbers of cases. In fourteenth-century Germany, for example, the famous rabbi, Yosef Weil, according to Asaf on page 102, recorded in his book of responsa that Rabbi Shimon from Braunschweig asked him whether it was permitted to put out the eyes of a Jew who violated the Sabbath and Yom Kippur (the Day of Atonement). Rabbi Weil answered that it was permitted and referred to talmudic evidence for his permission. In another case, reported by Asaf on page 104, the famous Rabenu Tam who lived in northern France in the twelfth century ordered that in the case of a Jew who beat another Jew the punishment should be the cutting off of the offender's hand rather than the usual punishment of flogging. Asaf recorded on page 103 that another rabbi had seen his father inflicting the punishment of flogging. Flogging was used in general in Germany as a punishment for lesser religious sins; the cutting of limbs was rare. The use of flogging even diminished with the passage of time; fines, excommunications and obligatory fasts were used by German Jews as almost the only punishments.

In the countries east of Germany, especially in Poland and after 1569 in the Polish-Lithuanian Commonwealth where Jewish autonomy was extensive, punishments inflicted by rabbis almost equalled those inflicted in Spain. Every Jewish community had its own prison and stocks, called "kuneh" in Yiddish, that were placed in the entrances to major synagogues. The stocks consisted of iron bars to secure the sinner's arms, compelling him to stand facing entering members of the congregation who would spit at him, slap his face and/or take other physical action against him. Flogging was freely practiced in the synagogue, usually during the reading of the law in the midst of the morning prayer. Asaf reported on page 122 that the famous sixteenth-century rabbi, Shlomo Luria, assured his questioners that a well-flogged sinner would not sin again and that the number of stripes in flogging should be determined by the court according to what is decided as fitting the sin. In serious cases the inflicted penalties were mutilation and death. A generation after Rabbi Shlomo Luria, another famous rabbi, Maharam (our teacher Rabbi Meir) of Lublin, according to Asaf on page 123, wrote about a case of a Jewish murderer caught by Polish authorities. Maharam insisted that such an offender should be executed by the rabbinical or Polish authorities. Maharam warned the rabbis against substituting mutilation for execution:

> I recall what occurred when I was young, in the time of Rabbi Shekhna R.I.P. In his time there was a most wicked Jew; the great rabbi permitted [the community] to put out his eyes and cut off his tongue. After having this done to him, he converted to Christianity, married a non-Jewish woman and had children. He and his [family members] were always enemies of the Jews.

In the seventeenth century, mutilation as a punishment, instead of death or flogging, tended to disappear among Jews of the Polish-Lithuanian Commonwealth. Expulsion from the town appeared as a new punishment. The autonomous Jewish community of a given town could determine which Jews would reside in the town. The privilege of residence was usually granted automatically only to the children of the old residents, their wives and the rabbis. All other Jews had to apply to the community authorities and receive, often after a payment and/or for a limited time, their residence rights. One of the cruellest punishments that a Jewish congregation could inflict, therefore, was expulsion, because an expelled Jew would have great difficulty acquiring residence rights elsewhere. This punishment, nevertheless, was increasingly employed in the seventeenth and eighteenth centuries. When Russia, Prussia and Austria thereafter divided Poland, these three conquering powers limited the autonomy of Jewish communities and forbade them to expel their members from towns. The expulsions in the seventeenth and eighteenth centuries were often immediate, regardless of the time of year, and were many times used as a weapon in religious disputes, such as the quarrel between the Hassids and their opponents, the Mitnagdim. The Union of Jewish Congregations in Lithuania, according to Asaf on page 127, ordered immediate expulsion from the town in addition to physical and financial punishment for any Jew who "behaved with contempt toward the rabbi." In another rule, cited by Asaf on pages 127 and 128, the Union ordered congregations to expel Jews who had previously been expelled from another town. The expelled Jews were usually compelled to sign a document, similar to the one quoted by Asaf on page 132, from the city of Krakow, stating that if they stay in the town for even one night they must accept any punishment imposed upon them by the community leaders, including "mutilation of ear or nose or of other places." In another case, cited by Asaf, a young Jew, who was expelled from Krakow for having taken part in a theft committed in the house of a notable, was sentenced to be flogged in front of the door to the synagogue; the youth additionally had to sign a declaration that if found again in Krakow he knew that "his two ears would be cut off, in addition [to his receiving] other punishments." The kuneh or stock was also used in this period as punishment especially for heretics but also for sinners who committed minor offences. In 1772, when the leaders of the Jewish community of Vilna began their struggle against the Hassidic movement, they first punished the Hassids in their town. Before the eve of the Sabbath prayer all Hassidic writings were burned near the kuneh so that the congregation members would see the ashes when they came to the synagogue. Before the burning the chief Hassid of Vilna, Meir Issar, was flogged privately in the "hall of the community." Following the flogging, Issar had to confess his sin, strictly following the formula prepared by the rabbinic court, in the synagogue during morning Sabbath prayers. He was then imprisoned for one week in the castle of Vilna. The chief rabbinic authority at that time, Haga'on Rabbi Eliyahu of Vilna, additionally wanted to put Issar in the kuneh, but the community leaders, apparently because Issar's family was important, refused. This story, mentioned by Asaf on page 139, was included in the detailed, Hebrew-language histories of this period.[9]

The story of Meir Issar is a typical example of persecution by Jewish authorities in eastern Europe of a Jewish religious dissident at the end of the eighteenth century. Fanaticism, religious disputes interposed with excommunications, burning of or sometimes burial in cemeteries of books and popular riots against heretics and dissenters characterized many European Jewish communities throughout most of the eighteenth century, with the exception of those in England and Holland. Towards the end of the century the zealotry decreased, first in Germany and Italy and then in the larger towns of eastern Europe; it continued during much of the nineteenth century among the bulk of the Jewish population in eastern Europe who lived in smaller towns. The great majority of Jewish immigrants to the United States, Britain and a few other places in the nineteenth century, having come from areas in which religious persecution of Jews by other Jews had been widely practiced for a long time, suddenly arrived in countries in which such persecution could not, at least not to nearly the same extent, be carried out.[10] The wish of many eighteenth-century Jews to persecute was seemingly greater than their actual ability to do so. An incident in the history of the Frankist heresy, which erupted in Poland in 1756 and continued for some years thereafter, provides a good example. When leaders of the autonomous Jewish community in Poland learned of this heresy, one of them, Rabbi Baruch from Greece, wrote a long letter to his friend in Germany and one of the greatest rabbis of that generation, Rabbi Ya'akov Emden.[11] In his letter Rabbi Baruch described the proceedings and aims of the main council of Jewish autonomy held in September, 1756, in Konstantinov. The council was called the 'committee of four lands', a name which referred to the four main Polish provinces. Rabbi Baruch reported details of the heresy and wrote that the committee of four lands decided "to bring the matter before the great Lord who rules over their [the Christian] faith, the Pope in Rome" and to struggle against the heresy. Rabbi Baruch wrote further that the committee asked "the help of [Polish] bishops so that the cursed ones would be condemned to be burned at the stake." Meir Balaban, the distinguished historian of Polish Jewry, remarked that the wish to see hundreds of "the cursed ones" burned at the stake by the Christian authorities, who at that very time were persecuting Polish Jews, indicated the depth of the hatred of the heretics felt by the Jewish leadership.[12] The committee's attempt failed. Rabbi Baruch went so far as to try to involve his patron, the powerful Minister Bruhl who was the favorite of the Polish King August III in this matter. Rabbi Baruch wanted Bruhl to arrange an interview for him with the papal nuncio in Warsaw. The Pope of that time period, Benedict XVIII, would almost certainly not have agreed to have a mass burning, but the heretics anyway obtained the help of powerful bishops and magnates and even of Countess Bruhl, the wife of the minister. The result was that the Jewish leaders could not, as they wanted to, pursue the persecution.

It may be instructive to compare the Frankist heresy incident with what Baruch Spinoza had to endure in Holland about a hundred

years earlier. Because of the relatively tolerant and more modern
Dutch regime, the Jewish community of Amsterdam could only
excommunicate Spinoza. As much as members of that community
desired to do so, they could not flog or kill Spinoza; they could not
compel Spinoza to make public confession in the synagogue that
he had sinned in his commentaries and statements about Judaism.
The Jewish community could only excommunicate Spinoza and
forbid him from attending the synagogue. A few years before
Spinoza's excommunication, the Jewish community of Amsterdam
excommunicated Uriel D'Acusta for similar reasons. D'Acusta,
however, was not endowed with Spinoza's firmness and could not
stand his exclusion from the synagogue and from Jewish community
life. D'Acusta asked the rabbis to reinstate him. The rabbis
sentenced him not only to the usual confession but also to lie at
the synagogue entrance so that congregation members could
trample on him before praying to God. D'Acusta accepted the
conditions and, after both confessing and being trampled upon,
was duly forgiven. He, however, again came thereafter to have
heretical views. Fearing another excommunication and something
even worse than being trampled underfoot as a recurrent sinner,
he committed suicide. A comparison between the fates of Spinoza
and D'Acusta suggests two lessons for contemporary Jews who do
not wish to submit to the tyranny often prevalent in Jewish
orthodoxy: 1) An intellectual compromise with Jewish orthodoxy
is no more possible than is an intellectual compromise with any
other totalitarian system. 2) An apologetic approach to the Jewish
past, which is in reality false beautification and falsification of one
part of Jewish history and is intended to remove the horrors and
persecutions that Jews suffered at the hands of their own authorities
and rabbis, only increases the dangers of a developing Jewish
"Khomeinism." In Israel such compromise increases the danger
of a Jewish state that could become dominated by rabbis who will
not hesitate to punish other Jews as did their revered predecessors
when not prevented from doing so by an outside power.

We have seen that formal and legal infliction of severe
punishments depended upon the amount of Jewish autonomy that
existed in specific places at specific times. Russia, Prussia and
Austria, as previously noted, after their conquest of Poland,
abolished Jewish autonomy and subjected Jews to the ordinary
criminal law of their countries. As bad as that criminal law was, it
was on balance better and more humane than the Jewish law as
applied by the rabbis.[13] Jewish communities that were suddenly
deprived of their power to persecute heretics found it difficult to
accustom themselves to a new situation. The relatively lax police
supervision that existed in Tsarist Russia during most of the
nineteenth century allowed Jewish authorities to persecute religious

innovators through riots, which were similar to what were called "pogroms" when committed by non-Jews against Jews. Until 1881 in Russia, the number of riots by Jews against other Jews probably exceeded the number of pogroms by non-Jews against Jews. The previously persecuted Hassids were the major and worst persecutors; they were especially active against the emerging Hebrew press of that time that appeared before the rise of the Yiddish press. The Hebrew press antagonized the Hassids mainly by reporting and protesting against the religious persecution by rabbis and their followers. In order to avert persecution by Jewish rioters, most of the Hebrew papers were printed and issued in St. Petersburg or behind the Prussian border, where the police were strong and the small Jewish communities mostly consisted of educated individuals.

The history of Jews in Russia until 1881 includes a great deal of persecution of Jews by Jews. The two following typical examples, one major and one minor, are illustrative: The major example is taken from the long article by David Asaf,[14] published in *Zion* (1994, number 4), the quarterly journal of the Israeli Historical Association. Asaf described the riot in Uman in the Ukraine, where one of the more famous Hassidic rabbis, Nahman of Braslaw, was buried and where his followers who came on pilgrimage to his tomb on the Jewish New Year were attacked and beaten year after year for decades by other Hassids. The annual beatings finally culminated in 1863 in an especially nasty attack by a coalition of Hassidic sects that was described by a contemporary Jewish writer in the Hebrew press of that time. The writer of the article noted the similarity between this Hassidic "pogrom" and those committed by the anti-Semites. He described how Hassids smashed the holy cupboard (Aron Ha'kodesh in Hebrew) where the scrolls of law were stored. The attacking Hassids considered the place to be heretical in and of itself; the alleged heretics were beaten and stoned; when they fainted, they were attacked again. The attackers used the occasion to beat the modernized Jews of the place as well, including women who wore what was considered to be immodest clothing. Fearful of other attacks, the Breslaw Hassids hired a company of Russian soldiers to defend themselves from other Hassids. The following year the collapse of the Hassidic coalition and another Jewish attack upon Jews in the town of Rzhishchev (south of Kiev) gave the Breslaw Hassids a temporary respite. The Rzhishchev riot erupted when a holy rabbi from another place had the temerity to visit Rzhishchev, where another holy rabbi resided, to collect money. As Asaf wrote in his article: "Of course, the Hassids of the local holy rabbi cursed and stoned the invader and he was almost killed." Many of the Hassids were wounded. The two holy rabbis then proclaimed that ritual slaughterers of each side were not kosher; each rabbi also proclaimed that the prayers of the other side were "an abomination to God." Scuffles ensured. The holy rabbi of Rzhishchev was denounced by his colleague as a forger of banknotes. A police investigation followed. Although the Breslaw Hassids attained a respite, they were, as Asaf showed, attacked periodically by other Hassids until 1914.

A minor example occurred in the town of Vyshegrad in 1886 and was recorded in the contemporary Hebrew press. Quoting research of new Jewish historians, Rosen in his previously cited article wrote:

> Hassids of Vyshegrad were opposed to the new cantor [of the synagogue] because his clothes are clean and he puts rubber shoes over his ordinary shoes. They therefore rioted in the synagogue against this cantor and beat their opponents until blood flowed. The police came quickly to separate the two sides. The rabbi who incited the riot was then arrested by soldiers and brought to the government house to explain the riot. The actual rioters will be criminally prosecuted.

After 1881 the situation in Russia began to change and Jewish attacks upon Jews decreased for several apparent reasons. First, in 1881 the government instigated Russian and Ukrainian pogroms began, and mass emigration of Jews from Russia began. In addition police supervision was tightened under the regime of Alexander III, who ascended to the throne after revolutionaries assassinated his father, Alexander II. Attacks by Jews against Jews, although diminished, nevertheless continued in Russia until 1914.

In Polish areas ruled by Austrian police, supervision was stronger and therefore direct attacks by Jews against other Jews apparently ceased. Orthodox Jews employed some secret forms of religious persecution against modern Jews, who called themselves "maskilim" (enlightened). In extreme cases, Jewish servants of the maskilim were suborned to kill their employers or other methods of assassination were employed. In his article Rosen related:

> Because of the approaching anniversary of Rabin's assassination, Professor Ze'ev Gris of the department of Jewish thought at Ben-Gurion University [in Be'er Sheva] sent us a story about what happened in Lemberg (now Lviv) in the nineteenth century. [In 1848 Lemberg was part of Austria.] A rabbi, named Avraham Cohen was assassinated by Jews for religious reasons. This was part of a confrontation between enlightened Jews, although relatively moderate since they kept the commandments, and the fanatical Hassids. An article about this was once published by the Hebrew press in Palestine in *Davar* one year after [the Labor leader] Arlozorov [was assassinated]. [The article] was severely attacked by the right wing Hebrew press of that time.

Rosen also quoted Professor Bartal who believed the attacks of the Hassids in the general confrontation to be the forerunner of the massacre committed by Baruch Goldstein. Bartal commented further that the maskilim usually only attacked the Hassids or other orthodox religious Jews by employing satire.[15] Only if provoked beyond endurance, Bartal asserted, would the maskilim attack or defend themselves by using physical violence.

Rosen's account of the poisoning assassination of Rabbi Cohen, as taken from what Professor Gris wrote, is worth relating:

In Lemberg in the 1840s hundreds of maskilim, after looking for a rabbi to head their congregation, found Rabbi Avraham Cohen, who was the rabbi in the small Austrian town of Hohenmass. Avraham Cohen was born in Bohemia to a poor Jewish peddler, but he became highly educated. After finishing his Yeshiva studies and receiving the authorization to become a rabbi, he went to study at and earned a degree from Prague University. The historian, Dr Ze'ev Aharon Eshkoli, who researched the story of Rabbi Cohen, published his account in 1934; he wrote that Cohen was a moderate but as "one educated in the German style of those times he was considered a modernist." In 1844, Cohen was appointed rabbi of the Lemberg congregation of maskilim; two years later he was the rabbi of all maskilim in the district of Lemberg. In this role he tried to introduce changes in Jewish life, but he soon encountered furious opposition of "the religious fanatics," as Eshkoli defined them. Cohen, for example, initiated the opening of Jewish schools that would serve as alternates to yeshivot, and he attempted to abolish the tests of Jewish religious subjects that Orthodox rabbis imposed upon all young Jewish couples at their betrothal. Cohen's most important initiative, according to Eshkoli, was his attempt to abolish the taxes on kosher meat and sabbath candles, which Lemberg Jews paid to [Austrian] authorities. These taxes were burdensome for poor Jews but were sources of income for many Orthodox notables. The method [of taxation] was as follows: A rich Jew for a certain lump sum obtained from the authorities the right to impose the tax on the Jews, from whom he took a much greater sum supposedly for his efforts. Five tax gatherers, all very pious, headed the opposition to Cohen. Their leader was Rabbi Hertz Berenstein, who came from a noted rabbinical family; the second was Rabbi Tzvi Orenstein, the son of the former Orthodox rabbi of Lemberg. In 1846, Cohen sent a memorandum to the emperor [of Austria] pointing out the injustice involved in the gathering of those taxes. Because of his connection with the authorities, he was twice invited to talk with the emperor. The five tax gatherers also sent a memorandum pointing out that the tax gathering provides a livelihood for thousands of Jewish families. The Austrian authorities, nevertheless, accepted Cohen's request and abolished those taxes in March, 1848.

The abolition of those taxes may not primarily have been due to Cohen's request. The 1848 revolution, which began in Vienna as a reaction against Hapsburg absolutism, probably prompted the tax abolition. Austrian liberals viewed those taxes as discriminatory and opposed them; they were supported by the enlightened Jews. Orthodox Jews, especially their rabbis, were the firm allies of absolutism and reaction, not only in Austria but throughout Europe and the Middle East. Rosen continued his story about Rabbi Cohen's misfortune:

> Whether for reasons of ideological opposition to Cohen or for economic reasons or for both, the five Jewish notables in 1848 began a total struggle against Rabbi Avraham Cohen. First, they put placards in the synagogues that incited Jews to spit in his face and stone him. When the persecution increased, Cohen's friends asked him to agree to his being guarded all the time; he refused, saying that he did not believe that Jews would kill him. The next step involved placards saying plainly that the "law of pursuer" [to be explained below] applies to Rabbi Cohen. [One placard said], for example: "He is one of those Jewish sinners for which the Talmud says their blood is permitted" (that is, every Jew can and should kill them). Another placard asked: "Will a Jew be found who will liberate us from the rabbi who destroys his congregation?" The fanatics first decided that the assassination would take place during Purim in 1848; they even cast lots to determine who would have the honor of murdering the rabbi, but their plans went awry. A month later during Passover of 1848 a crowd of Jews stoned Rabbi Cohen's home; only a large number of policemen saved him. On September 6, 1848, however, Avraham Bar-Pilpel, a Jewish assassin, successfully entered the rabbi's home unseen, went to the kitchen and put arsenic poison in the pot of soup that was cooking. Shortly thereafter, Rabbi Cohen and his family ate the soup; Rabbi Cohen and his little daughter died. The Hassids and their leaders did not attend the funeral; they celebrated. No Orthodox rabbi, moreover, uttered one word of condemnation, neither of murderous incitement before the murder nor of the murder itself. Many nationalistic Jews who were not Orthodox shared in being silent. The Jewish historian Graetz, author of the first history of the Jews, omitted this story from his history, which, by the way, [was published] later. Orthodox Jews took the murdered rabbi's corpse from the section of the notables of the cemetery and buried it in another section.

Professor Ze'ev Gris says: "My conclusion is, and I am sorry for it, that there is nothing new in Judaism." The de-legitimization, incitement, writing on the wall and especially the silence of the rabbinical leadership of Galicia of those times – everything was exactly the same as it was before the assassination of Rabin.

Was the murder of Rabbi Avraham Cohen an exceptional case? In December, 1838, the governor of southwestern Russia, General Dimitri Gabrielovitch Bibikov, issued a circular to district governors under his authority. He asked them to look carefully into what was happening in the synagogues and in Jewish houses of study. "In those places," he wrote, "Very often something happens that leaves dead Jews in its wake. Such crimes are especially grave since they occur in places dedicated to prayer and study of religious principles. They also are characteristic of autonomous judgment by the rabbinical courts, executed by their false views about extermination of 'informers' who reveal crimes of their co-religionists. The rabbis often succeed in obscuring the [official] investigation to such an extent that not only the identity of the assassins but even the identity of the victim remain unclear."

Many Israeli new historians believe that the forms of violence committed against both heretics and informers are intimately connected.

Two additional halachic laws are of special importance both generally and specifically when related to the Rabin assassination. These two laws, employed since talmudic times to kill Jews, were invoked by the assassin, Yigal Amir, as his justification for killing Prime Minister Rabin and are still emphasized by Jews who approved or have barely condemned that assassination. These are the "law of the pursuer" (din rodef) and the "law of the informer" (din moser).[16] The first law commands every Jew to kill or to wound severely any Jew who is perceived as intending to kill another Jew. According to halachic commentaries, it is not necessary to see such a person pursuing a Jewish victim. It is enough if rabbinic authorities, or even competent scholars, announce that the law of the pursuer applies to such a person. The second law commands every Jew to kill or wound severely any Jew who, without a decision of a competent rabbinical authority, has informed non-Jews, especially non-Jewish authorities, about Jewish affairs or who has given them information about Jewish property or who has delivered Jewish persons or property to their rule or authority. Competent religious authorities are empowered to do, and at times have done, those things forbidden to other Jews in the second law. During the long period of incitement preceding the Rabin assassination, many Haredi and messianic writers applied these laws to

Rabin and other Israeli leaders. The religious insiders based themselves on later developments in Halacha that came to include other categories of Jews who were defined as "those to whom the law of the pursuer" applied. Every Jew had a religious duty to kill those Jews who were so included. Historically, Jews in the diaspora followed this law whenever possible, until at least the advent of the modern state. In the Tsarist Empire Jews followed this law until well into the nineteenth century.

The land of Israel has been and still is considered by all religious Jews as being the exclusive property of the Jews. Granting Palestinians authority over any part of this land could be interpreted as informing. Some religious Jews interpreted the relations that developed between Rabin and the Palestinian Authority as causing harm to the Jewish settlers. In this sense, Rabin had informed. Influential rabbis, such as the Gush Emunin leader, Rabbi Moshe Levinger, publicly denounced as informers Rabin, some Labor and Meretz ministers and some Knesset members. Professor Asa Kasher of Tel-Aviv University, a widely respected person in Israel, tried to enlighten the public by writing a letter to the editor of *Haaretz* about the exact meaning of the term employed by Levinger and about the danger of assassination implied therein. His warnings were disregarded by everyone, including Rabin and the editors of *Haaretz*. Shabak, the branch of the Israeli secret police responsible for domestic affairs and the body responsible for guarding Rabin, also ignored the dangers implicit in a possible, and obviously probable, application to Rabin of the law of the informer. Shabak insisted until the actual happening that the danger of murder came only from Muslim extremists. Interestingly, by the end of August 1998, the Israeli media was filled with Shabak's warnings that Jewish religious fanatics intended to assassinate Netanyahu, Defense Minister Mordechai and other ministers because of their agreement in principle to Israeli withdrawal from an additional 13 per cent of the West Bank. These warnings were based upon the same fundamentalist logic that led to the assassination of Rabin; they indicated some of the danger posed by Jewish fundamentalism.

Rabin's murder followed logically from the religious premises of the 1984 Jewish underground. Members of the underground were then apprehended planting bombs under Arab buses near Jerusalem on a Friday. The bombs had timing devices so that they would explode after the Sabbath eve had commenced when under Jewish religious law, travel on a bus was prohibited and sinful. At that time, before the Intifada, many Israeli Jews rode in Arab buses. The only category of people not likely to use these buses when the bombs were due to explode were religious Jews. The pious members of the Jewish underground sought prior rabbinical approval for all their actions. Peres, Rabin and Shamir, acting together in accordance with the agreement that the national unity government then in power had devised, ordered the police to stop investigating the extremist rabbis. Not one rabbi opposed the religious reasoning that led to the planting of these bombs. The conclusion is inescapable that some rabbis approved and others did not oppose wanton killing of non-religious Jews, presumably because of their heretical opinions. *Yediot Ahronot* in its November 16, 1995, issue alleged that Rabbi Nahum Rabinowitz proposed the planting of mines and explosive devices around settlements threatened with evacuation by the Israeli army. This proposal followed the same line of reasoning. When asked about the danger inherent to lives of Jewish soldiers in his proposal, Rabbi Rabinowitz answered: "If they obey the order to remove a Jewish settlement, then they are wicked Jews" and as such, he implied, they deserve death. This should be seen within the context of the twofold hatred of non-Jews and secular Jews that settlement rabbis had preached for some time.

The reason for the willful ignorance of this danger, shared by many Israeli Jews, including Rabin himself, was in our view Jewish chauvinism, which is so prevalent among Jews. The chauvinists falsify the history of their nation in order to make it appear better than it really was. They also falsify the current situation by claiming that their nation is the best. This claim, often made by too many Jews, is especially dangerous when reinforced by a combination of religious fanaticism and willful ignorance. Jewish chauvinism is especially virulent, because the identification between Jewish religion and Jewish nationality has prevailed for so long and still prevails among many Jews. It should not be forgotten that democracy and the rule of law were brought into Judaism from the outside. Before the advent of the modern state, Jewish communities were mostly ruled by rabbis who employed arbitrary and cruel methods as bad as those employed by totalitarian regimes. The dearest wish of the current Jewish fundamentalists is to restore this state of affairs.

The information in the Talmud itself about killing and punishing Jewish informers is scanty and is anecdotal in nature. Fear of Roman and Sassanid authorities was at least partially responsible for this. The same situation existed during the time of the Ge'onim of Iraq, who lived from about AD 750 to 1050 under the strong rule of the Abassid Caliphate. The responsa of the Ge'onim rarely deal only with informers and impose at most only religious penalties. Rabbi Paltoi, according to Asaf on page 49 of *The Punishments*, stated in the mid-ninth century that an informer is not only a Jew who actually informs but one who during a quarrel in public with another Jew says that he will inform. Paltoi, nevertheless, imposed the mild penalty of designating such a person "wicked" and thus incapable of giving either an oath or testimony. In Muslim Spain, after the dissolution of the strong Ummayad Caliphate in the early years of the eleventh century, the situation was different, and informers were frequently executed. In Alicena, a city mostly inhabited by Jews in the mid-eleventh century, Rabbi Yosef Halevi Ibn Ha'migash, a famous scholar, according to Asaf on page 63 of *The Punishments*, ordered Jews to stone an informer during the Ne'yila prayer on Yom Kippur, which that year fell on the Sabbath. Stoning is usually considered to be a severe violation of both Yom Kippur and the Sabbath. The Ne'yila prayer, moreover, said only once a year at the close of Yom Kippur, is probably the most holy prayer in the Jewish calendar. The choice of that particular time must have been dictated by the need to explain to all Jews that the duty of killing a Jewish informer is more important than other religious considerations. Indeed, Maimonides wrote in his authoritative commentary to the Mishnah, as quoted by Asaf in *The Punishments* on page 63: "It happens every day in the west [Spain and North Africa] that informers who allegedly informed about money of the Jews are killed or are [themselves] informed against to non-Jews so that they [the Jewish informers] would be either killed or beaten by them [the non-Jews] or given to the wicked." This rule, widely quoted by later authorities, established an important precedent: informing is permitted, even enjoyed, when done by communal Jewish authorities in cases that they consider essential. Only individual Jews should be killed if they inform.[17]

In another part of his commentary Maimonides said that the obligation to kill both informers and heretics is a tradition that is applied in all cities of the west. After the reconquest of most of Spain by the Christians, except for the kingdom of Grenada, killings of informers continued and actually intensified in the kingdoms of Granada, Castile and Aragon. The number of cases recorded in the Spanish responsa is very large. The following few examples are representative: Rabenu Asher, as quoted by Asaf in *The Punishments* on page 73, answered a question about a Jew who was a notorious informer; the rabbinical court investigated the case. Rabenu Asher answered that the killing of informers does not need witnesses but only the expression of opinion by other Jews that a given person is indeed an informer. "Had we needed to take testimony of witnesses before the accused," Rabenu Asher opined, "we would never be able to convict them [the informers]." (This same reasoning was employed by the Inquisition, by modern totalitarian states and by the Israeli conquest regime in the territories occupied since 1967.) Rabenu Asher immigrated to Spain from northern France when already a famous rabbi; he was probably familiar with Ashkenazi customs as well as with those of Spanish Jews. Hence, he could probably comment with knowledge and sophistication that common practice in the diaspora was to punish with death an informer who informed three times on the Jews or their money. This was necessary, Rabenu Asher maintained, so that the number of informers among Jews would not increase. After reflecting upon all of this a bit more, he concluded that killing the informer as a punishment was a good deed. It would emphasize that all the Lord's enemies should perish.

In another responsa, cited by Asaf on page 74, Rabenu Asher dealt with a Jew, called either Avraham or Alot. Some Jews had charged that he had informed several times. Rabenu Asher insisted for all to know that the informer could be punished even on Yom Kippur when it falls on the Sabbath; he said that this had occurred in Germany and France. Rabbi Yehuda, the son of Rabenu Asher, opined, according to Asaf on page 79 of *The Punishments*, "[In the case of a Jew who had been an informer for years] every one who kills him will be rewarded by God. A Jew who could kill the informer and did not can be punished for all that the informer did as if he did it himself." In another case Rabbi Yehuda explained that the Jews themselves should kill the informers lest non-Jewish judges would refuse to inflict death penalties for informing. In some cases Jewish congregations literally bought the life of an informer from the king and then executed him publicly. This occurred for instance, in Barcelona in April, 1279. Rabbi Shlomo ben Aderet, according to Asaf in *The Punishments* on pages 65 to 67, reported this in his responsa. A Jew, named Vidalan de Porta, who belonged to a noble family, informed to King Pedro II of Aragon, who was also the Count of Catalonia. After being requested by the Jewish inhabitants of Catalonia, the king agreed (probably for a payment) to deliver him to the Jewish authorities of Barcelona, who had previously sentenced de Porta to death. Jews in Barcelona led him "to the street before the cemetery in Barcelona, and they opened the veins of both his arms. He bled to death." Three years after the execution, brothers of the victim protested against it. Rabbi Shlomo ben Aderet defended the verdict by noting that such verdicts were often carried out in Aragon and Castile. He also wrote to Germany seeking and receiving support for the verdict from the most important rabbi of that time, Meir of Rothenburg (Maharam). The law of the informer is clearly apparent in an anonymous Spanish responsa, important because it was quoted by the famous sixteenth-century Polish rabbi, Shlomo Luria. This is cited by Asaf in *The Punishments* on pages 83 to 87: "He [the informer] is not only killed by decision of the [rabbinic] court, but any Jew who himself is first to kill him will be rewarded by God." This same statement appeared in numerous rabbinical responsa.

Spanish Jews killed and/or mutilated informers as late as the fifteenth century. Jews in other communities, especially in North Africa and Portugal, who were influenced by Spanish Jews did likewise. Rabbi Shimon, the son of Rabbi Tzemach, who emigrated from Spain and went to Algiers in the early fifteenth century wrote in a responsa, as reported by Asaf on page 88 of *The Punishments*, about the sacred duty to kill an informer. In another responsa, according to Asaf on page 89 of *The Punishments*, Rabbi Shimon recognized that killing was not always possible. He advised in such cases that the informer should be branded on his brow or flogged but in any case should have his name as an informer publicized in all communities.

Information about the killing of reformers in early Ashkenazi communities in northern France and Germany is sparse before and non-existent after the thirteenth century. This was probably due to lesser Jewish autonomy and to the stronger power of non-Jewish states. Rabenu Asher, as previously mentioned, testified that in his time the killing of informers in Germany was common. He presented little evidence. Rabenu Tam, one of the chief rabbi of northern France, according to Asaf in *The Punishments* on page 107, reported that an assembly of French rabbis, held in Troyes, debated the problems "caused by the criminals of our nation," who either secretly or openly informed, and by the Jews who brought their cases against other Jews to non-Jewish judges, thereby flouting the exclusive authority of rabbinical courts. The only explicit punishment inflicted upon those criminals was excommunication, which included a prohibition against speaking to them. The rabbis tempered the prohibition somewhat by stating that those Jews who feared the anger of the king or the feudal lords could speak to the excommunicated informers but could not use such permission as merely an excuse to do so. Some rabbis said that an obscure ancient rule against informers could in addition be inflected. In the latter part of the thirteenth century, according to Asaf on page 107 of *The Punishments*, Rabbi Meir of Rothenburg wrote that Jews could kill or mutilate, by cutting out the tongue of an informer, who remained in a state of permanent excommunication. In only a few known informer cases in Germany in this time period were killing or mutilation inflicted. One such case concerned an informer in Strasbourg in the early fourteenth century. As reported by Asaf on page 108 of *The Punishments*, Rabbi Samuel Shlitzstat of Strasbourg sentenced an informer to death. The Jewish community applied to a non-Jewish judge who ordered the informer to be drowned in the Rhine. Some of the informer's friends then appealed to some powerful feudal lords and through them to the emperor. The friends testified in non-Jewish courts and gave signed testimony, apparently written in Latin. They testified that Rabbi Shlitzstat sent a letter to the Jews in which he said the informer should be killed. They also testified that he collected money from the Strasbourg and nearby Jewish communities to insure the drowning. The implication here was that the judge who gave the order to drown was bribed. The result in this case was that Rabbi Shlitzstat had to hide from the authorities for several years and thereafter escaped from Germany to go to Iraq. He told the president of the Iraqi Jewish community, David son of Hodaya, about the inequities of the Jews who had persecuted him. David son of Hodaya then solemnly excommunicated the offenders in writing. Rabbi Shlitzstat returned to Germany with the excommunication order. What happened upon his return, that is, the end of the story, is not known. From that time rabbinical sources reveal nothing about killings but much about excommunication of informers.

Detailed information about Ashkenazi Jews in sixteenth-century Poland is available. These Polish Jews, as previously indicated, enjoyed extensive autonomy in the relatively weak Polish-Lithuanian Commonwealth. Because of this, killings and other punishments of Jewish informers, for which evidence is abundant, were commonplace. Rabbi Shlomo Luria, as Asaf made clear on page 122 of *The Punishments*, stipulated that informers should be killed. He added:

> It is better to kill than to mutilate them, for example by cutting out their tongues, so as to remove the evil from our midst. It is also not only probable but nearly certain that a [mutilated] Jew would convert and, in order to take revenge, would tell incorrect things about Jews. I saw myself that by only mutilating them [the informers] Jews have greatly suffered.

After the early seventeenth century, Polish rabbis and the Jewish autonomous authorities tended to employ more cautious language when writing about killing Jewish informers. In a case of a certain Jewish informer who had been expelled from the town of Pinsk and from all Lithuania but who appeared in Lubavitch, the Committee of Lithuanian Jews in its ruling used the Hebrew phrase "hatarat dam" ("allowing the shedding of blood"). Asaf on page 128 and 129 of *The Punishments* discussed this ruling. This phrase, which became common in such rulings thereafter, was a bit less direct than an actual order to kill an informer. In this same case the Committee of Lithuanian Jews, after ruling that Jews who revealed Jewish secrets should be excommunicated even on Yom Kippur, stipulated, as reported by Asaf:

> In case of anybody who informs, even about Jewish money, and certainly in cases of bodily harm, every Jew knows the law and therefore there is no need to make any rules. We only are warning, we order every Jew who sees or hears such action, whether it concerns him or not, within three days to tell it to two notables

of the town who are not connected to the informer. Otherwise he [that Jew who sees of hears such action] will be excommunicated himself, and the punishment of the informer will be applied to him. The two notables will then do what they should do. But if the informer is powerful and for the time being they [the notables] cannot do anything to him, the rabbis and notables will write his name in the Chronicle [of the town] so that his [the informer's] sons will not be circumcised, no one will marry his daughters and he will be excluded from all sacred matters. The good chief rabbis will also keep watch so that the verse "and when I shall avenge" [a verse occurring several times in the Pentateuch that supposedly means that God's revenge has been delayed but will come] would apply to him.

Again, the language employed is more cautious and indirect than a direct order to kill an informer or a Jew who did not report an informer. The last sentence of the ruling is especially relevant.

A second Polish example is found in the preserved chronicle of the Jewish community in Krakow. This is discussed by Asaf on page 133 of *The Punishments*. This chronicle condemns Yisrael, son of Rabbi Aharon Welitshker, for informing on the Jews in regard to financial matters, robbing, using violence and committing religious offences that cannot be written. The condemnation continued:

We, the notables of the community and we the most honorable [rabbinical court], let the Lord guard them, considered the honor of his family and lessened his punishment. We therefore condemn him only to be excommunicated in all the synagogues and be incapable of either bearing testimony or swearing [in rabbinical court]. An iron collar should be put on his neck. He must also give back what he took by robbery, whether it was stolen from individuals or from communities. His property should be confiscated wherever found.

Additionally, he was ordered expelled from the town; not one of his descendents was ever allowed to live in that town. This tempered verdict was issued in the spring of 1772.

The third Polish example is taken from the preface to a talmudic book, *Taharat Kodesh*, published in 1733 and written by Rabbi Benyamin, son of the important Polish religious leader, Rabbi Matattya. This book, to which Asaf referred on page 133 of *The Punishments*, showed that informers increased in number over a period of time, in spite of killings and other ferocious punishments meted out to them. Rabbi Benyamin bitterly complained about the large number of Jewish informers in his time and added that many Jews helped or flattered them. He asked Jews to avoid the informers.

His proposed remedy was "to allow their blood [to be shed] so that we shall exterminate them totally." Rabbi Benyamin additionally prohibited accepting money from them for charitable purposes. He added that in an unspecified distant country the Jews had succeeded in exterminating the informers and thereby were secure in spite of their spending a goodly amount of money for their security. Rabbi Benyamin's recommendations were not cautious. More importantly, the Tsarist police investigations of the killing of Jewish informers and the many testimonies of enlightened Jews in the nineteenth century show that the problem of Jewish informers was not solved by these recommendations.

After the division of the Polish-Lithuanian Commonwealth between Russia, Austria and Prussia, finalized in 1795, and after the resultant abolition of autonomy of Jewish communities by the three conquering powers, violence inflicted by Jews, especially by Jewish authorities, on other Jews rapidly declined. Violence virtually disappeared in the Prussian part of Poland and remained at about the same level in the areas ruled by Russia. In the Russian area, violence, when practiced however, was often secret. In the area ruled by Austria (Galicia) the situation was a bit more complex; Jewish violence such as assassinations of modernist rabbis occurred under certain conditions.

The different levels of inter-Jewish violence in the three parts of divided Poland should be ascribed to the different levels of modern influences after the division. The Jews in the Prussian part of Poland were in an efficient absolutist monarchy, equipped with a good police and civil administration that were greatly influenced by modernist tendencies. The first partition of Poland occurred when Frederic II, the Great, the friend of Voltaire and other French philosophers of the age of the Enlightenment, ruled Prussia. The influences of the Enlightenment, at least in the ranks of Prussian administrators, remained strong for at least a generation after the death of Frederic II in 1786. Probably of equal importance was the fact that the Jewish Enlightenment began in Prussia, which possessed even before the partition of Poland a strong community of enlightened Jews, centered on Berlin, who at that time expressed themselves as much in Hebrew as in German. These enlightened Jews could thus be immediately understood by the majority of male Jews in areas annexed to Prussia.

The Jews in the Russian area of Poland were by contrast in a more backward regime that had a weak and inefficient administration in spite of the thin veneer of the Enlightenment provided by Catherine II, the Great. Russia had also been a country without Jews for hundreds of years. The first Jews allowed to live in the Tsarist Empire were the Jews who lived in the annexed Polish territory. The notorious "Pale," the only area of Russia where

Jews, with a few exceptions, were allowed to live until 1917, was simply the area of the Polish-Lithuanian Commonwealth annexed to Russia. The "old Russia" kept its "purity" of being forbidden to Jews. Because of the absence of Jews, Russians, especially Russian Church leaders, had a strong tradition of anti-Semitism. Anti-Semitism in Russia in 1800 was worse than in any other country at that time. The Tsarist regime, moreover, at the beginning of the Polish takeover introduced special taxes on Jews, in force until 1905, as well as other discriminations against Jews. The absence of large towns and cities, except for St. Petersburg and Moscow which were forbidden to Jews, and the undeveloped state of education enabled most Jews annexed to Russia to continue their old customs, especially in the smaller communities, until the 1880s. The old customs included the persecution of heretics and the killing of informers. Nevertheless, the small but growing group of enlightened Jews found it easier to oppose these and other old customs under Russian rule than under the conditions of Jewish autonomy in the Polish-Lithuanian Commonwealth. Russian rule, even with its deficiencies, afforded the enlightened Jews somewhat more protection than they previously had, enabling them at least to testify about killings of informers.

The Jews in the territories annexed by Austria were in an intermediate situation between Prussia and Russia. After 1848 and especially after 1867, when Austria granted a limited form of constitution and other civil liberties, the Jewish situation in Austria came to approximate more the Prussian and after the unification of Germany in 1871, the German model.[18] Austria and the Hapsburg dynasty had strong anti-Semitic tendencies that were prominent under Maria Theresa (1740–80), who was probably the most anti-Jewish ruler of eighteenth-century Europe and who was responsible for the largest expulsion of Jews before the Nazi era: she expelled about 70,000 Jews from Prague and other Bohemian towns in 1745. Maria Theresa had to reverse her decree and allow Jews to return within a short time because of the strong protests of her allies, Britain and Holland, upon whose subsidies she depended in the War of Austrian Succession. Her successor, Joseph II, reversed her policies and in 1782 issued a decree granting limited, but still significant, rights to Jews. He did this in the face of considerable opposition.[19] After Joseph's death in 1790, the two tendencies fluctuated until Emperor Franz Joseph decided to adopt a pro-Jewish policy in 1867.

The new Israeli historians have presented evidence showing that until the 1880s the killings of Jewish informers by Jews in the Tsarist Empire were numerous. In his article dealing with the new Israeli historians Rosen quoted the writer, Shaul Ginzberg, who wrote in his autobiography that during the nineteenth century hundreds of Jewish informers were drowned in the Dnieper, the largest river flowing in the "Pale." These informers were charged and convicted under the law of the informers simply because they were suspected of informing the authorities about something. Rosen wrote: "Like Avraham Cohen, some of them acted because of ideological reasons such as the wish to bring the Jewish community to a modern way of life." Dr David Asaf researched some of those affairs and said: "Some of the informers were professionals who gave the authorities information about tax concealment, but even in such cases, judging them by what amounts to rabbinical martial courts and their execution by what amounts to lynching help us to understand the conflict between the enlightened Jews and the Orthodox, particularly the Hassids." As previously shown, a Jewish informer was condemned to death in secret without being able to say anything in his own defense. This mode of execution was employed for hundreds of years until the recent time.[20] Rosen asked Asaf if the Jewish community regarded those informers as traitors. Asaf responded:

> They were not so regarded by the enlightened Jews. More than this, the enlightened Jews wanted the Jews to be citizens of the state. This included in their view paying taxes and serving in the army. Giving information to authorities was in many cases a necessary thing in their view. If you compare the situation to the one existing [in Israel] now [one year after the assassination of Rabin] then, with some changes, the present conflict is similar to what went on then.

To show what was involved, Asaf recounted an affair he had researched involving a famous Hassidic rabbi from the town of Rozin, Israel Friedman, who was known as the "holy man of Rozin." Friedman as a major Hassidic personage was important, because the Hassidic movement played a major role in those assassinations. Asaf related, as reported by Rosen:

> Friedman was one of the greatest Hassidic leaders. In Jewish history books he is represented as a person of small scholarly knowledge but also as a man of power who enjoyed the delights of life. He was instrumental in the issuing of the law of the pursuer against some informers from the town of Oshitz in the Podolia district of the Ukraine. In February, 1836, a corpse of one of the persons, Yitzhak Oxman, was found beneath blocks of ice on the frozen river. The corpse was so mutilated, apparently as a result of torture, that it was difficult to identify. Only some time thereafter, when the corpse was taken out of its grave, were new witnesses able to identify it. The corpse of the other murdered

person, Shmuel Schwatzman, disappeared. We now know that he was strangled while praying in the synagogue. His corpse was cut into pieces and burned in the oven that heated the community bath. Following a police investigation, in which even Tsar Nicolai I was interested, it was established that the Jews of the community where the murder was committed, including relatives of the murdered persons, knew perfectly well what had taken place and how it was carried out. Everyone stayed silent either because of strong discipline or because of fear. This case was one of the few in which a secret rabbinical court, which issues unwritten verdicts of the law of the pursuer and death punishments, was discovered. Yosef Perl, one of the chiefs of the enlightened Jews of Galicia, secretly supplied information to the Russian authorities in order to bring about the conviction of Rabbi Yisrael of Rozin.

Asaf, who also described other Hassidic murders, said that Perl, who hated the Hassids, acted for reasons that he believed to be ideological. Rosen, in interviewing the new historians, discovered that the various Hassids also struggled violently with one another mainly because of economic interests. He wrote: "Since the Hassids gave money to their holy men and some of the latter adopted a nineteenth century way of life that rivalled the luxuries of contemporary kings, they were interested in the places from which their incomes came."

Pre-modern Judaism was characterized by many cases of inter-Jewish violence, of which the few cases mentioned above are merely representative. These few cases, however, are sufficient to show that Jewish fundamentalism in Israel, both in its messianic and Haredi forms, is a reversion to a situation that existed before the onset of modernization and the loss of the type of Jewish autonomy with its arbitrary powers that allowed killing or otherwise severely punishing informers. What occurred in Jewish fundamentalism is not dissimilar to what occurred in other forms of fundamentalism. Some innovations have been made, largely to disguise true intent. The predominant wish ideologically is to return to the supposedly "good times" when everything was seen and kept in proper order. In the case of the Jewish messianic variety of fundamentalism, the idea is to use modern methods to achieve the power to re-establish the traditional way of life in an effectual manner. The dangers of Jewish fundamentalism being established in Israel as at least part of the ruling power are great. For non-Jews in the Middle East, the Arabs and especially the Palestinians, the main danger is in and with the messianic variety of Jewish fundamentalism. This is most apparent in the role of the Jewish religious settlers in the Occupied Territories. For Israeli Jews who will not accept the tenets of Jewish fundamentalism, however, all varieties are dangerous. The Jewish fundamentalist attitude towards heretics is much worse than is the attitude towards non-Jews. This is analogous to the situation in other religions. A contemporary example is the attitude of the Iranian regime to Baha'ists, regarded as Muslim heretics, which is much worse than the attitude towards Christians and Jews. Our firm belief is that a fundamentalist Jewish regime, if it came to power in Israel, would treat Israeli Jews who did not accept its tenets worse than it would treat Palestinians. This book is an attempt to provide wider understanding of Jewish fundamentalism and hopefully help avert the danger from becoming a reality.

Note on Bibliography and Related Matters

Serious books describing a social phenomenon usually contain a bibliographical listing or essay, detailing and perhaps briefly discussing the primary and secondary sources consulted by the authors. For some years we have read a significant number of books in English and Hebrew that are concerned with Judaism and the state of Israel. In our book we decided to refer only minimally to those books in English; we relied primarily upon the Israeli Hebrew press, basic Jewish religious (and in a few cases literary) texts and some learned Hebrew articles, published in Israeli journals and magazines. We identified these in our text. Our first reason for doing this is that Hebrew sources are, with few exceptions, the most pertinent in dealing with Jewish fundamentalism in Israel. We are nevertheless aware that the number of books that focus on aspects of or background to our topic, published in English and languages other than Hebrew, is large. We wish to offer an explanation about why we did not cite, and most often ignored, much of this voluminous literature.

We believe that the great majority of the books on Judaism and Israel, published in English especially, falsify their subject matter. The falsification is sometimes a result of explicit lying but is mostly the result of omission of major facts that may create what the authors consider to be an adverse view of their subjects. Many of the books that fit into this category are comparable to much of the literature produced in totalitarian systems, whether religious or secular and whether or not embodied in a state. We do not deny that books on Israel and Judaism published in English have value; they may, and often do, contain correct and valuable information. Books about the USSR under Stalin or his successors written by Stalinists, books about Iran written by followers of Khomeini, books on Christian fundamentalism written by its adherents often contain correct and valuable information. Many other analagous examples exist. What usually makes such books unreliable are not so much the lies but rather the purposeful omissions. Regarding Judaism and Israel, the omissions are more blatant and numerous in books published in English outside of Israel than they are in Israel's Hebrew literature. The omissions pertinent to our subject of Jewish fundamentalism exist for the same apologetic reasons as do the literary omissions in any totalitarian system. The information freely available in Hebrew can and should be used to redress apologia by omissions in English. The coverage in Hebrew of Jewish fundamentalism is more complete and is not riddled with omissions, because, as our book shows, Jewish fundamentalism poses an immediate threat to the beliefs and style of life of a majority of Israeli Jews. Jewish fundamentalism, if it increases in strength, could destroy Israeli democracy; this danger does not exist in the diaspora where Jews, even when supporting the worst aspects of Jewish fundamentalism, benefit from democracy and pluralism. In our view the state of Israel has faults that have been and still are caused by the nature of Zionism and by the open and hidden influences of Jewish fundamentalism. To exchange the present reality of the state of Israel for a Jewish fundamentalist state of either the Haredi or messianic variety would create a far worse situation for Jews, Palestinians and perhaps the entire Middle East. We believe that our book, based primarily upon Hebrew sources, correctly points out this danger for the first time in English.

To document our above comments, we shall present a short list of important issues in Israel and in Jewish history of the diaspora before the modern period, which are relevant for Jewish fundamentalism but are nevertheless omitted from the literature in English about Israel and Judaism. We shall first consider two issues, closely connected to Jewish fundamentalism, that are not specifically mentioned in our book. We shall thereafter present some issues that, although discussed in our book, are not mentioned in the voluminous literature in English. During the Labor Party primaries of the 1999 Israeli election campaigns, accusations appeared in the Hebrew press claiming that fraud in the vote counts occurred in Druze and Arab sectors of the party. The use of such expressions should raise concern. Political parties in the United States and Britain do not specify Jewish, non-Jewish or similar sectors. Readers of the Israeli Hebrew press know that an Arab or Druze, that is, a non-Jew who is an Israeli citizen, even if living in Tel-Aviv or Haifa, cannot belong to the Labor Party branch of her or his neighborhood; that person must belong to one of the two sectors that exist for Druze and Arabs respectively. Jews cannot belong to one of those sectors. Consequently, an Arab living in Tel-Aviv votes in the primaries of the Israeli Labor Party only as a member of the Arab sector and not together with her or his neighbors. Other types of sectors also exist, based upon social structure in the Labor Party. The kibbutzim sector is one example. In these other sectors membership fluctuates according to the natural movements of population, not according to racist criteria. A kibbutz member of the Labor Party who leaves the Kibbutz to settle in Tel-Aviv becomes a member of the party branch of that person's new neighborhood; conversely, a Tel-Aviv member of the Labor Party who joins a kibbutz automatically becomes a member of the kibbutz sector. In contrast, an Arab member of the Labor Party remains an Arab wherever that person lives, confined ethnically or more precisely religiously. Such a proposal for the operation of political parties in the United States or Great Britain would be quickly labeled and condemned correctly as anti-Semitic. Such a proposal would be roundly discussed in the press and in other literature concerned with the United States and/or Great Britain. In the voluminous descriptions in English of Israel, this phenomenon, although known in Israel, is almost never mentioned.

The probable reasons for the above omission are most likely the same as those for other similar omissions. The first and most important probable reason is that many Jews and those who sympathize with them wish to avoid comparisons between what rights Jews as a minority in the diaspora demand for themselves and what rights Jews deny to non-Jews in those areas where Jews are a majority and wield the power. We believe that Jewish fundamentalism justifies, explicitly and unconsciously as a believed survival tactic, both the discrimination and its cover-up. As noted in our book, Jewish fundamentalism in Israel influences most of society. Its influence is especially significant in regard to the principles of Israeli state policies, but its hidden and often clear-cut influence upon a majority of Jews in the diaspora is strong. Two additional reasons in our view account for omissions of vital facts in the English discussion of phenomena in Israel that could be disturbing to many people. A hidden, and sometimes not so hidden, assumption made in much of the English literature about Judaism and about Israel as a Jewish state is that Jews are morally superior to all other nations. This is the most important belief of Jewish fundamentalists who condemn almost everything "not Jewish" mostly because it is non-Jewish. Any discussion of the fact that many Jews, when they are able, practice the same kind of discrimination against non-Jews that some non-Jews practice against Jews could be detrimental to the theory of Jewish moral superiority. Although we believe this is part of racist theory, which we oppose, we understand that unfortunately human beings, including Jews, often have xenophobic tendencies influenced by historical circumstances. Thus, Jews can and should be viewed within the same context as other human beings and should in this regard work to eradicate Jewish xenophobia by exposing it in its present and past forms. The second reason emanates from writers who are apologists for and from other advocates of the Israeli political left. The Labor Party is Israel has consistently practiced blatant racism. Likud, the most important party of the Israeli right, has not practiced racism so severely and generally as has the Labor Party. As opposed to the Labor Party situation, Arabs have been, and still are, able to be members of Likud in their own neighborhood branches. The idea that the Israeli right wing is in this particular case better than the Labor Party is abhorrent to the dogmatists of and apologists for the left just as in the 1930s the idea that many practices in Great Britain were better than those of Stalin was abhorrent to fellow travelers. The refuge in both cases was and is a consistent omission of facts that do not fit into the dogma.

A similar case in point is kibbutz membership in Israel. The kibbutz is one of the most admired, especially by leftist apologists, Israeli phenomena. It is a fact, widely known and discussed in Israel, that only Jews can be kibbutz members. Non-Jews who wish to become kibbutz members must not only acquire the approval of the kibbutz members; they must, as a condition of joining, convert to Judaism. The Israeli Chief Rabbinate has established conversion schools for non-Jews who wish to join kibbutzim. One of the conditions for conversion to Judaism of women in this as in other situations is that the female convert must be observed naked in a purification bath by three rabbis. Some of the other conditions for conversion of those non-Jews desirous of joining kibbutzim are lighter than are conditions for other potential converts. The Israeli Hebrew press has often focused upon the degree of difference in conversion procedures and has also mentioned repeatedly that to date not one Palestinian has become a kibbutz member. This specific, clearly influenced by Jewish fundamentalism, is almost always omitted in English language books published about and media coverage of Israel. We need not emphasize the wide discussion that would ensue if a British or American institution allowed Jews to become members only if they converted to Christianity.

Scholars and news media people who purport to describe Israel authoritatively have, as previously indicated, systematically ignored by omission critical phenomena, discussed in our book. Some examples of this follow. In Chapter 1 of our book we mentioned that the concept of Jewish blood bound together the Israeli secular right wing and religious Jews. This concept, which deems the blood of a killed or wounded Jew to be infinitely greater in value than the blood of a killed or wounded non-Jew, is of supreme importance in Israeli politics. The Netanyahu government in 1998 refused, even when pushed by the United States government, to release Palestinian prisoners who had killed Jews, whether they were soldiers killed in a clash or civilians murdered in a terrorist attack. The Jewish blood concept was the only possible reason. The same Netanyahu government, as well as some previous Israeli governments, have not objected to freeing Palestinian prisoners who had killed other Palestinians. The Palestinians killed were usually presumed to be agents of the Israeli secret police. The same situation has existed in regard to the Israeli security zone in southern Lebanon and to the South Lebanese Army. The main reason for creating those entities, which have prevented a cease-fire occurring between Israel and Lebanon, was the Israeli desire, influenced by Jewish fundamentalism, to save "Jewish blood." A majority of Israeli Jews have paid little attention to Lebanese, who have been killed, whether they were members of the South Lebanese Army or simply inhabitants of this zone. Bursts of anguish and even protests, on the other hand, have accompanied almost every Jewish casualty. Israeli protesters demanding that Israel leave Lebanon have mentioned only the Israeli casualties. Usually, only those Israeli Jews who have openly opposed Jewish fundamentalism in all its aspects, such as Israel Shahak, one of the authors of this book, have mentioned the Lebanese casualties. The politically important distinction between Jewish blood and non-Jewish blood is well-known to most Israelis but is ignored by almost all those who write about Israel and its policies.

As also noted in Chapter 1, Rabbi Yoseph, who commands the unquestioned allegiance of ten Shas members of the Knesset, argued in a published article that Israel is not sufficiently strong to destroy Christian churches on its territory and should therefore return some of the occupied territory to the Palestinians. Otherwise, Rabbi Yoseph contended, Jews might be killed in a war that could erupt. We pointed out that most writers who discussed Rabbi Yoseph's alleged dovish leanings falsified by omitting his reasons for advocating concessions. In addition to emphasizing Israeli weakness, Rabbi Yoseph expressed willingness to command the destruction of idolatrous, Christian churches if Israel and the Jews were sufficiently strong to do this without serious damage to Jews. Rabbi Yoseph thus illustrated the fierce and visible hatred of Christianity and Christians so evident among fundamentalists Jews and, to a lesser extent, among many other Israeli Jews of the political right. Although discrimination against and persecution of Jews in Christian countries has helped to persuade some secular Jews to accept this fundamentalist attitude, it is not the sole explanation. Oriental Jewish rabbis, and to a lesser extent their followers who came from Muslim countries wherein they were generally not persecuted by Christians, have expressed more hate of Christianity and its symbols than the fundamentalist European rabbis and their followers who were persecuted by Christians. In dealing with political factors in our book, we did not specify many of the often petty forms of hatred of Christianity that are officially approved. One case in point is that Israeli educational authorities removed the international plus sign from the textbooks of elementary arithmetic used in the first grades of Israeli schools. Allegedly, this plus sign, which is a cross, could religiously corrupt little Jewish children. Instead of the offending cross, the authorities substituted a capital "T." This substitution was made some years after Israel became a state; the influence of Jewish fundamentalism was responsible. If this substitution had been made by the Taliban in Afghanistan, by the Iranian regime or by China during the cultural revolution, it would probably have been discussed at length. In contrast, this easily discoverable fact has been omitted in English-language articles and books concerned with Israeli Jewish society and Judaism. This omission is but one piece of the existent evidence that most books of this genre are unreliable.

In Chapter 2 we pointed to specific acts of discrimination against and abuse of women perpetrated by Jewish fundamentalists. Seemingly unimpressed by the Israeli Hebrew discussion of and the Israeli Jewish feminist criticism of this discrimination and abuse, writers of English-language books and articles about Israel have rarely mentioned this phenomenon. They have not acknowledged that until modern times most Jewish women were kept illiterate and denied education by command of the rabbis. They and others have condemned abuses of women in Iran and other countries but have refused to specify the even more abusive acts against women in Israel. Jewish feminists have instead celebrated in their writings the few important Jewish women mentioned in the Bible and the one woman mentioned in the Talmud, Bruria, the wife of the second-century AD sage, Rabbi Meir. The diaspora Jewish feminists and other English-language writers have neglected any reference to the disparaging stories about women in talmudic literature; they have also failed to admit that from the time of Bruria until the advent of modern influences upon Jews in western Europe in the seventeenth century not one Jewish woman was sufficiently important to be emphasized as a leading figure in Jewish history. (This can be compared to the numerous women who became leading figures in many areas, including religion, in Western Christendom in the same time period, in spite of Christianity's well-known discrimination against women.) The inescapable conclusion is that English-language sources are unreliable, not only in the study of the Jewish fundamentalist attitude towards women but also in the more general study of the status of women in historical Judaism.

In discussing the topic of Jewish blood in Chapter 2, we quoted both the previously mentioned Rabbi Yoseph and the former chief rabbi of Israel, Rabbi Mordechai Eliyahu, both of whom ordered pious Jews not to accept blood donations from non-Jews unless their lives were at risk. These two eminent rabbis, as well as others inside and outside of Israel who agree with this view did not invent this opinion. This and other similar opinions, existent from the beginning of blood transfusions, are based upon a talmudic prohibition that does not allow a non-Jewish nurse to breast feed a Jewish child. The cited reason for this prohibition is that the milk from a non-Jewish woman would have an adverse effect upon a Jewish child. In Chapter 2 we quoted the discussion of the Jewish blood topic that was published in 1995 not only in Israel's most widely read daily Hebrew newspaper but in other Hebrew newspapers as well. We can assume that readers of this book who are not literate in Hebrew and who were not previously told about such discussion in the Hebrew press would be unaware of this prohibition of pious

Jews accepting blood transfusions from non-Jews and sometimes even from secular Jews. This prohibition is not to be found in English-language articles or books about Judaism or Israeli Jewish society. (Some fundamentalist Jews may discuss this topic among themselves, but they limit that discussion to their own groupings and do not write about it for publication in English.) It would be absurd to suggest that in the last years of the twentieth century scholars, writers and others from around the world would not discuss and attack an analogous edict, issued by highest ranking Christian Church leaders, prohibiting Christians from accepting blood transfusions from Jews. The prohibition is not a secret; it has been openly discussed in the Israeli Hebrew press. This is yet another example of distortion by omission, which makes English-language coverage of various aspects of Israeli Jewish society unreliable.

In Chapter 3 we briefly discussed how followers of Rabbis Yoseph and Shach attempted to use magic against one another. This occurred after the struggle between these two leading rabbis became intense. The political significance here transcended the Yoseph–Shach disputation; the alleged use of magic is part of the deep division between Israel A and Israel B, which are defined previously in both our text and glossary. Members of Israel B, following some historic Jewish customs, believe in magic and witchcraft; they often practice it themselves or follow directives supposedly derived from it by rabbis and cabbalists. (Books in Hebrew detailing instructions for spells and witchcraft recipes have been best sellers in Israel for many years.) Individuals who are reputed to achieve success by use of magic frequently obtain political power in Israel. Most Israeli political pundits are agreed that one of the important reasons for Netanyahu's victory in the 1996 election was the exclusive blessing he received during the campaign from the cabbalist Rabbi Kaduri, and the firm refusals of many Jewish magicians and cabbalists to bless Peres. (Only the Hassidic Belzer rabbi said that he was neutral regarding Peres.) Rabbi Kaduri has remained to date a widely reported, highly visible Hollywood type star in the Israeli Hebrew press. He was at the center of media attention when he descended below the surface of the sea in Eilat in a device, usually used to allow tourists to see underwater sea life, and supposedly instituted spells in order to avert an earthquake that was predicted by scientists. He claimed to have diverted the earthquake from Jews to non-Jews. Many Israeli Jews believed this claim, because the predicted earthquake was light in Eilat but was much more severe in upper Egypt.

Another example of the popularity in Israel of magic was evident in the circumstances surrounding the 1999 trial in the District Court of Jerusalem of a major Shas Party politician, Aryeh Der'i. Der'i was convicted and sentenced for taking bribes in spite of tens of amulets hung on his body and blessed by the most outstanding cabbalists, who additionally engaged in other magic ceremonies on Der'i's behalf. At the same time of this trial a scientific congress on the use of magic and witchcraft in Judaism was held in Jerusalem. Tom Segev, a columnist for *Haaretz* and one of Israel's best known authors, wrote that the use of magic by Jews was nothing new in Judaism. In his March 26, 1999, Hebrew-language *Haaretz* article, Segev transcribed a magical recipe found in a book, composed in talmudic times (AD 200–500) but still popular in the Diaspora in the eighteenth century. This recipe, which was devised to confuse a judge and cause him to acquit unjustly a person who used magic, called for the following: "Slaughter a lion cub with a copper knife. Gather its blood; tear out its heart and put the blood into it. Then, write the names of angels on the cub's face, and wipe the names with three year-old wine. Mix the wine with the blood. Next, take three heaps of perfume (names omitted). After purifying yourself, stand before the planet Venus at night with the perfume and the blood, which must be put on fire." This act would supposedly compel the bewitched judge to acquit. Segev reported that the Israeli scientists participating in this Congress believed magic to be "an inseparable part of Judaism – used in past intrigues involving rabbis." To support this view, Segev quoted a saying in the Palestinian Talmud attributing the large number of High Priests during the Second Temple period to the fact that High Priests often killed one another by using witchcraft. This opinion expressed in the Palestinian Talmud is probably incorrect; the large number of High Priests during this period should most likely be attributed to bribery and other political actions of secular (mostly Jewish) authorities of time connected with making appointments. This opinion, which is not quoted in English-language writings on Judaism, nevertheless indicates the wide use of witchcraft by Jews' attempting to kill one another in this time period. The typical picture, presented in English-language works, of the pious Jews of the third period of Jewish history is on balance invalid. The picture of the pious Jew of talmudic times, standing at night before a planet and attempting to perform magic rites, is more accurate and can help us understand the reality of Israeli Jewish society better than the fictional description offered by apologists. The use of magic in everyday life is also common in certain Jewish neighborhoods of New York, London, Paris and other cities.

In spite of its obvious political importance and social significance, this aspect of Judaism in modern times remains as widely unreported in English, and thus as unknown to those who do not read Hebrew, as the past use of magic and witchcraft. In all known societies some individuals have indulged, and still do indulge, in magic. The misguided attempt to hide this past and present tendency, which is widespread in Israel, has infested the English-language histories of the Jews. The substitution of apologetics for historical fact renders these history texts at least unreliable and perhaps unfit for study.

In Chapters 4 and 5 we dealt with the religious Jewish settlers in territories occupied by Israel since 1967 and with Gush Emunim, the movement that produced the settlers. Despite the attention given to the issues of Israeli settlements in the territories, English-language coverage has almost totally neglected the two major considerations, without which proper understanding of this overall topic is impossible. The first consideration is that the urge to settle has been theologically motivated and is a manifestation of Jewish fundamentalism. In discussions of the obligations that people must obey in countries ruled or influenced by Muslim fundamentalists the religious reasons are highlighted. In most English-language discussions of Jewish religious settlements, however, the religious reasons are usually either totally missing or are replaced with biblical quotations, uttered by the settlers. In our text we showed that the real motivating factors for the religious settlers, some of whom have moved to improbable sites, have minimal connections to the Bible. The real reasons emanate instead from a special idea of Jewish fundamentalism. This idea asserts that the messiah will arrive soon and postulates that the world is already in the messianic age.

We began Chapter 4 by asserting that messianic ideology, as a radical part of Jewish fundamentalism, is based upon the differences and opposition between Jews and non-Jews rather than simply between Jews and Arabs (or Muslims). Writers of English-language books, articles and book reviews have rarely mentioned this basic tenet, the major exceptions being those writers who have composed the invalid, out-of-context, virulent and poisonous anti-Semitic literature. The published reviews of Yehoshafat Harkabi's book, *Israel's Fateful Hour*, provide a good illustration of this point. The original Hebrew edition of this book was first published in Israel; the English edition was published thereafter in the United States in 1988. Harkabi's book received wide attention in the United States because of its analysis of Israeli politics in the 1980s and its emphasis upon differences between the Labor Party and Likud in foreign politics. In one crucial chapter, from which we quoted and paraphrased in our text, Harkabi analyzed some major issues of Jewish fundamentalism and stressed the importance of messianic ideology within that context. Harkabi's book was extensively reviewed in American publications, but only one reviewer in a small circulation progressive publication referred to this crucial chapter. The other reviewers in American publications avoided any mention of this chapter and/or its substance. Reviewers in Israel emphasized this chapter in their comments. The difference in reviewing between the United States and Israel is telling.

In maintaining that differences and opposition exist between Jews and non-Jews, messianic ideology continues to be the primary motivating factor for Gush Emunim and its major supporter, the National Religious Party. Those who have written about Israeli

Jewish society and about Judaism but have avoided mention of this
have distorted understanding. The significance here is most striking
when the broad support, both direct and indirect, for Gush Emunim
is considered. About one-half of Israel's Jewish population supports
Gush Emunim. The support, especially monetary, from Jews in the
diaspora is also of great importance. Many Orthodox and other
Jews as well in New York City and elsewhere have been and are
encouraged to assist Gush Emunim by what they read in the largest
circulation American Jewish weekly newspaper, the *Jewish Press*.
Published in Brooklyn, the *Jewish Press* has been and continues to
be an editorial advocate of Gush Emunim, often presenting op-ed
articles written by leading Gush Emunim spokesmen. New York City
and New York State politicians regularly seek backing of the *Jewish
Press* during electoral campaigns. Not only have *Jewish Press* editorial
writers advocated messianic ideology; they have also expressed
admiration of Yigal Amir, the assassin of Yitzhak Rabin. The *New
York Times*, which is read and probably influences many American
Jews, has published in-depth analyses of Christian and Muslim fundamentalism but has refrained from presenting similar articles
describing Jewish fundamentalism or even advocacies printed in
the *Jewish Press*. Even so-called liberal American periodicals, such
as the *Nation* and the *New York Review of Books*, which have published
editorial comments and articles upholding and advocating Palestinian
rights, have neglected to present analyses of Jewish fundamentalism
in their own country. Readers of these and most other periodicals
in the United States, and in other countries as well, would not
know, unless they read books and articles published in Hebrew in
Israel, that Gush Emunim's goal is to build a "sacred society" whose
nuclei are the Jewish settlements in the occupied territories. It is
insufficient, if not folly, to advocate Palestinian rights without understanding and referring to the principal cause of the denial of those
rights: Jewish fundamentalism in general and the messianic variety
in particular.

The Goldstein massacre, discussed in Chapter 6, was inadequately
covered in the English press. That Israeli Jewish society was divided
in its attitude towards the massacre was evident in the Hebrew but
not in the English press and literature. Before the massacre,
Goldstein's refusal as a doctor on religious grounds to treat non-
Jewish patients, including soldiers serving with him in the army, was,
although mentioned briefly, treated lightly in the English coverage.
Goldstein clearly derived his views from fundamentalist interpretations of sacred Hebrew texts. The English coverage indicated that
he merely followed the teachings of Rabbi Meir Kahane, a whipping
boy of the American press. In reality, Goldstein's views were more
broadly based and centered in Jewish fundamentalism. Having
immigrated to Israel as an adult, Goldstein, prior to his arrival in
Israel, had been influenced by the "Lubovitcher Rebbe" and his

influential disciple, Rabbi Ginsburgh. His attitude, moreover, was condoned by important, Israeli politicians and the Minister of Defense. Articles in the Hebrew press, to which we referred in our text, discussed these points in depth; the English coverage avoided mention of much of this.

In Chapter 7 we showed how well-documented features of Jewish fundamentalism during the past 800 years, the third and longest period of Jewish history, have influenced and continue to influence contemporary Jews in the state of Israel and in the diaspora as well. Both the popular and more scholarly and renowned, standard Jewish histories, written in English, omit most of these features. The historic features of Jewish fundamentalism were manifest in the Rabin assassination and in the reactions to it. Because of omission, distortion and lack of criticism of Jewish fundamentalism, the English-language coverage could not and did not put the Rabin assassination in the correct context and thus was misleading.

Important issues are involved here, all of which are omitted in the standard Jewish histories. The first of these, well-known to serious students of the third period of Jewish history and especially to those who have knowledge of Jewish religious law and Orthodoxy, is that, before being affected by outside modern influences, Jewish society was not tolerant. On the contrary, autonomous Jewish authorities persecuted deviants, perhaps more than did Christian and Muslim authorities in their respective religions and certainly more than did pagan, Buddhist and Hindu authorities. The intolerant attitudes and activities, enshrined in the sacred texts of Jewish fundamentalism in all its varieties, influenced the behavior and politics of Jews, especially when they had autonomous power. To oppose the current dangers posed by Jewish fundamentalism, it is first necessary to expose its historical basis. As we have repeatedly stated, most writers of books on Judaism in English have not done this. Influenced by their heritage, many Jews have unfortunately either remained indifferent to the oppression of Palestinians in and by the State of Israel or have at times criticized acts of oppression as posing possible danger to Jews. Some of these individuals, for example, condemn the use of torture as being unconditionally inhumane when used by states other than Israel, but they argue pragmatically that its use by Israeli authorities is not in Israel's best interest because of worldwide public opinion. Many of these same people in the United States are zealous in advocating and fighting for the separation of religion and state in their own country, but they react differently in regard to Israel. They do not criticize, indeed they most often support, the Israeli Ministry of Religion, which is almost always controlled by Jewish religious parties influenced by Jewish fundamentalism, for allotting only 2 per cent of its budget to non-Jews when nearly 20 per cent of Israel's citizenry consists of Muslims and Christians. Both in Israel and in the diaspora the relatively few Jews who have attempted

to defend non-Jews against discrimination and oppression by Jews
have been those who have been influenced by modern theories of
justice. The fact that the majority of Jews do not protest against, but
actually support, Jewish discrimination against non-Jews, especially
in the Jewish state, indicates, at least to some extent, the conscious
and unconscious influence of Jewish fundamentalism. We believe
that attempts to hide historical reality in Judaism and Jewish societies
were wrong when Jews were discriminated against and persecuted
in most countries. By the end of the twentieth century, when Jews
have achieved greater power in many societies than any minority
group of comparable numbers and when a Jewish state with nuclear
weapons is protected by the United States, falsification by omission
of Jewish history is purely adverse and totally unacceptable. The
nearly total absence of discussion of the above intolerant aspects of
the Jewish past and present in English-language books caused us to
dispense with a traditional bibliographical listing or essay.

The issue of Jewish normalcy and the exceptions to it require
examination. Jews in many instances oppressed their own people as
other people did. During the same time period, for example, that rabbis
ordered the hands of Jewish offenders to be cut, Spanish judges, as
well as judges in most Christian and Muslim courts, did likewise.
Rabbis ordered Jewish offenders put into stocks in the Polish-
Lithuanian Commonwealth just as non-Jewish authorities used the
stock as a feature of regular punishment throughout Europe and in
the American colonies. The systematic killing of informers, enjoined
by eminent rabbis as a religious duty, has no parallel in other societies.
Killing of informers has nevertheless occurred and still occurs in other
societies and, as is the case in Sicilian society, is often well known.
Scholarly historical works, historical novels and the classical literature
in general of many countries and societies depict the sometimes-
employed punishment of killing informers. In contrary fashion, the
major Jewish historians who have written about the third period of
Jewish history, for example, Salo W. Baron, Simon Dubnow and
Yitzhak Baer, have omitted such references in their works. Other highly
regarded Jewish historians who have focused upon the Polish-
Lithuanian Commonwealth, Christian Spain and Germany have
done likewise. Numerous Israeli scholars, who have written in Hebrew
and from whom we quoted and paraphrased in our text, have in
contrast displayed more honesty in their scholarship by including
examples of the systematic killing by Jews of Jewish informers.
Consequently, those readers who are not literate in Hebrew (or have
not been told in detail about books in Hebrew about Jewish history)
must have distorted perceptions of this aspect of Jewish history. This
reflection solidified our resolve not to include a traditional bibliographical listing or essay.

The distortions, largely by omission, in the English-language
histories of the third period of Jewish history are greater and more

severe than are those of the first and second periods. The reason for
this is obvious. Because Judaism and Jewish history are so important
for the history and theology of Christianity until and shortly after
the time of Jesus, Christian historians and biblical scholars, often
critical in their writings, dealt with Jewish history and Israelite society
during the first two periods. The better Jewish historians of those
two periods have felt obligated to follow trends established in
scholarship in the nineteenth and twentieth centuries; they have
engaged in critical discussion, even while complaining about what
they regarded as hostile tendencies of Christians who wrote about
Jewish history. Few Christian or Muslim scholars have been or are
interested in Jewish history between AD 70 and modern times, the
third period. Apologetic writing of Jewish history is not unique.
Most national histories include apologetic writings. The writing in
English by Jews of Jewish history has remained far more retarded
than have the writings of other national histories. A comparison that
illustrates this point is the difference between the development of
historical writing by American historians of United States history and
the lack of development in the writing of Jewish history, especially
of the third period. In recent decades standard United States history
textbooks have included numerous negative features, previously
omitted, of past discrimination and oppression of African Americans,
Native Americans, women and other disadvantaged minority groups.
As previously reiterated, most books in English of Jewish history,
especially of the third period, continue to omit negative features of
discrimination and oppression of both Jews and non-Jews by Jews.
The harmful effects of these omissions remain.

We are finally troubled by the near unanimity in standard English-
language Jewish histories regarding issues involving "Jewish interest."
Whereas the Israeli new historians of the 1980s and 1990s have
sparked fruitful debate about basic issues not only of the past century
in regard to Palestine but of the entire course of Jewish history,
previous historians who wrote in English have omitted facts and
disputations over interpretations of sensitive items. Having already
detailed much of this in our bibliographical note, we, in attempting
to illustrate our point, shall here present only one additional example.
The famous scholar Gershom Scholem, early in his career raised an
important intellectual issue about the nature of Judaism; soon
thereafter he, together with numerous other scholars, dropped it.
This issue then became virtually unknown to people who did not
know Hebrew. In his first book in English about Jewish mysticism,
Major Trends in Jewish Mysticism, based upon a previous set of
lectures delivered in New York City, first published in 1941 and
reprinted many times, Scholem questioned whether Jews who
believed in Cabbala had preserved the belief in monotheism that had
been previously so characteristic of Judaism. In his seventh lecture
towards the end of section five of the book, Scholem, after describing

the process, which according to the Lurianic Cabbala takes place by Jewish initiative within God, wrote: "To reconcile this process with the monotheistic doctrine, which was dear to the Kabbalists as it was to every Jew, became the task of the theorists of Kabbalistic theosoply. Although they applied themselves bravely to it, it cannot be said that they were completely successful." These two convoluted sentences implied that the most popular form of Cabbala, still believed by many Jews in Israel and in the diaspora, is not monotheistic. Actually, Scholem refrained from mentioning that many Jewish opponents of Cabbala, before it became dominant around 1550 and during the Jewish Enlightenment, asked the same question more clearly and expressed more sharply their opposition to the predominant Lurianic form on the ground that it denied monotheism. Since then, scholars who have written in English about Judaism, including Scholem himself in later books, have not, with few exceptions, questioned whether Judaism in all its forms and all times was monotheistic and/or whether many pious Jews were believers in monotheism. (Raphael Patai was one exception. In Chapters 5 to 8 of his book, *The Hebrew Goddess*, published in 1967, Patai raised this question. Israel Shahak, another exception, did likewise in his more recent book, *Jewish History, Jewish Religion*.) The scholars who have written in English about Judaism have, again with few exceptions, not considered in their books the even more important question of whether Judaism throughout its entire history has had fixed tenets.

We are aware that the books we have not put into a bibliography contain useful data. We nevertheless believe that these books are guilty of purposeful omission resulting in grave distortion and do not necessarily deserve to be listed in a bibliography. These books anyway can be easily found in other bibliographies. We append this note in lieu of a traditional bibliography in protest against what too often happens in Jewish studies outside Israel.

Notes

Preface

1. Baruch Kimmerling, review of Yohanan Peres and Efraim Ya'ar Yukhtman, *Between Agreement and Dispute: Democracy and Peace in Israeli Society* (Jerusalem: The Israeli Institute for Democracy, 1998) in Hebrew. Kimmerling carefully reviewed and analyzed the data, assembled between 1993 and 1995 by Peres and Yukhtman.

Introduction

1. We explain this to some extent in this book. This is explained in greater detail in Israel Shahak, *Jewish History, Jewish Religion* (London: Pluto Press, 1994).
2. The Romans actually adopted the term Judea by employing the form of "provincia Judea" in describing Palestine, which in the Bible is called by other names.
3. The Hebrew word for gentiles is "goyim," a word which, as used in the Bible, simply means nations. The singular "goy" in the Bible was – and is – applied to the Israelites themselves.

Chapter 1

1. Some Israeli Jews refuse to enter a synagogue as a principled protest against the Jewish religion; this phenomenon is rarely found in non-Israeli Jewish communities but can be compared to the attitude of some radicals to Christianity, for example, in France.
2. The Kishinev pogrom in 1903 in the Ukraine section of the Russian Empire was the first major pogrom in eastern Europe after a lapse of many years. Kishinev became the symbolic term of and for murders of Jews everywhere.
3. The religious reasons centered upon the fulfillment of religious observance. Common to almost all pious Jews who emigrated to Palestine in pre-Zionist times was the belief that all religious observances connected with agriculture could not be fulfilled outside of but rather only in the land of Israel. Wanting to fulfill as many commandments as possible, therefore, these Jews thus emigrated to Palestine.

Chapter 4

1. Pollard, an American Jew very devoted to Israel, was in the 1980s a highly placed employee of US Naval Intelligence. He gave many intelligence secrets (not only concerning Middle Eastern affairs) to Israel. He received a severe prison sentence in the US. Many American and Israeli Jews, and since the

mid-1990s also the Israeli government, have tried to persuade the US President to reduce his sentence or give him a pardon. However, these attempts have been unsuccessful, due to the strong opposition of US intelligence chiefs.

Chapter 5

1. Hardelim is an acronym of two Hebrew words that translated into English are "Haredi-nationalist" and "mustard-like."
2. Some religious Jews acquire religious study deferments and are excused from military service.
3. After the Rabin assassination, Hesder Yeshivot colleagues of the assassin, Yigal Amir, told members of the press how Amir beat Palestinians in the worst manner. They did not disguise the fact that all members of their unit beat Palestinians more than did soldiers in regular units.
4. All NRP members do not adhere to the messianic religious right-wing trend.

Chapter 7

1. "Rabenu" is the Hebrew word for "our rabbi." It was an honorary title given only to a few of the most famous rabbis.
2. Before and during talmudic times, rabbis in the Holy Land who were empowered to teach authoritatively and to serve as judges were appointed by "laying of hands." A rabbi, already so appointed, laid his hands on the head of a candidate and pronounced a sacred formula designed to transmit a sacred power, supposedly derived from Moses although not mentioned in the Bible. Rabbis in other countries never were given this form of appointment. Even if diaspora rabbis came to the Holy Land and after a long stay of study received the "laying of hands" appointment, they were forbidden to transmit it to other diaspora rabbis not in the Holy Land. The students of diaspora rabbis, who themselves became rabbis but did not go to the Holy Land, were, therefore, unable to judge in many matters under the normal law. The last Palestinian rabbis with powers derived from "laying of hands" seemingly disappeared in the tenth century without leaving successors.
3. This rule, which was never abrogated, seemingly applies to Torah scrolls used by Conservative and Reform rabbis. Many Orthodox rabbis in Israel have proclaimed that Reform and Conservative rabbis are heretics. Some of these Orthodox rabbis have publicly stated that Reform Jews are worse than heretics.
4. One example of these freely discussed issues is: After the Great Flood, how did animals who could not swim well and far reach islands in the Mediterranean?
5. One example of such theological problems is: What is God by his very nature incapable of doing?
6. Israel Shahak, one of the authors of this book, was present as a child in Warsaw, Poland, in early 1939 at a funeral of a Jewish heretic, the second cousin of his father. (He also heard this story confirmed by family members later.) At the funeral the immediate family members, including the father, put on the white garments that pious Jews wear on the holidays and rejoiced. One of Shahak's friends who came from Alexandria, Egypt, after hearing this story, recalled a similar Jewish funeral in Alexandria in the early 1940s with the family dressed in white.
7. Rabbi Samuel the Prince was so called, because he was a minister and a general in the kingdom of Granada.

8.   The Karaites denied the authority of the Talmud and only accepted the Bible. Rabbi Yoseph ben Faruj, who was made the head of the Jews in Spain and given the title of Prince, expelled the Karaites.

9.   A punishment considered to be similar to the kuneh was the putting of an iron collar on the neck of a Jewish criminal. The criminal then would have to walk or pace with this iron collar.

10. This important background is unfortunately not mentioned in the major historical studies of the Jews in the United States or in other countries to which Jews immigrated in the nineteenth century. The background is likewise not mentioned in those romantic, apologetic works that purport to describe the lives of first-generation Jewish immigrants. Many characteristics of the Jews in the United States and elsewhere were probably affected by this background.

11. This letter is described and partially quoted in Meir Balaban, *The History of the Frankist Movement* (Tel-Aviv, 1934 in Hebrew, p. 128). The letter was published in full in Rabbi Yaakov Emden's *Sefer Hashimush*, a collection of documents about various heresies (part B, document B).

12. Ibid.

13. This important point is seldom acknowledged in the histories of Jews written in English.

14. David Asaf should be distinguished from Rabbi Simha Asaf who wrote *The Punishments After the Talmud was Finalized: Materials for the History of Hebrew Law* (Jerusalem, 1992).

15. Two most important sources should be consulted to gain an understanding of these satires and the nature of the Hassidic movement against which they were directed. The first source is Yitzhak Erter's satire, *Metempychosis* (*Gilgul Nefesh* in Hebrew). Erter, who died in 1852, was regarded as the best Hebrew satirist of his time; his works were widely read and republished again and again, the last time in 1996 in Israel. In his satire, Ertel dealt with the Hassidic belief in metempsychosis and the help given by holy rabbis to the soul as it passes from a human body to an animal and then back again. The author meets a soul of a recently deceased Jew that tells him about its seventeen changes of abode. In one of those adventures, the soul inhabited a body of an intriguing zealot who died of chagrin when one of his intrigues failed; the soul then passed into the body of a fox with an especially beautiful and long tail. The tail caused the fox to be noticed by fox hunters and killed. Because a blessing of a holy rabbi was not said at the moment of death, however, the soul became a disembodied ghost. A Hassid bought the fur made of the fox's tail and in turn made it into a collar for a coat that he offered to his holy rabbi. A miracle occurred when the holy rabbi put on the coat and the fur touched his (the rabbi's) holy flesh. Erter wrote: "The fox's late soul was born again in a body of another holy rabbi, a person as clever and deceitful as a fox."

The second source is an earlier work, *The Discoverer of Secrets* (*Megaleh Temirin* in Hebrew), published anonymously in 1819 by Yosef Perl, the most enlightened Jew in Galicia at that time. The book purports to consist of letters written (in atrocious Hebrew, imitated from the bad style and grammar common in Hassidic books) by one Hassid to another and supposedly edited by another Hassid who found the letters and added learned references from major Hassidic books for every absurdity piously related by the correspondents. In Letter 150, one of the Hassids related that his holy rabbi died and that his widow earned a great amount of money by selling his garments to Hassids. Clothes of holy rabbis have sacramental value and absolve even the greatest sins if worn. Putting on a shirt of a holy rabbi; for example, absolves a person of the sin of murder, while putting on a holy rabbi's trousers absolves a person of adultery. The supposed editor of this book added several authentic references from Hassidic books to substantiate this belief among Hassids of his time. Such beliefs continue to be common among Hassids of today.

Unfortunately many of the books written specifically about Hassidism and almost all general Jewish histories written in English do not mention such beliefs.

16. "Moser," the Hebrew word for informer, is a terrible insult for Jews, similar to the word "collaborator" for Palestinians.

17. This was feasible if the Jewish community was united in facing a single informer or heretic or even a few of them. Difficulty arose when the community was split; each group then thought the other was heretical and should be reported to the authorities. This happened often in Jewish history. The consequences of such quarrels in which the non-Jewish authorities became involved were sometimes localized but other times spread to and disturbed Jewish communities in several countries. One such controversy involved Maimonides, a most severe critic of heresy who in this case was accused of being a heretic himself. Maimonides' position as a doctor to Al-Abdal, the brother of Saladin and the governor of Egypt, and as the supervisor of Egyptian Jews, prevented any significant Jewish attacks upon him in Muslim countries. Some Iraqi rabbis, who presumably enjoyed the patronage of the Khalif A-Nasir (1180–1225), made cautious accusations against him. Even after his death, Maimonides' position as supervisor of Egyptian Jews, which was inherited by his descendants for six generations, greatly fortified his position in all Muslim countries. In Christian Europe, however, Maimonides was repeatedly accused of being a heretic. Rabbi Shlomo of Montpellier from southern France first made this charge in the 1220s. Some rabbis and notables defended him; others opposed him. The anti-Maimonidean faction informed the Christian inquisitors, who were busy persecuting the Albigenses in southern France, that the philosophical, as well as some halachic, writings of Maimonides also offended Christianity. The inquisitors probably knew neither Hebrew nor Arabic, the languages in which the supposedly offending books were written, but they collected and burned some of them publicly. The pro-Maimonidean faction appealed to feudal lords, who captured some of the anti-Maimonidean Jews and delivered them to their Jewish enemies, who punished them as informers by cutting out their tongues. The controversy, nevertheless, continued until about 1300. This controversy probably still exists. In spite of the enormous prestige Maimonides enjoys among Orthodox Jews as the first codifier of the Halacha and as the leading philosopher of Judaism, he remains suspect among the Haredim. Most Haredi rabbis keep the philosophical writings of Maimonides away from most of their pupils. Maimonides, in the opinion of some scholars and in the view of this book's writers, was in some ways a heretic according to his own definition of the term. The obscure writing of his philosophy makes his heresies difficult for most readers to perceive. On this point, see Leo Strauss, *Persecution and the Art of Writing*, Chapters 2 and 3. Strauss compared the style of writing employed by some writers under the Communist regimes of the 1950s with the style employed by Maimonides and other Jewish medieval thinkers. Both groups used a comparable style to obscure some points from many readers because of fear of persecution by zealots, while at the same time giving hints that could be understood by sophisticated readers.

18. This situation, which endured until the rise of Nazism, made the Jews of eastern Europe strong German sympathizers and contributed to the rise of modern Polish anti-Semitism. Contrary to what Goldhagen has propagated, Jews of eastern Europe, even during World War I, regarded the Germans and the German occupying army as philo-Semitic. They had good reasons for holding this view.

19. In addition to the standard works of Jewish history, see Ernst Wangermann, *The Austrian Achievement 1700–1800* (London: Thames and Hudson, 1973). Wangermann noted outbursts of anti-Semitic violence in the period after the

limited tolerance granted by Joseph II. He also noted that a conservative member of the Council of State, critical of the Jews of Vienna for beginning to dress in a modern way, remarked: "[The sight of] young Jewish men, contrary to all custom going in public dressed indistinguishably from Christians … some even with swords at their sides [presages dissolution of society]." Cardinal Migazzi, the Archbishop of Vienna and the leader of the Catholic Conservative Party, was one of the people who most warned against any toleration for Jews. After the death of Joseph II and at the request of some rabbis, the Austrian government instituted strict censorship of Jewish books and prohibited the printing and import of all books of the Cabbala. Eliezer Falklash, the rabbi of Prague and the personal friend of the censor appointed to carry out this "holy work," addressed a long responsa to the censor on this subject. Rabbi Falklash in his responsa praised the order and applauded the Emperors Leopold II and Francis II for upholding the purity of the Jewish religion. See Shmuel Vertes, *Enlightenment and False Messianic Tendencies: History of a Struggle* (Jerusalem: Shmuel Vertes, 1998, in Hebrew).

20.   This is unknown to many Jews living in English-speaking countries because of censorship and apologetic writing that leaves out negative aspects of Jewish history. In Israel today, the Hebrew press frequently reports the use by Haredim of the law of the informer and the law of the pursuer. On February 18, 1999, for example, *Haaretz* reported that Israeli prosecutors accused Yosef Prushinovsky, a Haredi Jew who lived in the Mea She'arim quarter of Jerusalem and was on trial for swindling tens of millions of dollars from Haredim around the world, of trying to intimidate Haredi witnesses with these two laws. Prushinovsky allegedly threatened to use these two laws against any Haredi witnesses who dared to testify against him in Israeli secular courts. Many Haredi rabbis have held that testifying in Israeli secular courts, in which Arabs can be judges, constitutes informing to non-Jewish authorities. Haredi Jews, such as Prushinovsky, are thus often able to commit crimes, usually swindling, with legal impunity so long as they do it in their own community and do not steal so much that their pious victims are influenced to commit a grave sin in order to retrieve their money. The same situation is prevalent in some of the Haredi Jewish communities in the United States, but the American press rarely reports the cases or offers any halachic explanation.

Index

influence of 55–6, 72, 83
involvement in society 68
and peace treaty 69–70
and redemption doctrine 20, 67
and secular clothing 68
settlements 56, 72, 78–95
support for 68, 159
Gutman Institute 7

Ha'ain Hashvi'it 32
Haaretz
 on Aloni scandal 35, 36
 on assassination 115
 on dangers of peace process 12
 and Goldstein massacre 106, 108,
  110
 Gush Emunim ideology 57, 69, 74,
  75, 86–9, 111
 on Jewish exclusiveness 43
 on military service deferment 30
 on zealots in army 90, 93
Habad movement 43
Hadashot 35, 66
Hadaya, Rabbi E. 64
Ha'i, Rabbi 125, 126
Hakah, Tohay 103
Halacha
 and assassination 137–8
 and death penalty 59, 77, 99–100,
  112, 118
 and dress 8
 and emergency law 127–8
 and homosexuality ix
 as law of Israel 43
 and non-Jews 59, 62, 77, 99–100,
  103, 112, 118
 and women 8–9, 38, 40
Halperin, Rabbi Levy Yitzhak 42
Halvertal, Dov 110
Ha'Meiri, Menahem 124
Ha'migash, Rabbi Yosef Halevi Ibn
 140
Hardelim 86
Haredi parties
 male monopoly 17
 'special money' 51
 structure 16–17
 see also Agudat Israel; Degel Hatora;
  Shas party
Haredim 7–9, 17–18, 23–43, 44–54
 attitude to secular Jews 34
 and education 23–4, 26, 27, 31, 51
 influence of 10–11, 23–4, 31, 40–1
 and military service 68
 and modern times 30–1
 and sacred studies 30

and symbols 34
and women 9, 10, 37
world outlook 14–16
and Zionism 17–18, 19
see also Ashkenazi Jews; Oriental
 Jews; Sephardi Jews
Harel, Israel 69
Harkabi, Yehoshafat 57, 62, 71, 72,
 73, 158–9
Ha'Shavua 32
Hasmonean dynasty 3
Hassidism xi, 58–9, 66
Hassids
 murders 115, 136, 147–8
 persecution 133–5
 punishment 130
Hatanya 59
'Hatikva' 10, 17
hatred
 of Arabs and secular Jews 86
 of Christians 154–5
 internecine 53–4
 of Western culture 65
Hebron 82, 96
heder 24
Hellenism 2–3
heretics 120, 124–5, 149
 burial of 123–4
 punishments 125–6, 130–3
 see also Cohen, Rabbi; idolatry
Herzl, Theodor 17
Hesder Yeshivot 91–2, 93, 103
Hillel 28
Hirsch, Rabbi Rafael 19
history xii, 1–4, 12
 distortion of 150, 162–4
 Israeli Jewish historians 14
Holland 131–2
Holocaust 31, 52
homosexuals and lesbians ix–x
Horowitz, Nerri 86
hypocrisy x, 12, 37

idolatry 120, 121, 122
indoctrination 17, 26
informers 138–45, 146–7, 162
Intifada 68, 76, 80, 84, 91
Iraq 3, 44, 125, 139
Ish, Rabbi Hazon 124–5
Israel
 conquest of 64
 expelling non-Jews 20, 22, 76
 extent of viii
 as kingdom of Heaven on earth 69
 as secular state 87
Israel A/Israel B 6, 7, 11, 12, 156